Real Dissent

Also by Thomas E. Woods, Jr.

The Great Façade (with Christopher A. Ferrara)
The Church Confronts Modernity
The Politically Incorrect Guide to American History
The Church and the Market
How the Catholic Church Built Western Civilization
33 Questions About American History You're Not Supposed to Ask
Sacred Then and Sacred Now
Who Killed the Constitution? (with Kevin R.C. Gutzman)
We Who Dared to Say No to War (with Murray Polner)
Meltdown
Nullification
Back on the Road to Serfdom
Rollback

Real Dissent

A Libertarian Sets Fire to the Index Card of Allowable Opinion

Thomas E. Woods Jr.

To my listeners at TomWoodsRadio.com

CONTENTS

Foreword by Ron Paul   xiii

Preface   xv

Introduction   xvii

Part I: War and Propaganda   1

  1. I Was Fooled by the War-Makers   3

  2. Twilight of Conservatism   8

  3. Who's Conservative?   17

  4. Do Conservatives Hate Their Own Founder?   26

  5. The Cult of Reagan, and Other Neoconservative Follies   30

  6. The Anti-Imperialist League and the Battle Against Empire   37

  7. Is John Yoo Trying to Deceive?   47

Part II: Capitalism and Anti-Capitalism   51

  8. My Anti-Capitalist Twitter Critic   53

  9. Does the Market Make Everything a Commodity?   65

  10. Were We Rich and Awesome When Taxes Were Higher?   69

  11. Plunder or Enterprise: The World's Choice   73

  12. The Misplaced Fear of "Monopoly"   84

Part III: Libertarianism Attacked, and My Replies   93

  13. Progressives: We Owe Everything to Government   95

  14. "The Question Libertarians Just Can't Answer"   98

  15. "The Question Libertarians Just Can't Answer," Part II   100

  16. Grow Up, Libertarians   104

  17. Thanks for Proving Our Point   108

  18. Some Americans Distrust Authority   110

  19. Meet An Enforcer of Approved Opinion   115

  20. Smashed Yglesias   122

  21. Be Happy With Your Cabbage and Navy Beans, Citizen   129

  22. Left and Right: Peas in a Pod   131

  23. My Subversive Book   135

Part IV: Ron Paul and Forbidden Truths   141
  24. Ron Paul and the Remnant   141
  25. Ron Paul Does Not Have a "Cult" Following   148
  26. 26 Things Non-Paul Voters Were Basically Saying   153
  27. Warning: Forbidden Truth Uttered   157
  28. Why Do They Hate Us?   160
  29. Ron Paul Not Allowed Here   164
  30. Thank You, Ron   169
Part V: End the Fed   171
  31. Life Without the Fed?   173
  32. The Lifeblood of the Empire   183
  33. Kill the Monster   188
  34. The President Will Protect You From Bubbles   191
  35. Why Do They Love the Fed?   195
  36. Conservatives and the Elephant in the Living Room   199
Part VI: History and Liberty   203
  37. Historical Distortion   205
  38. My Challenge to Mark Levin   209
  39. How I Sent Mark Levin Home Crying   212
  40. State Nullification: Answering the Objections   214
Part VII: When Libertarians Go Wrong   227
  41. We're the Sweetie Pie Libertarians   229
  42. The Central Committee Has Handed Down Its Denunciation 233
  43. Hey, Everyone, Look at Me: I'm Against Slavery!   237
Part VIII: Books You May Have Missed   241
  44. Christianity and War   246
  45. There Really Have Been Antiwar Conservatives   248
  46. James Madison and the Making of America   254
  47. Who Was the Real Thomas Jefferson?   258
Part IX: Talking Liberty: Selected Tom Woods Show Interviews   265
  48. Are There Any Good Arguments for the State?
    (with Michael Huemer)   267
  49. The Unfashionable Dissenter: Copperhead, the Movie
    (with Bill Kauffman)   277

50. The Myth of the Rule of Law (with John Hasnas)   287
51. War and the Fed (with David Stockman)   296
52. The American Revolution: The Real Issue (with Kevin Gutzman)   304
Part X: Back to Basics   313
53. Liberalism in the Classical Tradition   315
54. Interview with the *Harvard Political Review*   320
Afterword: How I Evaded the Gatekeepers of Approved Opinion   325
About the Author   335

FOREWORD BY RON PAUL

I've been delighted to endorse the work of Tom Woods over the years, beginning with *The Politically Incorrect Guide to American History* in 2004, and continuing with Tom's books *Rollback*, *33 Questions About American History You're Not Supposed to Ask*, and *Meltdown*. I actually wrote the foreword to *Meltdown*, Tom's book on the financial crisis. If you had told me even ten years ago that a book written from the point of view of the Austrian School of economics, and which showed that economic downturns are caused not by the free market but by the Federal Reserve's interventions into the free market, would spend ten weeks on the *New York Times* bestseller list, I wouldn't have believed it.

During my presidential campaigns, Tom wrote some of the most effective replies to some of my unkindest critics. Whenever a popular Internet site would run an article with a title like "Ron Paul's 15 Most Extreme Positions," I knew Tom was on the case. His responses, both on his YouTube channel and in writing, were always informed, funny, and devastating.

Tom and I have worked together closely over the years. I asked him to write the Mission Statement and Statement of Principles for Campaign for Liberty, the organization I founded after the 2008 campaign. I invited him to testify before Congress about auditing the Federal Reserve. I've invited him to be the opening speaker for me on many occasions, and he spoke at our great Rally for the Republic in 2008. Today, Tom is doing some of his most important work of all, because of the lasting impact it will surely have: he's designing courses for the Ron Paul Curriculum, my K-12 homeschool program.

The book you hold in your hands is great fun to read, but it's also filled with useful debating points that will come in handy as you make the case for the free society with friends and family. In endorsing one of Tom's previous books I called him one of the libertarian movement's brightest and most prolific scholars, and I am delighted to commend his new book to you. You will enjoy it, and profit from it.

Not long ago I was having lunch with my mother and was apparently itching to get back to the office so I could compose the definitive smash to a particularly obnoxious attack on libertarian ideas. She suggested I put together a book of the various replies to critics I'd written over the years. When she happened to hear in a recent interview that I was thinking of doing just that, she emailed: "You're welcome."

Not all of the chapters that follow are replies to critics, but a great many of them are. Among people who follow my work, this is generally their favorite genre: the full-throttle reply to a widely read attack on libertarianism. As people brought these attacks to my attention, I began to specialize in replies. I don't like to see an ill-informed critic go unanswered, not only because I don't want by-standers thinking we've been defeated, but also because it's a good opportunity to provide libertarians the intellectual ammunition they need to reply to similar critics when they encounter them.

This is the first book I've written in three and a half years. I've spent most of that time on three major projects – see the afterword for details – but I've managed to keep up my writing in what I laughingly call my spare time. Most of the material in this book has appeared in some print publication or online (LewRockwell.com being the most frequent outlet), but it's not always easy to find. This book brings it all together. I'm really pleased with the articles that appear here; I'm convinced that some of my best and punchiest writing can be found in these pages.

I'm grateful to Jacob Hornberger for allowing me to use material previously published in the Future of Freedom Foundation's *Freedom Daily* as chapters 1, 12, 44, and 47 of this book. Thanks are due also to Naji Filali and the *Harvard Political Review* for granting permission to reproduce the material in chapter 54, to *The American Conservative* for chapter 2, and to the Ludwig von Mises Institute for the material in chapters 6, 9, 11, 31, and 53. Finally, my thanks to *Taki's Magazine* (takimag.com) for permitting the use of material that became chapter 45.

As always, I want to express my deep appreciation for my wife, Heather, who is my biggest fan and supporter. She has helped make me the man I am today. (The good parts, anyway.) And of course much love to my five daughters: Regina, Veronica, Amy, Elizabeth, and Sarah. How impoverished my life would be without you.

And a special thanks to all those who helped make the Tom Woods Show, launched in 2013, a much greater success than I ever expected. This book is for you guys.

Thomas E. Woods, Jr.
August 2014
Topeka, Kansas

INTRODUCTION

The common link binding together the chapters of this book is more than just the libertarian perspective they share. Most of them also do something else: they challenge the narrow band of opinion that Americans are permitted to occupy. Should they stray from the spectrum running from Hillary Clinton to Mitt Romney – surely, citizen, any position you may want to take may be found within that compendious range! – they will be condemned, smeared, or ignored by the gatekeepers of permissible discussion.

Who are these gatekeepers? On the left, sites like ThinkProgress and Media Matters specialize in tendentious portrayals of those uppity peons who stray from the plantation, wisely overseen by the *Washington Post* and the *New York Times*. On the right it's neoconservative sites like the Free Beacon, who have built a nice little cabin on that plantation, and who rat out anyone who tries to run away. Why, we don't hold any of the dangerous views of those libertarians, good Mr. *New York Times* reporter, sir! And you know what? We'll go one better: we won't even talk about issues that Bill Buckley's *National Review* freely debated even a couple generations ago. We are nice and respectable, Mr. *New York Times* reporter, sir, and we'll be sure to keep a close eye on those awful subversives who, probably because of some mental defect, are unsatisfied with the Romney-to-Clinton spectrum.

The respectables of left and right do not deign to show where we're wrong, of course. The very fact that we've strayed from the approved spectrum is refutation enough. That's why I've called these people the thought controllers, the commissars, or the enforcers of approved opinion. It is against them and their attacks that most of this book is aimed.

Part I covers foreign policy and war. The regime has fostered more confusion among the public over these issues than any other. Conservatives, of all people, wind up supporting courses of action that (1) expand the power of the state over civil society; (2) are justified on the basis of propaganda they'd laugh at if it came from the mouths of Saddam Hussein or Nikita Khrushchev; and (3) violate the absolute standards of morality that conservatives never tire of telling us are under assault. The antiwar reputation of left-liberals, meanwhile, is almost entirely undeserved; the mainstream left supported every major U.S. war of the twentieth century.

Conservatives no doubt consider themselves cheeky and anti-establishment for supporting U.S. military interventions, yet virtually all major U.S. newspapers supported the two wars in Iraq and have called for a belligerent posture against Iran. If conservatives think they're sticking it to the *New York Times* by supporting the federal government's wars, they are deceiving themselves. It was the *New York Times*' Judith Miller, for instance, who later became notorious for her uncritical acceptance of war propaganda. Hillary Clinton and John Kerry were every bit as belligerent as George W. Bush – Kerry even said in 2004 that he would be less likely than Bush to withdraw troops from Iraq, and proposed sending an additional 40,000.

Against this bipartisan consensus, anyone advocating a consistent policy of nonintervention abroad – the correct libertarian *and* conservative position, if you ask me – can expect to be marginalized and ignored. Meanwhile, the interventions of the past dozen years have backfired spectacularly, as Ron Paul and other noninterventionists predicted they would. The radical Islam against which neoconservatives assure us they are protecting America by means of various kinds of interventions in Iraq, Iran, Afghanistan, Pakistan, Syria, Libya, and elsewhere has spread and grown stronger as the U.S. government has demonized and destabilized regimes that had been keeping the crazies at bay. That's why I titled a recent blog post, "Neocons Take Break From Spreading Radical Islam to Criticize Rand Paul."

Part II is a defense of the free-market economy against some of the most common arguments. Here my opponents don't necessarily fall into the thought-control category. But many of the arguments I'm replying to are of the only-an-ideologue-could-disagree-with-me variety. Why, "monopolies" would dominate if you libertarians had your way! Everyone would earn ten cents an hour! Advertisers would manipulate consumers!

Those arguments and many others are the first to go.

Part III looks at – and takes apart – some of the attacks on libertarianism launched by mainstream outlets over the past several years. It seems a week hardly goes by without one. I never get more feedback than when I take on critics like these and send them home crying to their mothers. This part of the book collects a bunch of these replies.

In Part IV I assess the significance of the Ron Paul phenomenon. Ron was everything the establishment fears: a plain-spoken truth-teller, a man without pretense, a fearless slayer of sacred cows. He refused to fit into any of the stultifying categories into which our opinion-molders try to pigeonhole anyone and everything. He was anti-state and antiwar – the very epitome of consistency, though most conservatives (and liberals, for that matter) found this an inexplicable contradiction.

"Ron Paul is crazy," the guardians of respectable opinion assured us. What they really meant was that Ron Paul defied traditional political categories and advanced positions outside the Clinton-to-Romney continuum. People whose minds have been formed in ideological prison camps for 12 years have learned to confine themselves within an approved range of possibilities. Tax me 35 percent or tax me 40 percent, but don't raise the possibility that taxation itself may be a moral issue rather than just a matter of numbers. Either bomb or starve that poor country, but don't tell me there might be a third option. The Fed should loosen or the Fed should tighten, but don't tell me our money supply doesn't need to be supervised by a central planner. As always, confine yourself to the three square inches of intellectual terrain the *New York Times* has graciously allotted to you.

The Federal Reserve is the subject of Part V. Talk about outside allowable opinion: opposition to the Fed was nowhere to be found within mainstream American political life for nearly one hundred years after the central bank's creation at the end of 1913. Today, enlightened opinion is appalled at having to acknowledge the existence of critics who question the wisdom of the wise custodians of their monetary system. But given the Fed's track record, the naïve confidence that mainstream left and right expect us to repose in the Federal Reserve would be misplaced.

Part VI corrects the historical record on topics ranging from labor unions to presidential war powers to state nullification. Here you'll find my much-discussed confrontation with radio host Mark Levin, whose idea of a debate is to call his opponent an idiot, and not let his supporters see for themselves what that opponent has written. I was more than happy to link to Levin's responses to me, especially since I was certain I had won our debate.

In Part VII, I have some fun correcting certain libertarians who spend their time assuring respectable opinion that they are altogether different from those extreme libertarians like Woods, and that they're really quite obedient and observant when it comes to issues Americans have been instructed not to discuss.

Part VIII discusses some helpful books in the libertarian tradition, broadly conceived, from the past several years. Part IX features some of my favorite interviews from the Tom Woods Show (TomWoodsRadio.com) so far in 2014. And Part X concludes with reminders of the basic claims of the liberty message, in the form of my foreword to a new edition of Ludwig von Mises' book *Liberalism,* and an interview I did with Naji Filali in the *Harvard Political Review,* in which I laid out some essential libertarian ideas.

We can't expect to live in a free society if we play by the establishment's rules. It's time we set that index card of allowable opinion on fire.

This book is a match.

PART I

WAR AND PROPAGANDA

1

I WAS FOOLED BY THE WAR-MAKERS

Twenty years ago, as I was completing my freshman year in college, I was a full-blown neoconservative. Except I didn't know it. Having concluded that I was not a leftist, I simply decided by process of elimination that I must be a Rush Limbaughian.

Like most people, I was unaware that any alternative to those two choices existed, or that in some ways they were two sides of a common statist coin. In particular, I embraced a neoconservative foreign policy with gusto. The way to show you weren't a commie was by supporting the U.S. military as it doled out summary justice to bad guys all over the world. And frankly, it was exciting to watch it all unfold on TV.

I never gave the human cost of war a second thought and became impatient with anyone who did. War was like a video game I could enjoy from the comfort of my home. Devastation and human suffering were quite beside the point: the righteous U.S. government was dispensing justice to the wicked, and that was that. What are you, a liberal?

The Persian Gulf War of 1991 was the first U.S. conflict of my college career. During the months-long U.S. military buildup in the Gulf known as Operation Desert Shield I eagerly promoted the mission to anyone foolish enough to listen.

When war came, it was swift and decisive. Very few American casualties were suffered, while the Iraqi forces were destroyed, many burned alive by a chemical agent or buried in the desert while making a retreat.

Believe it or not, that actually bothered me, in spite of how voracious a consumer of war propaganda I was. No one defended Saddam Hussein's invasion of Kuwait, which he launched in response to that country's slant oil drilling, but was the outcome of the Persian Gulf War not a terrible tragedy for the Iraqi people – virtually none of whom had had anything to do with Saddam Hussein's fateful decision – all the same? A far poorer country than ours suddenly had a lot more widows and orphans, not to mention a great many civilian deaths to grieve over and much destruction to repair.

Mothers and fathers were crying themselves to exhaustion over children they had lost, or who, worse still, were dying agonizing deaths before their very eyes. Was it really right that we Americans should meanwhile be celebrating with a Bob Hope special, and – on cue – flattered by the ceaseless reminders that ours was the awesomest country ever?

It later transpired that the Kuwaiti government had hired a public-relations firm in the United States to sell the idea of military invasion to the American people. We later learned that the major atrocity story – that Iraqi troops had removed Kuwaiti babies from incubators and thrown them onto hospital floors – had been a fraud: the emotional young woman who testified to that effect in Washington turned out to be the daughter of the Kuwaiti ambassador to the United States.

Although I had strongly favored military action by the U.S. government from the start, in the wake of George H.W. Bush's declaration of victory I could not stop thinking about the lopsided casualty counts, the waves of killing rained down on a ramshackle army facing the greatest military machine in the world. Now these were soldiers, not civilians, so by the logic of war I was supposed to hate them or at least not care about them, their deaths being cause for celebration rather than regret.

I was having trouble doing that.

I went to see my European history professor at Harvard, Charles Maier, to discuss my misgivings about the war. Maier, a left-liberal in the *New Republic* mold, suggested I read a recent article in that magazine making the case for the war. I did, and (believe it or not) that helped to suppress any contrary thoughts for a while.

I was already beginning to read libertarian literature by the early 1990s because of my support for the market economy. My reading of the economic works of Murray Rothbard led inevitably to his philosophical works. The Rothbard essay "War, Peace, and the State" leaves an impression on the mind one can never quite shake.

Rothbard famously observed that one could uncover the libertarian position on X by imagining a gang of thugs carrying out the state action in question. If thugs can't just grab your money, for instance, neither can a well-dressed group of thugs calling itself "the state."

"War, Peace, and the State" takes that analysis and applies it to war. If you steal my television, I can take it back from you. But I may not walk down the street firing a gun every which way and harming third parties in order to make you surrender my television. Likewise, even assuming a war-making state to be absolutely in the right, it has no greater moral entitlement to harm third parties in pursuit of its ends than a private individual does.

Simply because some politician utters the word "war," we have been conditioned to believe it just and good that the rights of everyone within the confines of an arbitrary border are abruptly cancelled. What would in any other circumstance be murder and atrocity becomes an antiseptic matter of public policy.

The lingering effects of war can inspire callousness even after the guns have fallen silent. Many of us have seen the notorious clip from *60 Minutes* in which Madeleine Albright, then U.S. ambassador to the United Nations and soon to be U.S. Secretary of State, declared that the price of half a million dead children as a result of the sanctions against Iraq during the 1990s had been "worth it." Note that she did not dispute the figure. She looked the interviewer in the eye and said that the deaths of half a million kids were worth it in pursuit of one man she and her colleagues didn't like.

Now suppose the Soviet Union, during the height of the Cold War, had killed half a million children in the course of a sanctions policy. We would never have heard the end of it.

One of the great triumphs of the government propaganda machine in self-described democracies is the "we are the government" line. It makes the subject population somewhat more compliant than it might be if a particular family passed down the power to govern from one generation to another, with no chance (short of outright revolution) that anyone else will ever hold the reins of power. More important, criticisms of their government's foreign policy now come to be seen as personal affronts. We are the government, after all, so how dare you criticize "our" foreign policy!

For that reason, opponents of American foreign policy should, when speaking on this topic, eliminate the pronoun "we" from their vocabulary. "We" did not kill those Iraqi kids. In 2002 and 2003 "we" did not repeat transparent untruths about the alleged threat posed by a devastated Iraq. "We" did not lay waste to an already suffering country, killing hundreds of thousands and displacing four million others.

They did this. The American political class. We did not.

What some Americans did do, though, was to make sorry excuses for their political overlords. Some Americans defended a series of policies which, if pursued by the Soviet Union 30 years ago, they themselves would have condemned as grotesque violations of basic standards of morality. But with the U.S. government as the perpetrator, everything was different. They were as gullible on foreign policy as left-liberals are on domestic policy. They dutifully searched for evidence to corroborate their leaders' claims, even when their leaders had long since abandoned those claims. They accepted the most transparent propaganda without batting an eye.

Until 1991, I had done pretty much the same thing. But following the Persian Gulf War I began to have doubts. Within a few years I had come to regret my laziness, and the readiness with which I accepted foreign-policy propaganda from the very people I knew I couldn't trust when it came to the economy, the Constitution, or pretty much anything else.

The 19th-century writer Elihu Burritt noted the great sympathy the human race extended to those who have been the victims of misfortunes: famine, shipwreck, railway accidents, whatever. He then invited his readers to "compare the feeling with which the community hears of the loss or peril of a few human lives by these accidents with which the news of the death or mutilation of thousands of men, equally precious, on the field of battle is received."

How different is the valuation! how different in universal sympathy! War seems to reverse our best and boasted civilization, to carry back human society to the dark ages of barbarism, to cheapen the public appreciation of human life almost to the standard of brute beasts.... And this demoralization of sentiment is not confined to the two or three nations engaged in war; it extends to the most distant and neutral nations, and they read of thousands slain or mangled in a single battle with but a little more humane sensibility than they would read of the loss of so many pawns by a move on a chessboard. With what deep sympathy the American nation, even to the very slaves, heard of the suffering in Ireland by the potato famine! What shiploads of corn and provisions they sent over to relieve that suffering! But how little of that benevolent sympathy and of that generous aid would they have given to the same amount of suffering inflicted by war upon the people of a foreign country! This...is one of the very worst works of war. It is not only the demoralization, but almost the transformation, of human nature. We can generally ascertain how many lives have been lost in a war. The tax-gatherer lets us know how much money it costs. But no registry kept on earth can tell us how much is lost to the world by this insensibility to human suffering which a war produces in the whole family circle of nations.

I was once blind to the effects of war on my own moral compass and to how callous I had become toward entire countries and the fellow human beings who inhabited them. When I collaborated with Murray Polner on *We Who Dared to Say No to War: American Antiwar Writing from 1812 to Now* (Basic Books, 2008), it was in a spirit of contrition and reparation for having once cheered on what I now know to be evil.

"I am getting more and more convinced that the war-peace question is the key to the whole libertarian business," Rothbard noted privately in 1956. I am equally convinced. If we can't get this right, who cares about the Department of Education or the minimum wage?

June 24, 2012

2

TWILIGHT OF CONSERVATISM

"War and the military are, without question, among the very worst of the earth's afflictions," an American conservative of distinction once wrote, "responsible for the majority of the torments, oppressions, tyrannies, and suffocations of thought the West has for long been exposed to. In military or war society anything resembling true freedom of thought, true individual initiative in the intellectual and cultural and economic areas, is made impossible – not only cut off when they threaten to appear but, worse, extinguished more or less at root. Between military and civil values there is, and always has been, relentless opposition. Nothing has proved more destructive of kinship, religion, and local patriotisms than has war and the accompanying military mind."

That was Robert Nisbet in 1975. In *The Conservative Intellectual Movement Since 1945*, George Nash identified Nisbet, along with Russell Kirk and Richard Weaver, as one of the three most noteworthy of those intellectuals he identified as traditional conservatives. Of the three, Nisbet probably remains the least known among modern conservatives – a shame, and one that we can hope Brad Lowell Stone's very good biography of Nisbet may help to rectify.

Robert Nisbet was born in Los Angeles in 1913, and spent much of his youth in the Golden State. He did his graduate and undergraduate work at Berkeley, whose faculty he joined in 1939; he would later teach in both the history and sociology departments at the University of Arizona and Columbia University. By the time of his death in 1996, he had written 17 books and gained a reputation (in the words of his biographer) among "his admirers and detractors alike as one of the most original and influential American social theorists of his generation."

Throughout his life, he managed to travel in a variety of conservative circles. He spent 1978-80 at the American Enterprise Institute, and enjoyed adjunct scholar status there well into the 1980s. His articles occasionally appeared in neoconservative periodicals like *Commentary*.

How could an anti-militarist have maintained such connections? As well as being an exceptionally personable figure, Nisbet was a man of enormous influence. In addition to his other achievements, he was the social-science editor at Oxford University Press, and it is said that when he received the Albert Schweitzer chair at Columbia he was the most highly paid professor in America. (It is probably also true to say that both AEI and *Commentary* were better and less ideologically rigid institutions a quarter century ago than they are now.)

This year marks the 30th anniversary of Nisbet's *Twilight of Authority*, long considered something of a minor classic, and it is from that book that most of Nisbet's words that follow have been taken. Most interesting are three things: Nisbet's warnings about the ongoing growth in executive power, his prescient critique of American conservatism, and his skepticism and caution about the growth of the warfare state that has long since vanished from establishment conservatism.

Nisbet's 1953 classic *The Quest for Community* argues that for the most part, every major modern political philosopher in the West, from Hobbes to the present, has taken as his starting point the idea of a unitary, all-powerful central state ruling over an undifferentiated aggregate of individuals, and which is legally and temporally prior and superior to all subsidiary associations. This became the model for political association throughout the West since the French Revolution. Every competing center of authority – family, local community, church, or any number of others – was increasingly subordinated to the central state.

Part of the reason that totalitarianism enjoyed such triumphs during the 20th century, Nisbet suggested, was that deracinated men, stripped of the traditional social identities that these intermediary associations had once provided, longed for something to put in their place. That sense of belonging was fulfilled, for some, in the totalitarian state, which developed upon the ruins of those very associations and which offered men both a source of meaning and a sense of belonging, thus serving as a crude substitute for the social identities that smaller associations, suppressed or marginalized by the massive bureaucracy at the center, had once forged for them.

Much as he deplored the centralization of power that continued apace in the U.S. during his lifetime, Nisbet would never have confused his country with a totalitarian state of the sort with which the last century was riddled. Still, Nisbet noticed analogous trends toward the centralization of power in Washington – and in the hands of the president in particular – at the expense of smaller and more immediate associations. The conservative movement today, on the other hand, convinced that one of its own is in the White House – even those conservatives who have something critical to say about the president always wind up rallying to him as soon as Ted Kennedy utters an unkind word – has exhibited no discernible concern over the growth in executive power.

The modern-day cult of personality that surrounds the president probably originated with the ebullient and idiosyncratic Theodore Roosevelt, whose great variety of interests along with his sheer energy attracted the rapt attention of so many Americans. In addition to these accidents of personality, TR also brought with him a full-fledged philosophy of the presidency, not entirely dissimilar to that of his supposed archenemy, Woodrow Wilson.

TR contended that the burden of proof was on those who would restrain presidential power; for him, it was enough that a proposed presidential action was not prohibited by the Constitution. He described the executive branch in general and himself in particular as the unique spokesman of the entire American people, since he alone occupied an office in whose election all Americans participated. (John C. Calhoun, on the other hand, had memorably observed that, strictly speaking, there was no such thing as "the American people," since such an aggregate had no place in our decentralized order of self-governing states.)

These principles, combined with TR's anxiousness to have a hand in everything, led to a dramatic elevation in the vigor and visibility of the presidency. For instance, TR once convened a conference at the White House to discuss how rough play in college football might be addressed. We would think nothing of such an incident today, and of course in the grand scheme of things it is of no importance at all. But in 1903, the fact that the president would involve himself in a matter so trivial, a matter that until that time all Americans would have assumed fell to the organs of civil society to resolve, was of no small significance.

It is no coincidence that the number of executive orders issued by the president exploded under TR's watch, since they comported so well with his philosophy of the presidency. Presidents Rutherford Hayes and James Garfield had each issued none. Chester Arthur issued three, Grover Cleveland (first term) six, Benjamin Harrison four, Cleveland (second term) 71, and William McKinley 51. In his nearly two terms in the office, TR issued 1,006.

At least some conservatives were heard to complain when the Clinton administration's Paul Begala, speaking of executive orders, gleefully squawked: "Stroke of the pen, law of the land. Kinda cool." (Clinton once described Teddy Roosevelt as his favorite Republican president.) But the number of conservative critiques of executive power run amok that we have heard since the accession of Bush 43 can safely be rounded off to zero. Whatever the explanation for this silence, it is probably not this president's scrupulous restraint and modesty in his exercise of presidential power.

Nisbet deplored this. But what particularly disturbed him was the almost grotesque mystique that had come to surround the American president. "Not only what the President thinks on a given public issue," Nisbet wrote, "but what he wears, whom he dines with, what major ball or banquet he may choose to give, and what his views are on the most trivial or cosmic of questions – all of this has grown exponentially in the regard lavished by press and lesser political figures upon the presidency during the past four decades." There were monarchical pretensions in all this, he said, for the first care of royalty "is that of being constantly visible, and naturally in the best and most contrived possible light for the people."

Nisbet likewise spoke of "a regard for the monarch that makes him virtually sacred in presence, that thereby gives his person a privileged status in all communications and that creates inevitably the psychology of constant, unremitting protection of the President not merely from physical harm but from unwelcome news, advice, counsel, and even contact with officers of government." Apart from the last point, which may be a reference to the special relationship Nixon had with Kissinger when it came to foreign policy decisions, the resemblance of Nisbet's description to the reality of the Bush presidency is too great to escape notice.

In case comparing the president to the kings of yore seems overwrought, Nisbet invites us to consider the nature of the official iconography, ceremony, and architecture that has come to surround the American presidency. He quotes the *New York Times*' Russell Baker: "[The Rayburn Building] dwarfs the forum of the Caesars. Mussolini would have sobbed in envy. ... [But] the Kennedy Center nearly succeeds for bare-faced oppression of the individual spirit. Poor Lincoln, down the road a piece in his serene little Greek temple, would be crumpled like a candy wrapper if the Kennedy Center could flex an elbow. The Pentagon of the warlike forties is matched by a monstrous new Copagon, home of the FBI, astride Pennsylvania Avenue. The vast labyrinths bordering the mall would make a minotaur beg for mercy."

"My misgivings are not about the wretched architects," continued Baker, "who must give Washington what it pays for, but about their masters who have chosen to abandon the human scale for the Stalinesque. Man is out of place in these ponderosities. They are designed to make man feel negligible, to intimidate him, to overwhelm him with the evidence that he is a cipher, a trivial nuisance in the great institutional scheme of things."

In 2005, Baker would be dismissed as an incorrigible America-hater, but Nisbet, a genuine conservative, replied with sympathy. "It has always been thus," he began. "Merely compare the public architecture of Greece before and after the rise of Alexander; of Rome, before and after Augustus, and before and after the eruption of, first, Renaissance despots in Italy and then divine right monarchs. The change in American government that has taken place during the past several decades is almost perfectly evidenced by the change in the style and character of its buildings in Washington."

Writing in the wake of Watergate, Nisbet took note of "a good deal of resentment against royalism in the White House." He knew it would not be permanent. "There are too many powerful voices among intellectuals – in press, foundation, and elsewhere – that want a royal President provided only that he is the right kind of individual." He feared that the only lessons that had been learned from Watergate were "to avoid such idiocies as tapes and illegal, unwarranted break-ins. ... I would be astonished if the real lesson of Watergate – the Actonian principle that all power tends to corrupt, absolute power absolutely – were other than forgotten utterly once a crowd-pleasing President with the kind of luster a

John F. Kennedy had for academy, press, and the world of intellectuals generally comes back into the White House."

For much of the Left, Nisbet explained, a strong president as a unifying force was too central to their idea of the American polity to be dispensed with just because a Republican had disappointed them. "There are those, such as Arthur Schlesinger, who argue indeed that only a strong and richly visible President can hold the fabric of democracy intact, that the President is the only vital symbol of unity and consensus." (That these words of a center-left social democrat might just as easily have come from practically any neoconservative is not without its significance.)

Nisbet also argued that it wasn't just executive power that conservatives showed little interest in limiting; it was federal-government power in general. "The prospects for conservatism are hardly bright," he concluded in 1975. "It became great by virtue of its fight against power, which now is being converted into a fight for capture of power, central power."

Eleven years later, in *Conservatism: Dream and Reality*, that bleak assessment had not improved:

> The Far Right is less interested in Burkean immunities from government power than it is in putting a maximum of governmental power in the hands of those who can be trusted. It is control of power, not diminution of power, that ranks high. Thus when Reagan was elected conservatives hoped for the quick abolition of such government 'monstrosities' as the Department of Energy, the Department of Education, and the two National Endowments of the Arts and Humanities, all creations of the political left. The Far Right in the Reagan Phenomenon saw it differently, however; they saw it as an opportunity for retaining and enjoying the powers. And the Far Right prevailed. It seeks to prevail also in the establishment of a 'national industrial strategy,' a government corporation structure in which the conservative dream of free private enterprise would be extinguished.

Some people were not prepared to render quite so harsh a judgment in 1986. But apart from Nisbet's misleading use of the term "Far Right," if the experience of five years of George W. Bush and the lukewarm-to-nonexistent conservative opposition to the greatest budget-buster since LBJ doesn't begin to vindicate him, what would?

We also see in the work of Robert Nisbet far more caution about the warfare state than can be found in just about any mainstream conservative organ today. There was, first of all, a connection between war and the growth in executive power that we have already seen him deplore. "The day is long past," he warned, "when this phrase ['national security'] was restricted to what is required in actual war. As everyone knows, it has been, since World War II under FDR, a constantly widening cloak or umbrella for governmental actions of every conceivable degree of power, stealth, and cunning by an ever-expanding corps of government officials."

> As we now know in detail, the utilization of the FBI and other paramilitary agencies by Presidents and other high executive department officers for the purposes of eavesdropping, electronic bugging, and similarly intimate penetrations of individual privacy goes straight back to FDR, and the practice has only intensified and widened ever since. Naturally, all such royalist invasions have been justified, right down to Watergate, under the name of national security. The record is clear and detailed that national security cover-up has been a practice of each of the Presidents since FDR.

Of all the misapplications of the word "conservative" in recent memory, Nisbet wrote in the 1980s, the "most amusing, in an historical light, is surely the application of 'conservative' to … great increases in military expenditures…. For in America throughout the twentieth century, and including four substantial wars abroad, conservatives had been steadfastly the voices of non-inflationary military budgets, and of an emphasis on trade in the world instead of American nationalism. In the two World Wars, in Korea, and in Viet Nam, the leaders of American entry into war were such renowned liberal-progressives as Woodrow Wilson, Franklin Roosevelt, Harry Truman and John F. Kennedy. In all four episodes conservatives, both in the national government and in the rank and file, were largely hostile to intervention; were isolationists indeed."

It would be difficult, said Nisbet, to imagine a combination more at odds with traditional conservatism than military adventurism and ideological crusading.

Nisbet could find much to disturb a traditional conservative even in the rhetoric of Ronald Reagan: "President Reagan's deepest soul is not Republican-conservative but New Deal-Second World War Democrat. Thus his well noted preference for citing FDR and Kennedy as noble precedents for his actions rather than Coolidge, Hoover, or even Eisenhower. The word 'revolution' springs lightly from his lips, for anything from tax reform to narcotics prosecution. Reagan's passion for crusades, moral and military, is scarcely American-conservative."

Nisbet recalled that contrary to popular opinion, the political Left for the most part had not opposed war per se. Hard leftists have historically found much revolutionary potential in war. "Napoleon was the perfect exemplar of revolution as well as of war, not merely in France but throughout almost all of Europe, and even beyond. Marx and Engels were both keen students of war, profoundly appreciative of its properties with respect to large-scale institutional change. From Trotsky and his Red Army down to Mao and Chou En-lai in China today, the uniform of the soldier has been the uniform of the revolutionist."

War, argued Nisbet, is "by nature revolutionary in its impact upon a people.... Its values...are antithetical in the extreme to the values of kinship-based society with its consecration of tradition, conventionality, and age or seniority."

Nisbet suggested further that the revolutionary and the military man both possessed a disdain for "traditional civil society, its privileges, immunities, and conventional authorities." For both, this society, particularly in its modern capitalist form, "can seem egoistic, venal, needlessly competitive, often corrupt, and fettered by privilege unearned. Careful reading of the memoirs of the great generals in history will, I am sure, reveal as much distaste for all this as one finds in the memoirs of revolutionists."

Less extreme leftists have been no less enthusiastic for war's potential to transform the home front, Nisbet added. Leftist intellectuals were practically unanimous in favoring U.S. entry into World War I since they understood the opportunity it presented for institutional change at home. Wartime economic planning, they were convinced, would help to erode Americans' conservative beliefs in the limits of government and the inviolability of private property.

The experience of wartime planning never entirely faded from the national consciousness, and certainly not from that of the Left. When the Depression came, the Left jumped at the chance to revive the spirit of government planning it had so assiduously cultivated during the Great War. The rallying cry was "We planned in war"; now, therefore, we shall plan in peace. War symbolism was ubiquitous in the imagery adopted by Franklin Roosevelt's New Deal. "In terms of frequency of use of such symbols by the national government," wrote Nisbet, "not even Hitler's Germany outdid our propagandists."

Needless to say, this was no anomaly. "It is in time of war that many of the reforms, first advocated by socialists, have been accepted by capitalist governments and made parts of the structures of their societies," Nisbet pointed out. "Equalization of wealth, progressive taxation, nationalization of industries, the raising of wages and improvements in working conditions, worker-management councils, housing ventures, death taxes, unemployment insurance plans, pension systems, and the enfranchisement of formerly voteless elements of the population have all been, in one country or another, achieved or advanced under the impress of war."

Nisbet, therefore, as even this brief survey reveals, was altogether different from the interchangeable automatons and mediocrities who pass for conservative commentators in 2005. Among the worst aspects of the collapse of traditional conservatism is that my children will grow up in a world in which vulgar and belligerent nationalism will be presented to them as the alternative to leftism. Nisbet would not have been surprised at this unfortunate situation. But he would surely have continued to employ his talented and incisive pen against it, reminding his fellow Americans that in the midst of the right-wing noise machine there still existed, if somewhat chastened and neglected, a humane and principled conservatism to which civilized men could repair.

December 5, 2005

3

WHO'S CONSERVATIVE?

"The United States needs to go to war with Iraq," wrote *National Review*'s Jonah Goldberg in 2002, "because it needs to go to war with someone in the region and Iraq makes the most sense." Elsewhere, he wrote: "Every ten years or so, the United States needs to pick up some small crappy little country and throw it against the wall, just to show we mean business."

If you're wondering if these are the words of a conservative, try to imagine Russell Kirk uttering them.

But it is the various forms of Wilsonianism, uttered apparently in all seriousness, that most decisively disqualify neoconservatism from any place within the conservative intellectual tradition. When writing for Internet outlets, I inevitably received email from people who condemned me for not wanting to bring democracy to Iraq, and/or to "liberate" the Iraqi people. One man actually told me that if I weren't a "liberal" I would be more eager to liberate this oppressed people.

It says a great deal about the state of conservative thought in America that messianic utopianism could be confused with conservatism. To the contrary, such an ideology, whereby there exists some moral obligation to spread democracy and to "free" the various unfree peoples of the world, is precisely what the great conservative Edmund Burke meant when he spoke of the "armed doctrines" of the French Revolution. Mesmerized by the universalisms of the Enlightenment, the Jacobins were ready to spread revolution throughout Europe – for why should only the French enjoy the blessings of liberty?

Let us assume for the sake of argument that modern democracy is the best form of government, and let us also assume that the War Party is being sincere in its professed desire to bring democracy to Iraq. Let us also assume that the Iraqis will eventually reconcile themselves to being invaded by American and "coalition" forces, and won't engage in sabotage against the U.S.-installed regime. Let's even assume that the U.S. will support a democracy in Iraq even when it becomes obvious, as it should be already, that free elections will of course yield an anti-American government. Let's assume all of this.

There are still problems. First of all, majoritarian democracy is just about the worst arrangement for a place like Iraq. Although followers of the War Party tend to be more familiar with the conservatism of Sean Hannity than that of John C. Calhoun, whom they've never read, it is Calhoun whose wisdom is especially valuable here. Calhoun warned that majority rule, which can be justified only on the basis of convention and utility rather than on any strictly moral foundation, can work only in places where there exists a basic commonality of interests among the people. Otherwise, majority rule becomes just another form of tyranny, as interest groups with mutually exclusive goals use their electoral strength to oppress each other.

This is why Calhoun believed in the concurrent majority. He believed that distinct groups should be able to resist the oppression of electoral majorities. He appealed to ancient examples of such arrangements, in which measures did not pass unless they had the approval of majorities in each group, rather than simply requiring a majority of the entire people taken in the aggregate.

If someone wanted to establish a democracy in Iraq, surely Calhoun's principle of the concurrent majority is the model to be followed. The Kurds, the Sunnis, and the Shi'ites would be at each other's throats under any other arrangement (and possibly even under this one as well). Naturally, of course, our global democrats consider Calhoun to be unacceptably reactionary, and insist on the French revolutionary model of political organization: a single aggregated people in whose name the government operates.

Yet this is almost nit-picking. The real difficulty with neoconservative ideology is the alleged imperative to spread democracy in the first place.

A conservative recognizes a hierarchy of concerns: I owe my children, my neighbors, and my co-religionists much more than I owe anyone in Iraq or anywhere else. Cicero, like so many figures in our classical past, held that "the union and fellowship of men will be best preserved if each receives from us the more kindness in proportion as he is more closely connected with us." The Bible confirms the wisdom of the ancients, instructing us that "if any man have not care of his own, and especially of those of his house, he hath denied the faith, and is worse than an infidel" (1 Tim. 5:8).

The calling of the monk or missionary to serve distant peoples is often confused with a general Christian obligation to have equal concern for every individual in the world, and might be cited by globalists in support of their call for ceaseless wars of "liberation." But no such general obligation exists. For one thing, what the missionary does in leaving family and friends behind is known in theology as a supererogatory work. It is not an instruction binding upon the great mass of mankind. In fact, it would be positively harmful and disruptive if every Christian devoted himself to works of supererogation.

Thus, for example, when in the late thirteenth and early fourteenth centuries some of the stricter Franciscans insisted that their lives of absolute poverty must be binding upon anyone who wished to call himself Catholic, the popes absolutely denied this universal obligation at the same time that they praised it among those whom God had called to adopt it. Likewise, when socialists in the nineteenth and twentieth centuries began to appeal to the common property of certain early Christian communities as a biblical mandate for communism, Catholic moral theologians were unanimous in responding that disorder and chaos would result if works of supererogation – expressly intended only for the few – were transformed into binding legal and social norms.

St. Thomas Aquinas had this to say in support of patriotism and against the suggestion that all people everywhere have an equal claim on our sympathy and assistance:

> Our parents and our country are the sources of our being and education.
> It is they that have given us birth and nurtured us in our infant years.
> Consequently, after his duties toward God, man owes most to his parents and his country. One's duties towards one's parents include one's

obligations towards relatives, because these latter have sprung from [or are connected by ties of blood with] one's parents...and the services due to one's country have for their object all one's fellow-countrymen and all the friends of one's fatherland.

Elsewhere St. Thomas remarked that "people's charitable activities towards one another are to be exercised in accordance with the varying nature of the ties that unite them. For to each one must be given the service which belongs to the special nature of his connection with him that owes it."

Over 100 years ago, Fr. F.X. Godts spoke of those who "take the name of 'Internationalists,' boasting that they have no country and no fellow-countrymen." "Their unholy doctrine," he concluded, "is as much opposed to nature as it is to religion."

Edward Cahill, S.J., echoing Cicero, explained in *The Framework of a Christian State* (1932) that "obligations of piety extend in due proportion, directly or indirectly, to parents, relatives, fellow-countrymen, and to all persons closely connected with these." He continued:

> Hence, when St. Paul says that in the Church 'there is neither Gentile nor Jew...Barbarian or Scythian, bond or free, but Christ, all in all'... he does not imply that the Church wishes to abolish or ignore the natural ties which bind individuals to their own country, no more than she would wish to abolish family ties or distinction of sex, or even reasonable distinctions of class, all of which are necessary for the good of the human race. He means rather, that just as the Church, while consecrating and upholding domestic ties and obligations, nevertheless, receives equally into her fold the members of every family, so also she receives and cherishes impartially the citizens of all nations, for all are equally dear to her Founder.

It is the Stoics of ancient Rome with whom the idea of world citizenship has been historically associated, but the idea was given still greater impetus much more recently by the eighteenth-century Enlightenment. The Enlightenment tended to encourage the idea that the ideal man was a citizen of the world, his affections not limited by the merely immediate. In his book *The Brave New World of the Enlightenment*, Professor Louis Bredvold, speaking about William Godwin, noted that he "absolves man from all ties of attachment to individuals so that he may devote himself to the pursuit of universal benevolence."

That is quite a perceptive summary of the temper of the Enlightenment: a denigration of the natural obligations that a man incurs by virtue of being a father, husband, and friend in favor of the obligation he is now said to owe without discrimination to the entire human race. Thus, for example, when John Lennon lectured the world on peace and brotherhood even though in his own life he went years without seeing his son from his first marriage, he was only one in a long series of universalist humanitarians dating back at least to Jean-Jacques Rousseau, the eighteenth-century political thinker who was all broken up at the news of the suffering caused by the earthquake in Lisbon, but who placed all five of his own children in a foundling asylum, thereby condemning them to lives of hard labor and misery.

South Carolina Senator Robert Y. Hayne elaborated on this point in his famous 1830 debate with Daniel Webster. He spoke of those who exercised what he called "false philanthropy":

> Their first principle of action is to leave their own affairs, and neglect their own duties, to regulate the affairs and the duties of others. Theirs is the task to feed the hungry and clothe the naked, of other lands, whilst they thrust the naked, famished, and shivering beggar from their own doors; to instruct the heathen, while their own children want the bread of life. When this spirit infuses itself into the bosom of a statesman (if one so possessed can be called a statesman), it converts him at once into a visionary enthusiast. Then it is that he indulges in golden dreams of national greatness and prosperity. He discovers that "liberty is power"; and not content with vast schemes of improvement at home, which it would bankrupt the treasury of the world to execute, he flies to foreign lands, to fulfill obligations to "the human race," by inculcating the principles of "political and religious liberty," and promoting the "general welfare" of the whole human race.

Hayne's description of false philanthropy eerily anticipates the views of President Woodrow Wilson, the anti-conservative. Wilson was eager to involve the United States in World War I, one of the worst conflagrations in human history, even though the safety of the American people was in no way threatened. Oh, the president tried his best to trump up some reasons for intervention, of course. But they generally made no sense. To paraphrase historian Ralph Raico, Wilson insisted that every American had the right, in time of war, to travel aboard armed, belligerent merchant ships carrying munitions of war through declared submarine zones. No other professed neutral had ever dared put forth such a doctrine, let alone gone to war over it.

Wilson's mind was elsewhere: he was looking ahead to the peace settlement, at which he believed a genuinely disinterested United States would be able to forge a just and lasting peace. More importantly, under American leadership a League of Nations would be established to provide collective security against aggression. To those who protested that national sovereignty might be compromised by the kind of supranational organization that he proposed, Wilson replied that a time would come "when men would be just as eager partisans of the sovereignty of mankind as they were now of their own national sovereignty."

This is a recipe for endless warfare and ceaseless strife. Moreover, military intervention is always an uncertain undertaking, fraught with danger and unforeseen consequences, such that the genuine statesman of conservative inclinations determines upon it only after the most serious reflection and after the exhaustion of all alternatives. Woodrow Wilson truly and sincerely believed he would "make the world safe for democracy" by getting the U.S. into World War I even though he effectively admitted we had no national interests at stake. (He spoke of our "high, disinterested purpose.") The result was 120,000 dead Americans, 250,000 wounded, our government transformed forever, and one of the most disastrous peace settlements in history, which gave rise to the Nazis less than a generation later.

Whoops.

As Professor Raico explains, "Instead of letting the European nations find their own way to a compromise peace, American power had swung the balance decisively in favor of Britain and France. Among the consequences was the fall of the Kaiser and the old Germany, which Wilson, believing his own propaganda, considered the epitome of evil." The catastrophe of Wilson's policy becomes still clearer when we consider the testimony of George Kennan, writing just after World War II: "Today if one were offered the chance of having back again the Germany of 1913 – a Germany run by conservative but relatively moderate people, no Nazis and no Communists – a vigorous Germany, full of energy and confidence, able to play a part again in the balancing-off of Russian power in Europe, in many ways it would not sound so bad."

Isn't that like saying that Wilson, in chasing after his visionary schemes, ultimately wasted all those American lives? I leave that to the reader to decide.

A conservative would never have entertained the saccharine expectations that Wilson appears to have had, or been so eager to sacrifice the sovereignty of his nation for the sake of an abstraction called "humanity." Leftists, not conservatives, deal in abstractions. Marx and Lenin wanted to save "humanity" – though, perhaps not coincidentally, they showed far less solicitude for the actual human beings they encountered. (There is no evidence that Marx, for all his braying about alleged mistreatment of workers, even once visited a factory.) Americans have been well wishers of freedom everywhere but defenders only of their own. That was the posture of Washington, Jefferson, John Quincy Adams, and indeed all of our early statesmen.

Senator Robert A. Taft, whom I recently profiled for *American Conservatism: An Encyclopedia*, published by the Intercollegiate Studies Institute, appreciated the prudent, limited, finite, and sensible foreign policy of American tradition, since it was so naturally appealing to the conservative instinct. Known in his day as "Mr. Republican," Taft explained in *A Foreign Policy for Americans* (1951): "No foreign policy can be justified except a policy devoted without reservation or diversion to the protection of the liberty of the American people, with war only as the last resort and only to preserve that liberty."

To those "who talk about an American century in which America will dominate the world" and encourage our country to "assume a moral leadership in the world to solve all the troubles of mankind," Taft replied with the prudence and caution that are supposed to be the conservative's trademark. "I quite agree that we need that moral leadership not only abroad but also at home.... I think we can take leadership in providing of example and advice for the improvement of material standards of living throughout the world. Above all, I think we can take the leadership in proclaiming the doctrines of liberty and justice and in impressing on the world that only through liberty and law and justice, and not through socialism or communism, can the world hope to obtain the standards which we have attained in the United States."

It is not true that any moral obligation exists for those fortunate enough to live under politically stable regimes to spend their blood and treasure from now until the end of time to bring liberty to the peoples of the world. Harry Elmer Barnes used the apt phrase "perpetual war for perpetual peace." The relatively small number of livable places in the world would simply exhaust themselves in conflict and nation-building, and the constant warfare would doubtless have countless unpredictable consequences – as any government intervention has. Over two centuries ago, Charles Pinckney held out the more modest goals for which republican governments should strive: "If they are sufficiently active and energetic to rescue us from contempt, and preserve our domestic happiness and security, it is all we can expect from them – it is more than almost any other government ensures to its citizens."

Even if perpetual wars to install what would inevitably be perceived as alien regimes were in fact desirable, the fact remains that nations, even our own, possess finite resources. In the nineteenth century, Henry Clay, explaining why America had contributed neither arms nor funds to the Hungarian cause for which there was so much American sympathy, raised this very point:

> By the policy to which we have adhered since the days of Washington…
> we have done more for the cause of liberty in the world than arms
> could effect; we have shown to other nations the way to greatness and
> happiness…. Far better is it for ourselves, for Hungary, and the cause
> of liberty, that, adhering to our pacific system and avoiding the distant
> wars of Europe, we should keep our lamp burning brightly on this
> western shore, as a light to all nations, than to hazard its utter extinction amid the ruins of fallen and falling republics in Europe.

Likewise, William Seward, Abraham Lincoln's Secretary of State, declared: "The American people must be content to recommend the cause of human progress by the wisdom with which they should exercise the powers of self-government, forbearing at all times, and in every way, from foreign alliances, intervention, and interference." In 1821, John Quincy Adams declared most famously of all that America "has abstained from interference in the concerns of others, even when the conflict has been for principles to which she clings.... She goes not abroad in search of monsters to destroy. She is the well-wisher to the freedom and independence of all. She is the champion and vindicator only of her own."

"National greatness conservatism," as the alternative presented to conservatives is at times clumsily known, bears no resemblance to historic conservative thinking in America. If anything, it has far more in common with leftism than with conservatism, for it was the Left that was always unsatisfied with the prosaic pursuit of bourgeois life. The conservative who wishes to preserve the republic given to him in the eighteenth century must be an abiding skeptic of executive power, a vigorous supporter of states' rights, and contemptuous of saccharine promises about remaking the world. Woodrow Wilson, in short, was not a conservative.

The conservative temperament shuns all appeals to utopia, and seeks instead those finite but noble (and attainable) virtues we associate with hearth and home. These are the things that the conservative delights in and defends. Nathaniel Hawthorne once observed that a state was about as large an area as the human heart could be expected to love, and Chesterton reminded us that the genuine patriot boasts not of how large his country is, but always and of necessity of how small it is. Now that is all very mundane and uninteresting to those who would urge "greatness" upon us, but if conservatism is less exciting than ideological crusades waged from now until eternity, it is also more realistic and more sober, and less likely to set the world ablaze.

March 27, 2003

4

DO CONSERVATIVES HATE THEIR OWN FOUNDER?

Toward the end of his life, Russell Kirk, one of the great founders of American conservatism, became contemptuous of Republican militarism. Didn't know that? Neither do most readers of *National Review*, for which Kirk wrote for so many years.

Kirk's opposition to relentless war makes him a "liberal" in NR's lexicon. Now it'd be kind of hard to describe the key founder of modern American conservatism as a liberal – harder even than NR's task of making Rudy Giuliani seem like something we should want in a U.S. president. So the whole Kirk problem is simply passed over in silence.

Young conservatives, take note: what you are about to encounter is the voice of the real thing, whose opinions are worth more than those of a million talk-show ignoramuses put together. That these views would never, ever get published in the typical "conservative" magazine today tells you all you need to know about the state of the "conservative movement": so remote is it from the genuine article that Kirk himself would be unwelcome.

The remarks from which I draw here are taken from a 1991 speech to the Heritage Foundation. What a difference a decade and a half can make: these opinions would *never* be permitted at Heritage today. Of that you can be sure. (Now remember, this is 1991, so Kirk is speaking of George H.W. Bush, not George W. Bush, for whom these remarks could be amplified many times over.)

Oh, once in a while you'll still get tributes to the great Kirk, but his foreign-policy views will be ignored – or greeted with awkward smiles and a cough, if anyone is so discourteous as to break the silence on the subject.

"Presidents Woodrow Wilson, Franklin Roosevelt, and Lyndon Johnson were enthusiasts for American domination of the world," Kirk said in his speech. "Now George Bush appears to be emulating those eminent Democrats. When the Republicans, once upon a time, nominated for the presidency a 'One World' candidate, Wendell Willkie, they were sadly trounced. In general, Republicans throughout the twentieth century have been advocates of prudence and restraint in the conduct of foreign affairs."

President Bush, Kirk said, had embarked upon "a radical course of intervention in the region of the Persian Gulf. After carpet-bombing the Cradle of Civilization as no country ever had been bombed before, Mr. Bush sent in hundreds of thousands of soldiers to overrun the Iraqi bunkers – that were garrisoned by dead men, asphyxiated."

And why, exactly? "The Bush Administration found it difficult to answer that question clearly. In the beginning it was implied that the American national interest required low petroleum prices: therefore, if need be, smite and spare not!"

Kirk then recalled Edmund Burke's rebuke to the Pitt ministry in 1795, when the British government seemed to be on the verge of going to war with France over the issue of navigation on the River Scheldt in the Netherlands. "A war for the Scheldt? A war for a chamber-pot!" Burke said. Today, said Kirk, one may as well say, "A war for Kuwait? A war for an oilcan!"

Since a war for an oilcan turned out to be not so popular, President Bush "turned moralist; he professed to be engaged in redeeming the blood of man; and his breaking of Iraq is to be the commencement of his beneficent New World Order." Kirk said Bush had embarked on what Herbert Butterfield called "the war for righteousness." "It has been held by technicians of politics in recent times," Butterfield wrote in *Christianity, Diplomacy, and War,* "that democracies can only be keyed up to modern war – only brought to the necessary degree of fervor – provided they are whipped into moral indignation and heated to fanaticism by the thought that they are engaged in a 'war for righteousness.'"

"Now indubitably Saddam Hussein is unrighteous," said Kirk,

but so are nearly all the masters of the "emergent" African states (with the Ivory Coast as a rare exception), and so are the grim ideologues who rule China, and the hard men in the Kremlin, and a great many other public figures in various quarters of the world. Why, I fancy that there are some few unrighteous men, conceivably, in the domestic politics of the United States. Are we to saturation-bomb most of Africa and Asia into righteousness, freedom, and democracy? And, having accomplished that, however would we ensure persons yet more unrighteous might not rise up instead of the ogres we had swept away? Just that is what happened in the Congo, remember, three decades ago; and nowadays in Zaire, once called the Belgian Congo, we zealously uphold with American funds the dictator Mobutu, more blood-stained than Saddam. And have we forgotten Castro in Cuba?

And now Russell Kirk – conservative among conservatives – makes the obvious point that the loudmouths today ridicule and condemn: perpetrating large-scale violence can make people angry.

Now here is Kirk: "*We must expect to suffer during a very long period of widespread hostility toward the United States* – even, or perhaps especially, from the people of certain states that America bribed or bullied into combining against Iraq. In Egypt, in Syria, in Pakistan, in Algeria, in Morocco, *in all of the world of Islam, the masses now regard the United States as their arrogant adversary*; while the Soviet Union, by virtue of its endeavors to mediate the quarrel in its later stages, may pose again as the friend of Moslem lands. Nor is this all: for now, in every continent, the United States is resented increasingly as the last and most formidable of imperial systems." (Emphasis added.)

Well, away with Russell Kirk, then: he "blames America" for terrorism!

Oh, and what kind of leftist said the following? "Perpetual War for Perpetual Peace comes to pass in an era of Righteousness – that is, national or ideological self-righteousness in which the public is persuaded that 'God is on our side,' and that those who disagree should be brought here before the bar as war criminals."

The founder of American conservatism, that's who.

These are the words of a civilized man. I have my differences with Kirk on important questions, to be sure, but this is a learned, serious thinker whose work and thought anyone can and should respect – which is more than can be said for the sloganeering Ministry of Propaganda that now dominates official conservative media.

So who plans to be first in line to denounce even the deceased Russell Kirk as an "unpatriotic conservative"?[1]

May 18, 2007

---

[1] David Frum wrote a notorious article in *National Review* in 2003 called "Unpatriotic Conservatives," in which he attacked the handful of conservatives who opposed the war in Iraq.

5

THE CULT OF REAGAN, AND OTHER NEOCONSERVATIVE FOLLIES

Some time ago *The American Spectator*'s Jeffrey Lord claimed Ron Paul's foreign policy of nonintervention was "liberal," and that conservatives are supposed to be hawkish on foreign policy. Now to some extent, no one really cares about these labels, and who qualifies as what. But it is obviously false to say that supporters of nonintervention must be left-liberals. I showed this in my YouTube response ("*American Spectator* Dead Wrong on Ron Paul"), which dismantled Lord's entire position.

I figured that would be it. There is no wiggle room left for Lord after that.

Yet he came back for more. So here I go again:

1) I pointed out in the video that the anti-imperialist movement in the late nineteenth and early twentieth centuries was dominated by conservatives, as historian William Leuchtenberg has noted. I likewise pointed out that we may count on one hand the number of Progressives who opposed U.S. entry into World War I. I further noted that the recent interventions Lord supports were likewise supported by Hillary Clinton, Howard Stern, the *New York Times*, and the *Washington Post* (among others I mentioned). Before Lord goes attacking other people for their tactical alliances, he might make note of the beam in his own eye.

Lord does not acknowledge any of this. I wouldn't, either, were I in his shoes.

2) Lord is obsessed with Ronald Reagan, and again condemns Ron Paul for opposing Reagan's expansion of government power. The weird cult of personality around the deceased former president reveals that Reagan has become the Right's Obama: a man whose every action is to be treated as ipso facto brilliant, perhaps even divinely inspired. Critics are mere heretics whose arguments need not actually be refuted; the mere fact that they have disagreed with the Great Leader is enough to condemn them forever.

How dare you say Ronald Reagan wasn't free-market enough! He supported the free market to the precisely correct extent, says the Supreme Neocon Council.

That Lord is more interested in someone's loyalty to a man than he is in loyalty to the principles that the man was supposed to represent, is the classic expression of a cult of personality.

3) In pointing out that Felix Morley, one of the founding editors of the weekly conservative newspaper *Human Events*, was himself a noninterventionist, it was obviously not my intention to argue that *Human Events* favors nonintervention abroad as an editorial position. I myself have been published and interviewed numerous times in *Human Events*, so I'm quite familiar with its editorial line. The point is that Lord describes nonintervention as a "liberal" (as in left-liberal, not classical liberal) position. As long as I can find some indisputably non-liberal supporters of nonintervention, I win. No one in his right mind would consider Morley a left-liberal. But Morley is simply Exhibit A.

4) Here's Exhibit B: Lord's own superior at *The American Spectator*, senior editor Angelo Codevilla. Speaking on the Mike Church Show about the bipartisan foreign-policy consensus to which Lord subscribes, Codevilla said:

> This is a radical departure from the way that America's status in the world was built in the first place. It was built by a founding generation and the statesmen of the nineteenth century who adhered to the

traditional view that the governors of any country are the stewards of the interests of that country only, and they are not entitled in any way to interfere in the affairs of other countries....

Beginning in the early part of the twentieth century, people like Woodrow Wilson began supposing that we had the right and duty to be the world's keepers, and they have proceeded to mess things up around the world ever since.

What I try to do in this book [*A Student's Guide to International Relations*] is to explain...that the world really is filled with people who are really different, who really do think differently, and that they work in an international system which gives them full rein, full capacity to be what it is they want, and that makes it impossible for foreigners to conduct their affairs.

In other words, imperialism has always been something of a losing proposition, especially in the modern international system, and our ruling class's attempt to nation-build the world in their own image is doomed to failure and to creating one disaster after another....

[Other countries] have, according to our Founding Fathers, every right to be as benighted, backward, and nasty to one another as they want. The Declaration of Independence says all men are created equal, all nations have the right to be who they are.... The Declaration of Independence claimed no special rights for the American people. It claimed for the American people the rights that the American people recognized in the rest of mankind....

Americans, like the rest of mankind, have an inalienable right to self-determination. Now that's not simply a theoretical statement. It's also a practical one. Because it is utterly impossible for one people to transfer its own ethos, its own notion of good and evil, its own way of doing things, to another. The Afghans, the Arabs, are who they are; they have grown up in a particular culture. It is what they know, what they love. As John Quincy Adams would have put it, who has appointed us as judges over them?

Codevilla also shot off a one-liner against the chickenhawk phenomenon; when Church asked him about neoconservative Bill Kristol, Codevilla replied: "And by the way, I served in the armed forces.... Billy didn't at all."

5) For Exhibits C, D, E, and on through the alphabet, see Bill Kauffman's book *Ain't My America: The Long, Noble History of Antiwar Conservatism and Middle American Anti-Imperialism*, which I review in chapter 45 of this book.

6) Catholic University's Claes Ryn, who is more conservative than Lord and his entire circle of friends put together, has explained the difference between conservatism as classically understood on the one hand, and the militant Jacobin universalism to which Lord and the neoconservatives subscribe on the other. It should hardly be necessary to point out that the "global leadership" propaganda and the endless "democracy" project GOP candidates urge us to embrace is completely foreign to the finite goals and expectations of a conservative. A sample from Ryn's speech to the Philadelphia Society:

> One current assumption about conservatives is nothing less than weird: that they are hawks, always looking for prey and always bullying. Conservatives are in reality normally doves, looking for ways to settle conflicts peacefully. They view war differently from neo-Jacobin desk-warriors. The suffering and destruction of war are frightful realities involving actual human beings. War is the very last resort.

> Conservatives harbor no illusions about the international arena. Bad people behave badly. So conservatives want to be prepared to handle threats to their own society and civilization or to international peace. But their normal way of interacting with other peoples is to try to defuse conflict and to pursue a common human ground. This is the cosmopolitan way.

In domestic affairs, American conservatives have always feared unlimited power, partly because of their belief in original sin. Fallen creatures must be restrained by law. Government must be limited and decentralized, hence the separation of powers and federalism. The sprit of constitutionalism forms the core of the American political tradition. Unchecked power is an invitation to tyranny. The framers even wanted the U.S. Congress, which was to be the preeminent body of the national government, to have divided powers. Needless to say they disdained democracy.

Jacobins see no need for restraints on virtuous power. Today American neo-Jacobins are promoting presidential ascendancy and great leeway for the executive. Old restraints and liberties must yield to the needs of the virtuous national security state.

Ryn has just described the difference between Jeffrey Lord and a conservative. No one who listens to neoconservative talk radio has ever heard these distinctions before, which is why Lord can get away with pretending all his opponents are left-liberals.

7) Lord's discussion of the Cold War reads like something from 1974. It's as if the Soviet archives were never opened. As Sir Michael Howard (rather a credentialed historian) has noted, no serious historian any longer makes claims about Stalin's intentions abroad – claims I myself once believed, before the archives were opened and the evidence forced me to change my mind – that Lord repeats as if out of a Richard Nixon campaign brochure.

For example, we are told, breathlessly, about the communist threat to Greece in the late 1940s. In fact, Stalin specifically instructed Yugoslavia – which is where the aid to Greece was coming from, not from the Soviet Union – not to aid the Greek communists, who were not allowed to join the Cominform and whose Provisional Government was not recognized by the Soviet Union or indeed any other communist government. Senator Taft didn't see any U.S. interest involved in Greece in any case.

As for Turkey, long before the Bolshevik Revolution the Russians had sought control of the Straits. There was no military threat to Turkey at all, as George Kennan, the man who famously called for "containment" of the Soviets in his Long Telegram and his 1947 *Foreign Affairs* article, tried in vain to point out. In Lord's party-line world, we are evidently not even allowed to agree with George Kennan.

Throughout the Cold War, Soviet capabilities were consistently, almost ludicrously, inflated. It is hard to believe that so-called conservatives could in effect have shared the rosy view of Soviet productive capacity put forth by the likes of John Kenneth Galbraith and Paul Samuelson, but share them they did. It is as if they didn't actually believe the free-market rhetoric they otherwise used. They expected a gigantic, socialistic basket case to conquer the world. What it wound up doing was accumulating basket cases in Africa and elsewhere that in no way helped and surely intensified its own economic backwardness.

But Lord, never one to question the bipartisan foreign-policy consensus – we heretics, on the other hand, dissent from every bipartisan consensus – takes Truman, a middle-of-the-road Democrat, to be a model statesman. Question Truman and his grandiose statements and strategy? What are you, some kind of commie?

I realize that in questioning the Cold War consensus I am violating one of the long list of unforgivable sins in the official conservative movement. The Cold War, like Ronald Reagan, is one of those topics on which mainstream conservatism will admit no dissent. There is the Official Version of Events, and there are the heretics who question it.

The Cold War apparatus gave birth to a military-industrial complex that is evidently impossible to rein in, and which is constantly in search of further justifications for ever-greater levels of spending. This is the one government program conservatives may never question. This one is run by omniscient angels who don't need to be audited. This one has no entrenched interests of its own that it might pursue at the expense of the common good. That's true only of the farm lobby and the education bureaucracies. This is the Department of Defense, citizen. Trust them. USA! USA!

8) Russell Kirk, one of the most important conservative thinkers of the twentieth century, was critical of libertarians. I assumed everyone knew that. But just as interesting is that Kirk was no neocon like Lord. (See chapter 4.)

More to the point: although Lord doesn't mention it, by the 1990s Kirk was praising libertarians for having "an understanding of foreign policy that the elder Taft represented."

That's right – the iconic Kirk praised libertarians for their foreign-policy views.

What other conclusion can we draw, then, except that Lord must now expel Kirk from the conservative canon? We can hope Lord's sense of the ridiculous is developed enough to stop him.

October 1, 2011

6

THE ANTI-IMPERIALIST LEAGUE AND THE BATTLE AGAINST EMPIRE

In April 1898 the United States went to war with Spain for the stated purpose of liberating Cuba from Spanish control. Several months later, when the war had ended, Cuba had been transformed into an American protectorate, and Puerto Rico, Guam, and the Philippines had become American possessions.

When the U.S. government decided not to grant independence to the Philippines, Filipino rebels led by Emilio Aguinaldo determined to resist American occupying forces. The result was a brutal guerrilla war that stretched on for years. Some 200,000 Filipinos lost their lives, either directly from the fighting or as a result of a cholera epidemic traceable to the war.

That American forces were engaged in a colonial war to suppress another people's independence led to a great deal of soul-searching among important American thinkers, writers, and journalists. What eventually became the American Anti-Imperialist League began at a June 1898 meeting at Boston's Faneuil Hall, where people concerned about the colonial policy that the U.S. government may choose to adopt in the wake of the war gathered to speak out against the transformation of the United States into an imperial power. The League was formally established that November, dedicating its energies to propagating the anti-imperialist message by means of lectures, public meetings, and the printed word.

Those who later became anti-imperialists could be found both among supporters and opponents of the Spanish-American War of 1898. William Jennings Bryan was a good example of the former, and Moorfield Storey of the latter. It is on this latter group of anti-imperialists that I wish to dwell for a moment, since what they had to say about war is liable to sound eerily familiar.

Storey was quite an interesting figure: an accomplished lawyer and graduate of Harvard Law School as well as president of the American Bar Association, he was a supporter of laissez-faire and a well-known advocate of the gold standard and free trade. Storey, who was white, was also the first president of the National Association for the Advancement of Colored People (NAACP) from 1909 until 1915. He spoke at the Boston meeting presided over by Bradford, and went on to become both a vice president of the New England Anti-Imperialist League and, later, president of the national organization.

Now consider Storey's words in April 1898, on the eve of the Spanish-American War, for it was these sentiments that animated his and so many others' anti-imperialist work:

> This Club [the Massachusetts Reform Club] never met under circumstances more calculated to create the gravest anxiety in every patriotic man than tonight, and by patriotic man I do not mean him who measures his country's greatness by the extent of her territory, the size of her armies, the strength of her fleets, or even by the insolence with which she tramples upon her weaker neighbors, but him who knows that the true greatness of a nation, as of a man, depends upon its character, its sense of justice, its self-restraint, its magnanimity, in a word upon its possession of those qualities which distinguish George Washington from the prize-fighter – the highest type of man from the highest type of beast.

Carl Schurz, who among other things was the first German-born American to serve in the U.S. Senate, was likewise deeply involved in the League as an officer as well as firmly opposed to the Spanish-American War. He wrote in April 1898:

The man who in times of popular excitement boldly and unflinchingly resists hot-tempered clamor for an unnecessary war, and thus exposes himself to the opprobrious imputation of a lack of patriotism or of courage, to the end of saving his country from a great calamity, is, as to "loving and faithfully serving his country," at least as good a patriot as the hero of the most daring feat of arms, and a far better one than those who, with an ostentatious pretense of superior patriotism, cry for war before it is needed, especially if then they let others do the fighting.

Schurz recalled a verse from James Russell Lowell, writing about the Mexican War of 1846-48:

The side of our country must ollers be took.
An' President Polk, you know, he is our country.

"Again in our own time," Schurz reported, "we hear with the old persistency the same old plea to the voters of the nation to be loyal to the country, right or wrong. And when we probe the matter – nor is much probing necessary – we find that we are being urged to be loyal not to the country right or wrong, but to President McKinley right or wrong." To fit the present situation, Schurz suggested amending Lowell's lines to read,

The side of our country must ollers be took,
An' Mister McKinley, you know, he is our country.

We can fill in Lowell's verse today easily enough.

Among the best-known members of the Anti-Imperialist League was Mark Twain, who served as vice president from 1901 until his death in 1910. One of Twain's most compelling antiwar writings, a short story called "The War Prayer," was considered too radical to be published in Twain's lifetime. "I don't think the prayer will be published in my time," Twain said. "None but the dead are permitted to tell the truth."

"The War Prayer" was a vivid commentary on the misappropriation of religion on behalf of nationalistic causes. It begins with a church service in which the pastor calls down the blessings of God upon American military forces and concludes with, "Grant us the victory, O Lord our God!"

> A frail old man makes his way into the church and, waving the pastor aside, explains that he has spoken with God Himself, who wishes to hear the other half of that prayer – the half that was only in their hearts and uttered but implicitly.

> O Lord our Father, our young patriots, idols of our hearts, go forth to battle – be Thou near them! With them – in spirit – we also go forth from the sweet peace of our beloved firesides to smite the foe. O Lord our God, help us to tear their soldiers to bloody shreds with our shells; help us to cover their smiling fields with the pale forms of their patriot dead; help us to drown the thunder of the guns with the shrieks of their wounded, writhing in pain; help us to lay waste their humble homes with a hurricane of fire; help us to wring the hearts of their unoffending widows with unavailing grief; help us to turn them out roofless with little children to wander unfriended the wastes of their desolated land in rags and hunger and thirst, sports of the sun flames of summer and the icy winds of winter, broken in spirit, worn with travail, imploring Thee for the refuge of the grave and denied it – for our sakes who adore Thee, Lord, blast their hopes, blight their lives, protract their bitter pilgrimage, make heavy their steps, water their way with their tears, stain the white snow with the blood of their wounded feet! We ask it, in the spirit of love, of Him Who is the Source of Love, and Who is the ever-faithful refuge and friend of all that are sore beset and seek His aid with humble and contrite hearts. Amen.

The story ends abruptly, with the people considering the man a lunatic – and, presumably, carrying on as before.

It is sometimes said of the anti-imperialists that they cared more about the effects that colonialism would have on the character of America and Americans than they did about its effects on the peoples who were held as colonies. This is not entirely fair to the anti-imperialists, who were genuinely horrified at the treatment the Filipinos received at the hands of American forces and who sought to investigate conditions there.

The Nation's E.L. Godkin, for instance, declared that the U.S. government had substituted "keen effective slaughter for Spanish old-fashioned, clumsy slaughter." William James was astonished that his country could "puke up its ancient soul…in five minutes." Andrew Carnegie wrote to a friend who favored expansion: "It is a matter of congratulation…that you have about finished your work of civilizing the Fillipinos [sic]. It is thought that about 8000 of them have been completely civilized and sent to Heaven. I hope you like it."

In 1901, the League passed a resolution instructing its executive committee "to use its best efforts in promoting a petition to the President of the United States that General Aguinaldo should be permitted to come to this country under safe conduct, to state the case of his people before the American Congress and nation." Needless to say, Theodore Roosevelt ignored this appeal.

Over the next several years the League focused on discovering and disseminating the truth about the fate of the Filipinos under American occupation. They publicized firsthand testimonies of tortures like the "water cure" that U.S. forces employed. Thus according to Private A.F. Miller of the Thirty-second United States Volunteers,

"This is the way we give them the water cure; lay them on their backs, a man standing on each hand and each foot, then put a round stick in the mouth and pour a pail of water in the mouth and nose, and if they don't give up pour in another pail. They swell up like toads. I'll tell you it is a terrible torture."

George Kennan, the special investigator of the *Outlook*, wrote in 1901:

The Spaniard used the torture of water, throughout the islands, as a means of obtaining information; but they used it sparingly, and only when it appeared evident that the victim was culpable. Americans seldom do things by halves. We come from here and announce our intention of freeing the people from three or four hundred years of oppression, and say "We are strong and powerful and grand." Then to resort to inquisitorial methods, and use them without discrimination, is unworthy of us and will recoil on us as a nation. It is painful and humiliating to have to confess that in some of our dealings with the Filipinos we seem to be following more or less closely the example of Spain. We have established a penal colony; we have burned native villages near which there has been an ambush or an attack by insurgent guerrillas; we kill the wounded; we resort to torture as a means of obtaining information.

These were the kinds of things the anti-imperialists wanted to bring into the public eye.

By and large, however, the American public was unmoved. One anti-imperialist writer pondered the meaning of this indifference: "What is the significance of such silence? Do we realize that amidst all the sunshine of our rich, prosperous life we are being weighed in the balance of a true civilization, of eternal justice – and are being found wanting? It is the product of arbitrary government authority without justice, force from which the lifeblood of righteousness and truth has run out."

Some were in fact quite hostile to the League and its mission. According to the commander of the New York chapter of the Grand Army of the Republic, all League members should have their citizenship stripped from them and be "denied the protection of the flag they dishonor." Teddy Roosevelt described the anti-imperialists as "simply unhung traitors, and…liars, slanderers and scandalmongers to boot."

The League carried on all the same. Edward Atkinson, who had been involved in the League since the Faneuil Hall meeting, actually inquired with the War Department to get a list of soldiers serving in the Philippines in order to send them some of his antiwar writings. He wrote:

In this morning's paper a correspondent of the *Boston Herald* states that the Departments are going to "expose" the Anti-Imperialist League and others who have as alleged stirred up discontent among the troops in Manila. I do not think the Executive Committee of the Anti-Imperialist League has yet taken any active measures to inform the troops of the facts and conditions there. The suggestion is, however, a valuable one and I have sent to Washington today to get specific addresses of officers and soldiers to the number of five or six hundred so that I may send them my pamphlets, giving them my assurance of sympathy. I shall place the same lists in charge of the Executive Committee of the League to keep up the supply.

He never heard back.

So he went ahead and sent some at least to a limited group of officers and American officials and others in the Philippines, as a start. The Postmaster General ordered that all Atkinson pamphlets heading for Manila be seized from the mails. Atkinson then thanked the government for all the attention, pointing out that interest in his pamphlets had risen dramatically throughout the country. He wrote: "I think the members of the Cabinet have graduated from an asylum for the imbecile and feeble-minded. They have evidently found out their blunder because the Administration papers suddenly ceased their attacks on me all on the same day, and I miss the free advertisement. I am now trying to stir them up again to provoke another attack."

Some sectors of the League were reluctant to support Atkinson's activities, though some individual anti-imperialists did, as did the League's Chicago branch. But he continued his work, observing in 1899 that his latest pamphlet was his "strongest bid yet for a limited residence in Fort Warren."

As early as 1896, Atkinson had written to the *New York Evening Post* with a suggestion for a petition to be drawn up to the U.S. Congress along the following lines:

> It is requested that an act may be passed to the effect that any citizen of the United States who proposes to force this country into a war with Great Britain or with any other country on a dispute about boundaries or any other similar issue, shall be immediately conscripted or entered upon the army roll for service from the beginning to the end of any such war when it shall occur. It is suggested that Senators of the United States shall be assigned to the position of general officers in this addition to the army upon the ground that their military capacity must certainly be equal to their political intelligence.... It is next suggested that Representatives in Congress shall be assigned to the command

of brigades.... Of course, men who in high public position have...expressed such an earnest desire to assert and defend the honor of the country at any cost, would most enthusiastically vote for this enactment and would immediately enroll themselves for active service in the field.

This proposal for the immediate enrollment of the Jingo army will at once develop the sincerity of purpose of the advocates of aggression and violence by their enlistment. An indirect but great benefit would then ensue by the removal of these persons from the high positions in which they have proved their incapacity to deal with questions of peace, order and industry and to given them the opportunity to exert and prove their military prowess.

Atkinson, like Storey, was for laissez-faire – an important strain in anti-imperialist thought. Here was the old liberal tradition in all its wonderful consistency: in favor of private property and peace, and against looting and empire. George E. McNeill put it more simply: "Wealth is not so rapidly gained by killing Filipinos as by making shoes." Andrew Carnegie even offered to purchase the independence of the Philippines with a check for $20 million – the amount the U.S. government had paid Spain for the islands. The *New York Times* denounced the offer as "wicked." (Is the *New York Times* ever right about anything?)

At the same time, labor leaders like Samuel Gompers belonged to the League, as did other people who by some standards belong to the Left, like Jane Addams and William James. It was a cross-ideological organization against empire.

And yet, for all their tireless work, the anti-imperialists by and large failed to spark the national discussion about the role of the U.S. government in the world that we have needed to engage in ever since. Today, that debate takes place only between neoconservatives and "realists," both of whom agree on the need for some kind of major U.S. military presence over much of the globe. Not only is nonintervention not even considered, but it is also enough to get you written out of polite society.

(It may be worth considering someday exactly what opinions do get you branded an extremist, and what don't. It's evidently all right to favor incinerating innocent people in all kinds of scenarios, from Hiroshima to Vietnam – no one who favored those things has since been considered beyond the pale in mainstream political and media circles – but if you resolutely refuse to inciner- ate anyone, you're selfish and irresponsible, and so of course will not appear on television alongside such luminaries as Newt Gingrich and Joe Biden, in whose selflessness and statesmanship you are unworthy to bask.)

In *Freedom and Federalism* (1959), Old Right journalist Felix Morley suggested that the process of empire-building was

> essentially mystical. It must somehow foster the impression that a man is great in the degree that his nation is great; that a German as such is superior to a Belgian as such; an Englishman, to an Irishman; an American, to a Mexican: merely because the first-named countries are in each case more powerful than their comparatives. And people who have no individual stature whatsoever are willing to accept this poison- ous nonsense because it gives them a sense of importance without the trouble of any personal effort.

Morley, a co-founder of *Human Events* newspaper, added that empire-build- ing amounted to

> an application of mob psychology to the sphere of world politics, and how well it works is seen by considering the emotional satisfaction many English long derived from referring to "the Empire on which the sun never sets." Some Americans now get the same sort of lift from the fact that the Stars and Stripes now floats over detachments of "our boys" in forty foreign countries.

(Ah, the old days, when it was only forty.)

States have successfully managed to persuade their subject populations that they themselves are the state, and therefore that any insult to the honor of the state is an insult to them as well, any questioning of its behavior or intentions a slap in their very own faces. It becomes second nature for many people to root for their state in a way that does violence to reason and fact. As I noted in chapter 1, they will defend the most contorted, ludicrous claims –claims they themselves would have dismissed with scorn had they come from Saddam Hussein or the 1980s Soviet Union – if necessary to vindicate the honor of the men who rule them.

The few noble exceptions aside, just flip through a few modern right-wing magazines to see what I mean. It is impossible to speak sensibly about foreign policy when a third of the population (at least) is absolutely committed to digging up anything it can find to vindicate arguments even its own leaders no longer bother to defend. How is conversation possible with someone who contends that hundreds of thousands of casualties, a Shiite-dominated regime, and regional chaos were worth it because we found a negligible amount of chemical agent in Saddam's Iraq?

President Polk, he is our country – that was bad enough. President McKinley, he is our country – that was much worse. But what genuine American patriot, in the sense to which Moorfield Storey referred, could bring himself to say, "George W. Bush, he is our country"? That alone reminds us of how important it is to oppose empire with every ideological tool at our disposal.

December 15, 2006

7

IS JOHN YOO TRYING TO DECEIVE?

Law professor John Yoo is known primarily for his tenure as Deputy Assistant U.S. Attorney General under George W. Bush, during which time he claimed to find constitutional justification for pretty much everything the Bush Administration wanted to do, domestically or overseas, to prosecute the War on Terror. Kevin Gutzman and I answered Yoo pretty decisively, if I may say so, in our book *Who Killed the Constitution?*

I can be fairly tough on my intellectual opponents, but I rarely accuse them of outright lying. In Yoo's case we have to come close. Professor Gutzman, who is an expert on colonial, revolutionary, and early republican Virginia, once told Professor Yoo about documentary evidence he had come across in his research on Virginia that showed Yoo's views on presidential war powers under the Constitution were incorrect. Yoo expressed interest in seeing it, and Gutzman obliged. And Yoo simply continued on as before.

I'm not going to go through all of Yoo's arguments in this most recent article, since I've already done so in that book and on my special page on war powers, to which I direct the interested reader. (See TomWoods.com/warpowers.)

You can guess where Yoo stands on the president's power to bomb Syria without congressional authorization. In a recent article at the FOX News site – you can read it at bit.ly/YooOnSyria – he trots out all the usual arguments (my own personal favorite, that presidents have initiated force on their own "more than 100 times," makes its predictable appearance), most of which are answered at the link above, and the rest in our book.

But I was struck by this particular distortion. He quotes Alexander Hamilton in support of the idea that the colonists did not in fact repudiate the example of King George III, and did grant their president the power to initiate non-defensive military action without congressional approval. (And non-defensive is precisely the issue here: no one in his right mind thinks the bombing of Syria involves saving Americans from an imminent danger.)

Here's Yoo:

> As Alexander Hamilton wrote in Federalist 74, "The direction of war implies the direction of the common strength, and the power of directing and employing the common strength forms a usual and essential part in the definition of the executive authority."

> Presidents should conduct war, he wrote, because they could act with "decision, activity, secrecy, and dispatch." In perhaps his most famous words, Hamilton wrote: "Energy in the executive is a leading character in the definition of good government.... It is essential to the protection of the community against foreign attacks."

Note that Yoo has changed the subject. Now he's talking about "conducting war." No one disputes that the commander-in-chief power gives the president constitutional authority to *conduct* war, *once Congress has declared it*!

And here's what he leaves out from Hamilton, who absolutely *does* repudiate the example of George III, contrary to Yoo. Hamilton writes in Federalist #69 that the president's power

> *would be nominally the same with that of the King of Great Britain, but in substance much inferior to it.* It would amount to nothing more than the supreme command and direction of the military and naval forces, as first general and admiral of the confederacy; while that of the British king extends to the declaring of war, and to the raising and regulating of fleets and

armies; all which by the constitution under consideration would apper-
tain to the Legislature. (Emphasis added.)

Can any reader come up with an explanation for how someone could leave
out this passage when discussing Hamilton's views on presidential war powers —
that is to say, an explanation that doesn't involve deception?

September 4, 2013

PART II

CAPITALISM AND ANTI-CAPITALISM

8

MY ANTI-CAPITALIST TWITTER CRITIC

One day in 2011 I awoke to a barrage of criticisms on my Twitter feed (@ ThomasEWoods) from a progressive who was quite appalled that I would exonerate the free market of blame for child labor, poor working conditions, and the like. She was responding to a blog post in which I linked to a presentation I had made to a group of high school students at the Mises Institute. (It's a useful talk, by the way, which you can find on YouTube under the deceptively boring title "Applying Economics to American History.")

Her tweet read, "How right-wing Ayn Rand disciples INDOCTRINATE high school students" (capitalization hers). Subtle, she isn't.

As I clicked on her various links, I discovered scores, perhaps even hundreds, of common fallacies about the free market. I found very few I hadn't seen numerous times before. I decided to take some of them on – not to persuade my critic, who has already made up her mind, but to help other people respond to arguments like these and to show people on the fence how backward and easily refuted these claims are.

(1) Among her criticisms was the familiar "survival of the fittest" accusation – why, the market rewards the strongest and grinds everyone else into the dust!

But it is precisely in a *pre-capitalist* economy – where the division of labor is poorly established and where capital investment is practically nil – that only the fittest survive. As F.A. Hayek pointed out, before the Industrial Revolution those who could not make a living in agriculture and lacked the tools to support themselves in a craft had no way to integrate themselves into the economy at all. The wealth (and employment opportunities) that the market economy creates makes possible the sheer survival of countless millions of the world's weakest and most vulnerable people, for whom the necessities of life would not previously have existed in sufficient abundance to keep them alive.

It is the capital investment that the unhampered market economy encourages that increases people's real incomes over time and makes the necessities of life less expensive over time, relative to wage rates.

When firms increase and improve the equipment and machinery at the disposal of workers, their labor becomes more productive. Imagine someone using a forklift, as opposed to stacking pallets with his bare hands, or producing books with modern equipment as opposed to a sixteenth-century printing press. The amount of production the economy is capable of is thereby increased, often dramatically, and this increase in production puts corresponding downward pressure on consumer prices (relative to wage rates).

There is nothing natural or inevitable about the availability of this productivity-enhancing capital equipment. It does not fall out of the sky. It comes from the wicked capitalists' abstention from consumption, and the allocation of the unconsumed resources in capital investment.

This process is the only way the general standard of living can rise. Only in this way can the average laborer produce the tiniest fraction of what today he is accustomed to producing. It follows that only under these conditions can he expect to be able to consume the tiniest fraction of what today he is accustomed to consuming.

The increases in the productivity of labor that additional capital brings about push prices down relative to wage rates. By increasing the overall amount of output, such increases raise the ratio of consumers' goods to the supply of labor. Put more simply, improvements in the production process that lead to an increased supply of output make that output cheaper and easier for people to acquire.

That's why, in order to earn the money necessary to acquire a wide range of necessities, far fewer labor hours are necessary today than in the past. Thanks to capital investment, which is what businesses engage in when their profits aren't seized from them, our economy is far more physically productive than it used to be, and therefore consumer goods exist in far greater abundance and are correspondingly less dear relative to wage rates than before.

As I've shown in *Rollback*, the poverty rate in the United States fell from 95 percent in 1900 to around 12-14 percent in the late 1960s – a period in which government antipoverty measures were fairly trivial. By the late 1960s, when Lyndon Johnson's War on Poverty programs began receiving substantial funding, the poverty rate stagnated. By 1994 it was about the same as it had been in the late 1960s, even though the federal government was by that time spending four times as much per capita as it had under LBJ.

Now suppose the situation had been reversed. Suppose the dramatic fall in poverty had occurred under the War on Poverty, and that it was under the free market that the poverty rate had stagnated. We would never hear the end of it: the free market does nothing to eradicate poverty, and only our wise overlords in the political class can do the job! But when exactly the opposite is the case, the facts are simply passed over in silence.

(2) We read in one of her links: "In the ideology of the free market, freedom is conceived as the absence of interference from others. There are no common ends to which our desires are directed. In the absence of such ends, all that remains is the sheer arbitrary power of one will against another. Freedom thus gives way to the aggrandizement of power and the manipulation of will and desire by the greater power."

Let's take this odd paragraph apart one sentence at a time.

(2)(a) "In the ideology of the free market, freedom is conceived as the absence of interference from others."

Correct. Freedom means no one has the right to initiate aggressive force against anyone else. What else could it mean without becoming Orwellian?

(2)(b) "There are no common ends to which our desires are directed."

I'm not entirely sure what this means. True, no one has the right to force anyone else to pursue any particular end he does not wish to pursue, but why is that a bad thing? Would it be better if we could all be coerced into pursuing particular goals? Are we sure the goals of the coercers would always be laudable? Where do the coercers derive the right to decide for everyone else what their goals should be?

And of course it is not true that, just because guys with guns can't order peaceful people around, we have no common ends in a free market. In the market economy we cater to each other's needs. We fit ourselves into that place in the division of labor where our abilities best serve the most urgent needs of our fellow men. Without any commissar having to dictate what to produce, in what quantities, and in what location, we devise structures of production in which labor, capital, and nature-given factors proceed through a series of stages until the finished consumer good is finally reached. It is an astonishing phenomenon, entirely missed by critics.

There are limitless ways business firms can combine factors of production to produce an equally limitless potential array of goods. Thankfully, firms do not have to grope around in the dark amid these trillions of choices.

If their production process uses an input more urgently needed elsewhere, that input gets bid away from them and they find a substitute. If they produce too much of something, their resulting losses prompt them to produce less, thereby releasing resources for the production of another good that consumers value more highly. At all times, resources are directed, in light of consumer wants, to those production processes in which they are most urgently demanded.

No dictators are necessary to force us into the coerced pursuit of common goals in order to bring about this happy outcome.

And far from dog-eat-dog, the resulting structures are fundamentally co-operative, with the industries in lower-order stages of production depending for their success on the output of the higher-order stages, and the higher-order stages depending on the demand of the lower-order ones. Our critic thinks we can't have common goals unless someone holding a monopoly on the initiation of violence – i.e., a government official – forcibly imposes them on us. This strange proposition is contradicted in a billion ways every day the market economy operates – even in the hampered market economy of today. The title of Frédéric Bastiat's book *Economic Harmonies* reflects a central though unjustly neglected insight into the true nature of the market economy.

(2)(c) "In the absence of such ends, all that remains is the sheer arbitrary power of one will against another."

This is supposed to be a description of the market economy. It is instead a description of government. How else do we describe the exercise of force by a privileged class against peaceful individuals, in order that the peaceful individuals be expropriated and ordered about by that privileged class?

No one forces you to buy a Twinkie. But governments do force you to fight in their wars and pay for their bailouts. Some people might consider *that* "sheer arbitrary power."

(2)(d) "Freedom thus gives way to the aggrandizement of power and the manipulation of will and desire by the greater power."

Again, this has things exactly reversed. It is government that does these things. Ever see governments propagandize for war? They manage to turn their populations against peoples they have never even heard of, much less actually met. If it is manipulation of the public our critic opposes, she might start with the political class in which she reposes so much misplaced confidence.

(3) She linked to this quotation from Abraham Lincoln: "Corporations have been enthroned and an era of corruption in high places will follow, and the money power of the country will endeavor to prolong its reign by working upon the prejudices of the people until all wealth is aggregated in a few hands and the Republic is destroyed."

Unfortunately for her, that quotation is a fake. Lincoln never said that.

(4) Another of her tweets read, "Our main enemies: Corporatocracy, American Empire…."

Supporters of the free market agree with her here, so I do not understand what she could be thinking. Meanwhile, her Twitter avatar includes the logo for Obama 2012. This is cognitive dissonance of an unfortunately very common kind. She believes herself to be an opponent of "corporatocracy" and the "American Empire," while lending support to a candidate and a political party that have done as much as anyone else in this country to bring those very things about.

As Anthony Gregory noted in a recent essay, Obama

> shoveled money toward corporate America, banks and car manufacturers. He championed the bailouts of the same Wall Street firms his very partisans blamed for the financial collapse. He picked the CEO of General Electric to oversee the unemployment problem. He appointed corporate state regulars for every major role in financial central planning. After guaranteeing a new era of transparency, he conducted all his regulatory business behind a shroud of unprecedented secrecy. He planned his health care scheme, the crown jewel of his domestic agenda, in league with the pharmaceutical and insurance industries.

As for foreign policy, my critic evidently thinks the American empire, which is the product of a thoroughly bipartisan foreign policy extending over sixty years, is the exclusive creation of wicked Republicans. To the contrary, as Andrew Bacevich shows in his book *Washington Rules*, the foreign-policy differences between people like Hillary Clinton and John McCain are essentially trivial. Hillary was a major supporter of the Iraq war, as were the *New York Times*, the *Washington Post*, and pretty much all the major U.S. newspapers. My critic's own heroes are just as responsible for the morally and economically disastrous American empire project as anyone else.

Again Gregory:

> [Obama] continued the war in Iraq, even extending Bush's schedule with a goal of staying longer than the last administration planned. He

tripled the U.S. presence in Afghanistan then took over two years to announce the eventual drawdown to bring it back to only double the Bush
presence. He widened the war in Pakistan, launching drone attacks at
a dizzying pace. He started a war on false pretenses with Libya, shifting the goal posts and doing it all without Congressional approval. He
bombed Yemen and lied about it.

He enthusiastically signed on to warrantless wiretapping, rendition-
ing, the Patriot Act, prison abuse, detention without trial, violations of
habeas corpus, and disgustingly invasive airport security measures. He
deported immigrants more than Bush did. He increased funding for
the drug war in Mexico. He invoked the Espionage Act more than all
previous presidents combined, tortured a whistleblower, and claimed
the right to unilaterally kill any U.S. citizen on Earth without even a nod
from Congress or a shrug from the courts.

By supporting Obama instead of taking a principled stand against the system, my critic lends aid and comfort to the very "corporatocracy" and "American
empire" she claims to oppose.

(5) "Another problem with the idea of the free market is that humans make decisions based upon the short term rather than the long term."

Assuming this dubious psychological generalization to be true, why would
it not apply equally well to the political class itself? Why would it not apply
equally to the voters who will elect the political class? No one ever answers
this question.

And since the unfunded liabilities of the major transfer programs are greater
than $200 trillion, I think my suspicions are vindicated.

Here her criticism of the market misses the idea of capital value. Does she go
80,000 miles between oil changes? I'll assume not. But if it is some kind of psychological law that "humans make decisions based upon the short term rather
than the long run," then why doesn't she? She can save money today, in the short
term, by neglecting the maintenance of her car and therefore its performance in

the long run. Who cares about the car's condition two years from now? That's the long term! Human beings, she says, don't care about that.

When you own a car, you own the rights to the flow of services it can render over the course of its useful life. That alone gives you ample incentive to think about the long term. The longer a durable good's useful life is, the more services it can render its owner. Therefore, property owners have an interest in taking actions that will increase the lifespan of the good in question.

Do governments operate under such incentives? Of course not. As Hans-Hermann Hoppe has frequently pointed out, the caretakers who operate the machinery of state in a democratic system do not own the resources they employ. Unlike private owners, therefore, they have no economic incentive to preserve the capital value of the country. It does not matter to them how long its capital stock lasts, how much debt it accumulates, or how many of its citizens it conscripts and leads to slaughter. These are all long-term questions. Their effects will be felt long after the politicians in question are retired.

(6) "This [alleged psychological law according to which people act only with very short time horizons] enables shrewd individuals or groups to manipulate markets and exploit individuals for their own gain. The invisible hand Smith described is either too slow or becomes too entangled to effectively make corrections to the market in sufficient time to prevent real, long term, harm from occurring. Consequently free-market corrections can produce enormous misery for the many while they take their sweet time to correct the market."[1]

I do not understand this passage. Evidently individuals or groups "manipulate markets" and "exploit individuals," though no examples or definitions of these terms are provided. This anti-social behavior apparently causes the entire market economy to suffer, such that a wrenching recovery process is necessary. These recoveries take too long, and cause further suffering.

Assuming for the sake of argument that these market manipulations, which are never defined or illustrated, really are the cause of recessions – and with the

---

[1] These lengthier and clearer passages are not my critic's words, but words she borrowed without attribution.

relevant terms not defined and a causal mechanism not even hinted at, I think I am ascribing more dignity to this position than it deserves – we are left to wonder why the economy is not in a state of permanent recession. Aren't greedy manipulators everywhere? If so, why does greed manifest itself only in cyclical patterns, rather than constantly?

Nowhere in my critic's brief is the Federal Reserve System even mentioned. (That is revealing but unfortunately rather typical: an alleged opponent of "corporatocracy" cannot bring herself to mention the institution that backstops some of the fattest of American cats.) She is not even curious enough to wonder what supporters of the free market – whom she imagines as little men with white mustaches, running about carrying sacks of money with dollar signs on them – might think causes economic downturns.

Our position actually involves a full-fledged theory, not merely a vague pointing of fingers at economic malefactors. In our theory, the central bank, the very institution our critic neglects as if it had absolutely nothing to do with the condition of the economy, interferes with credit markets to push interest rates to below-market levels, thereby setting the stage for a series of consequences that produces first an artificial boom and then an inevitable bust. I explain it in greater detail in my 2009 book (and *New York Times* bestseller) *Meltdown*.

The boom-bust cycle, according to the Austrian School of economics, is caused not by the market economy per se but by this intervention into the market. The bust, in turn, is brief or prolonged depending on the response by government. The first time government responded to a depression with a ceaseless program of intervention, namely the Great Depression, was also the first one to last so long.

Again, suppose the situation were reversed. Suppose the depression of 1920-21, in which the federal government and the Federal Reserve did next to nothing, had persisted for a decade, but the Great Depression had lasted only a year or two after the New Deal programs were instituted. We would never hear the end of it: why, this proves the stupid free market can't correct itself! We need our wise overlords!

But when the truth of the matter is exactly the opposite, we hear only crickets.

(7) "FREE MARKET ENCOURAGES the elimination of the weak."

Then why have population figures and life expectancy exploded under capitalism? Why do the poorest enjoy the greatest material advantages in those countries where the free market is least hampered by violent intervention?

(8) "It quickly became apparent that humans could be sold products with lower or even negative utility by appealing to the consumer on a deeper emotional level…. This discovery along with mass advertising enabled by mass communication effectively destroyed the free market observed by Adam Smith."

This is a bastardized version of John Kenneth Galbraith's critique of the market. According to this argument, the market isn't really free because advertising brainwashes consumers into buying whatever product a clever firm offers them. But as Murray Rothbard noted long ago, if this critique were correct we would have a hard time accounting for how much money firms devote to marketing research to try to ascertain whether consumer demand exists for the product they seek to develop. Why bother spending so much time and money figuring out what consumers want if a clever advertisement is enough to snooker them into buying almost anything? Why would any firm or industry ever suffer losses?

All the advertising in the world couldn't save New Coke or the Edsel, and once people can download music in mp3 format or watch streaming movies, no amount of celebrity endorsements is going to prop up Sam Goody's or Blockbuster.

(9) Capitalism creates inequality!

As Ludwig von Mises observed, in the old days the rich traveled in a coach-and-four while the poor traveled on foot. That is inequality. Today the rich travel in fancy cars while the poor travel in run-down cars. That is a dramatic reduction in inequality. This is all the more true when we consider that the amenities many poor people now have *in their cars* would have been unheard of in the richest people's *homes* just four generations ago.

The American middle class and poor take for granted amenities that the greatest kings and queens of Europe could scarcely have imagined. Over the course of the twentieth century the real incomes of the poor increased by 1900 percent, a far greater increase than any other economic group enjoyed.

Most arguments about income inequality are based on static analysis. They speak of the "lowest quintile" earning a certain amount in 1990 and a certain amount in 2000. We are then supposed to grieve over these numbers. But the numbers are so static as to disconnect them from reality. They neglect to add that people in the lowest quintile in 1990 are not the same people as those in 2000. Robert Murphy, quoting a 1995 report from the Dallas Fed, points out that fully 29 percent of those in the bottom quintile of income in 1975 had moved to the very top quintile by 1991. This movement among quintiles is not captured at all in the standard figures.

More interesting still is that the top 25 most economically free countries have more equal income distributions than the bottom 25, using the Gini coefficient that economists use to measure inequality.

Finally, the market economy has repeatedly tried to cut the most politically connected men of wealth down to size, but my critic's own political hero, Barack Obama, has supported bailing them out. That is not the free market's fault.

(10) Her complaints included a tweet directing me to the "Catholic Church condemning free-market philosophy."

Well, I have written an entire book on this, after all – the prize-winning 2005 book *The Church and the Market: A Catholic Defense of the Free Economy* – not to mention quite a few articles, so presumably there is a teensy bit to be said for my side of things.

(11) Unhampered capitalism yielded the terrible "robber barons" of the late nineteenth century.

First of all, it is clear from her other posts that my critic thinks unhampered capitalism is pretty much what we have now. We are supposed to overlook the 80,000 pages of regulation – all of which is innocently aimed at protecting the common good, of course – in the Federal Register added to the Code of Federal Regulations every year. We are not supposed to think about the hundreds of federal agencies (not to mention those of state and local governments), the millions of federal employees whose salaries are paid out of the productive labor of the rest of the population, and the trillions of dollars in taxes.

She likewise thinks the banking system is pretty close to a free market – after all, hasn't she seen news reports about bank "deregulation"? To the contrary, the banking system is perhaps the least free-market sector of the entire economy. The whole system is overseen by the government-created Federal Reserve System, which presides over a system-wide cartel. It involves monopolistic legal tender laws, a monopoly of the note issue, artificial disabilities on other media of exchange apart from the depreciating dollar, and various forms of bailout guarantees. For a sense of what a free market in banking would actually look like, read Murray N. Rothbard's *The Mystery of Banking*.

And that's not to mention the layers of cronyism all through the federal apparatus, most obviously within the military-industrial-congressional complex. That's another area I cover in *Rollback*. What does any of this have to do with capitalism?

(As for the robber barons themselves, see chapter 12.)

It is not easy to understand the hostility toward a system that has made possible the greatest explosion in wealth and living standards in human history, and which has done more to eradicate poverty than all the rock stars and government transfer programs put together.

July 8, 2011

9

DOES THE MARKET MAKE EVERYTHING A COMMODITY?

More clichés have been directed at the market economy than at just about any other social phenomenon. Reading through the proceedings of an international symposium from 1982, edited by Walter Block and Irving Hexham, I came across this remark: "The free market philosophy and social reality makes us look at the whole of social life as a market.…. It leads people to regard everything that surrounds them as merchandise, as having a price, as an object to be used."

Now it doesn't matter who said this, though I owe it to the editors at least to note that neither of them was the guilty party. (I doubt Walter Block would say something like that even under threat of torture.) It is not an unusual argument: the free market allegedly "commodifies" everything, and reduces all of life to a matter of dollars and cents.

But is that really what the market does?

Murray Rothbard described the free market as simply "the social array of voluntary exchanges of goods and services." In titling one of his books *Power and Market* (originally intended to be the closing section of *Man, Economy and State*) Rothbard was positioning "power" and "market" as antinomies. The market consists of voluntary transactions between willing parties; the state, or "power," introduces compulsion into human relations, bringing about coerced outcomes that people would not voluntarily have chosen.

If power and market are opposites, let us contrast the pure market economy with a pure exertion of power – the military draft. The draft consists of a group of people who comprise the state declaring the right to employ the physical bodies of its subjects in a conflict involving the infliction of violence and the serious risk of death. The moral hazard involved in the draft is obvious: the state will be more prepared to wage wars, and to engage in tactics likely to involve significant loss of life, if the cost of such activity is socialized and the soldiers they use are, from the state's point of view, essentially costless. If there are plenty more where that hundred thousand came from, and none of the authorities must bear any direct cost for the loss of life, we can expect more recklessness with human life than would otherwise exist.

Now our critic says that the market "leads people to regard everything that surrounds them as merchandise, as having a price, as an object to be used." But isn't that exactly what the *state* does in the case of the draft, this most non-market of transactions? It views the populace as raw material to be employed, involuntarily, in perilous and violent pursuit of the state's goals – in other words, as "an object to be used." Except the state doesn't even pay a mutually agreeable price for the labor it conscripts!

This is how the state behaves all the time. It need not interact with people justly or with any concern for their preferences or rights at all, much less actually arrive at mutually satisfactory terms with them. It may act unilaterally, and the individual has no recourse other than to accept whatever the state determines with regard to how much of his property will be expropriated, what his children will be taught in school, or where he must be sent to fight and die.

Market prices serve an important function, apart from making possible both economic calculation and the indefinite extension of the division of labor. Market prices imply ownership, which in turn implies the right of disposal over the thing owned. If I don't meet your price, you need not perform your labor service for me. If I don't meet your price, you need not relinquish your property to me. They remind us that social cooperation must involve genuine *cooperation*, which means that no one side of a transaction has the right to cheat or steal from the other. Instead, they must reach terms that are mutually satisfactory in order for a transaction to take place.

Market prices, in other words, are not artificial, wicked things that discourage social cooperation. They make social cooperation, properly understood, possible in the first place. They convey the rule that we may not simply walk around as self-absorbed savages, taking whatever we want from whomever we want, as if nothing and no one can trump our demands and desires. We must be willing to offer something in exchange for the things we acquire, such that the person providing them – instead of being exploited by us, with no thought to his well-being at all – can see his own condition improved as well.

With the state, on the other hand, the price is whatever the state says it is. It will provide services you do not want, will never use, and may even find morally repugnant, and then tell you what you must pay for them. In the case of eminent domain, where the state confiscates your property for its own purposes, you will be paid *something*, but the state itself will decide exactly what it will pay you. How is this preferable to a world in which each individual is allowed to declare the terms on which he will dispose of his person and property, and in which no exchange takes place unless both parties voluntarily agree to it?

It is the *state*, then, and not the market, that "regards everything that surrounds [it] as merchandise...as an object to be used." Precisely because it acts outside of the market, the state can devise arbitrary prices for its services, make those prices vary across different classes of people, and then threaten physical force against anyone refusing to pay them. Who in civil society is allowed to behave like that?

Now our critic may say that he does not wish to dispense with the market altogether,

but that he wishes to see the market play less of a role in society, and to foster a more democratic and communitarian approach to property and its use. But neither voting nor flowery language affects the moral question in the slightest. If a majority of voters vote to expropriate me or to send me to fight one of the state's battles overseas, the situation is morally no different than if the state had done these things according to its own whims.

And to the extent that the market plays less of a role in society, to the very same extent do arbitrariness and force take its place. If the free interaction of property owners is not permitted to determine the terms on which individuals will interact with each other, the barrel of a gun must do so instead. Then we'll see which system treats everything as "an object to be used."

Nothing is easier or more fashionable than to condemn the alleged materialism of the market, but this kind of rhetoric is the enemy of rational thought. It is private property and market prices or the law of the jungle, and no amount of fashionable cynicism about the market or romantic delusions about how nice life would be without it can obscure this fundamental choice.

September 18, 2006

10

WERE WE RICH AND AWESOME WHEN TAXES WERE HIGHER?

John Kenneth Galbraith said in 1965 that there was no problem in New York that couldn't be solved by doubling the city's budget. By the 1970s the budget had been tripled, and the city's problems were worse than ever.

That embarrassing moment came to mind when I read this bit of nonsense circulating on the Internet: "In the 1950s and 1960s, when the top tax rate was 70-92%, we laid the interstate highway system, built the Internet, put a man on the moon, defeated Communism, our education system was the envy of the world, our middle class thriving, our economy unparalleled. You want that back? Raise taxes on the rich."

Now for the truth.

(1) Via loopholes or outright tax evasion, these tax rates were not paid, as tax accountants can tell you.

(2) Big spending programs are not evidence of prosperity; the U.S. government could duplicate any of these programs today.

(3) Left out is that when our education system was supposedly "the envy of the world," it was spending *far* less per capita, adjusting for inflation, than it does

today. From the early 1970s to 2003 alone, spending per capita doubled. So the Left has actually gotten its wish, though it pretends it hasn't. Meanwhile, Japan, spending one-third as much per capita, and with much larger class sizes, vastly outperforms the U.S.

Moreover, there is no connection between higher education spending and higher SAT scores. In fact, some of the highest scores are earned in states that spend the least on education. Washington, D.C., which spends the most, is dead last.

(4) The prosperity of the 1960s was fueled in good measured by the inflationary policies of the Federal Reserve. In John F. Kennedy's three years as president, M2 growth averaged about 8 percent per year, far higher than in the 1950s. This produces resource misallocation that can look like prosperity. This false prosperity is self-reversing. By 1970, just as Arthur Okun, influential White House economist throughout the 1960s, was boasting that the business cycle had been tamed forever, the recession began.

Americans paid for that false prosperity with a decade of inflation and stagnation. As economist Mark Thornton points out, "From the beginning of 1946 to the beginning of 1965 the consumer price index increased by 71.4%, but then increased 20% by the end of the decade. From 1965 – when the experiment began in earnest – to the end of 1980 the CPI increased by 176.6%. The experiment had tripled the rate of inflation experienced by consumers."

It's not just price inflation and unemployment we should look to for the full story, though. Again Thornton:

> A better indication is to be found in the fact that in May 1970, a portfolio consisting of one share of every stock listed on the Big Board was worth just about half of what it would have been worth at the start of 1969. The high flyers that had led the market of 1967 and 1968 – conglomerates, computer leasers, far-out electronics companies, franchisers – were precipitously down from their peaks. Nor were they down 25 percent, like the Dow, but 80, 90, or 95 percent. This was vintage 1929 stuff, and the prospect of another great depression, this one induced as much by despair as by economic factors as such, was a very real one.

The stock market as measured by the Dow did decrease 25% between 1969 and 1971 and then…lost another 20% by mid-1975. However, the real losses in the stock market were larger and longer lasting than an ordinary chart of the Dow might suggest…. Stocks tended to trade in a wide channel for much of the period between 1965 and 1984. However, if you adjust the value of stocks by price inflation as measure by the Consumer Price Index, a clearer and more disturbing picture emerges. The inflation-adjusted or real purchasing power measure of the Dow indicates that it lost nearly 80% of its peak value.

No wonder the tax-raisers want to talk about the 1960s, but then pretend that the equally high-tax 1970s never occurred.

(5) Kennedy used the economy of the 1950s against Vice President Richard Nixon in the election of 1960. Economic growth averaged 2.4% per year under Dwight Eisenhower — not a bad record, to be sure, but hardly the earth-shattering, historically unique figure one might expect in light of the constant references to the 1950s.

(6) It was not unthinkable in the 1950s that a family might not have a telephone, a refrigerator (some still had iceboxes), or a television. (Bearing in mind that Ralph was a cheapskate, the Kramdens in *The Honeymooners* lacked all these things, and the program was not laughed out of court as silly or implausible.) Anyone wanting to live at that standard of living today can do so with precious little effort. Today, by contrast, 85% of Americans own cell phones, a technology that would have seemed out of science fiction in the 1950s.

(7) Government and its predation on the economy have grown far greater in the meantime. The overall tax burden for ordinary families has grown dramatically. "The most important change in the balance sheets of middle-class households over the past three decades is a dramatically higher tax burden caused by the progressive nature of the American tax system," writes law professor Todd Zywicki. "For the typical 1970s family, paying 24% of its income in taxes works out to be $9,288. And for the 2000s family, paying 33% of its income is $22,374."

(8) Reducing taxes on "the rich" means more funds available for capital investment, which is the central mechanism by which poverty has been alleviated and living standards have been vastly improved all over the world.

(9) Even if we were to accept that the 1950s were the summit of human happiness, correlation does not prove causation. How do we know there wouldn't have been even greater prosperity had taxes been lower? Supporters of this view would have to provide us with a causal mechanism explaining why the violent seizure of property and its expenditure on economically arbitrary projects would make a country more prosperous than employing those funds in capital investment to increase the productivity of labor.

I can point to plenty of relatively limited-government places around the world that are doing very well economically. My critics would refuse to accept that this proves anything. They are partly right. Without a theoretical understanding of what produces prosperity, we can't know if country A is prosperous because of or in spite of policy B.

(10) The U.S. "defeated communism" in the 1950s and 1960s? The timing seems a bit off. And when the system did collapse, it collapsed because it defeated itself, as free-market economists had predicted it would.

April 16, 2012

11

PLUNDER OR ENTERPRISE: THE WORLD'S CHOICE

I delivered these remarks at the Cato Institute in early 2007, after having won the first prize in the books category of the Templeton Enterprise Awards for The Church and the Market. *All book and article winners were invited to address a special Cato event.*

Although supporters of the market economy often have good reason for pessimism, it is important, especially in this age of globalization, not to lose sight of the genuine victories that the classical liberal tradition can boast. Half a century ago, Gunnar Myrdal could declare: "The special advisers to underdeveloped countries who have taken the time and trouble to acquaint themselves with the problem, no matter who they are...all recommend central planning as the first condition of progress." At that time, development economists who dissented from this consensus could have fit inside a phone booth. Today, economists who still favor central planning for the less-developed countries may as well hold their convention in a phone booth.

Public protests against globalization – protests that occur by and large in the prosperous West – denounce free trade and the mobility of capital as instruments of exploitation and oppression. The great development economist Peter Bauer used to say that if that were the case, then we should find the greatest prosperity among those less-developed countries that have the fewest economic connections to the West, and that those places that are altogether isolated – and therefore suffer from none of this alleged exploitation at all – should be paradise on earth. Needless to say, that is not even close to what we find, and most serious observers know it.

Today practically everyone agrees that some kind of market economy is essential if the less-developed countries are to progress to developed status. There are differences of opinion, to be sure, and the so-called "new development economics" of the past decade holds far more peril than promise. But that the terms of the debate have shifted there can be little doubt.

As globalization has proceeded, the subject of the market economy has attracted more and more attention, with friend and foe alike seeking to understand the implications of the creation of a truly global marketplace. One of the market's virtues, and the reason it enables so much peaceful interaction and cooperation among such a great variety of peoples, is that it demands of its participants only that they observe a relatively few basic principles, among them honesty, the sanctity of contracts, and respect for private property.

This is not to say that the philosophical principles the market embodies come naturally to every cultural milieu. Peter Bauer always insisted that a people's religious, philosophical, and cultural values could have important consequences for their economic success or failure. A people who believe in fatalism or collectivism, rather than in personal responsibility, will be less likely to undertake the risks associated with capitalist entrepreneurship, for example.

Or consider the example of tenth-century China. Rodney Stark points out that a substantial iron industry was beginning to flourish there at that time, producing an estimated thirty-five thousand tons of iron per year – a figure that ultimately grew to a hundred thousand. This abundance of iron translated into better agricultural tools, which in turn meant increased food production. Great wealth was being created, and China's economic prospects seemed excellent.

The imperial court, on the other hand, decided that all this accumulation of wealth by mere commoners amounted to an intolerable departure from pure Confucian principle, which imagined great wealth in the hands only of society's elite, and demanded that commoners be satisfied with their lot. The government simply seized the entire industry, and this wonderful example of innovation and wealth creation was crushed. Here is an example of cultural values that were incompatible with a market economy.

But I want to go even further, and suggest that morality and the market are mutually reinforcing. It isn't merely that the market requires certain moral attributes in order to function properly. The market itself encourages moral behavior.

It takes little imagination to surmise how critics of the market would respond to such a claim. Doesn't the market encourage greed, rivalry, and discord? Does it not urge people to think only of themselves, accumulating wealth with no thought to any other concern?

That human beings seek their own well-being and that of those close to them is not an especially provocative discovery. What is important is that this universal aspect of human nature persists no matter what economic system is in place; it merely expresses itself in different forms. For all their saccharine rhetoric, for example, communist apparatchiks were not known for their disinterested commitment to the common good. They, too, sought to improve their own well-being – except they lived in a system in which all such improvements came at the expense of their fellow human beings, rather than, as in a market economy, as a reward for serving them.

Communism brought out the worst in human nature, and crippled people's ability or ambition to participate in a market economy. "Traveling around the country," wrote American reporter Hedrick Smith in 1990, "I came to see the great mass of Soviets as protagonists in what I call the culture of envy. In this culture, corrosive animosity took root under the czars in the deep-seated collectivism in Russian life and then was cultivated by Leninist ideology. Now it has turned rancid under the misery of everyday living."

> The Soviet ruling class, with their cushy cars, clinics, and country homes, are a natural enough target for the wrath of the little people. But what is ominous for Gorbachev's reforms is that this free-floating anger, the jealousy of the rank and file, often lights on anyone who rises above the crowd – anyone who works harder, gets ahead, and becomes better off, even if his gains are honestly earned. This hostility is a serious danger to the new entrepreneurs whom Gorbachev is trying to nurture. It is a deterrent to even modest initiative among ordinary people in factories or on farms. It freezes the vast majority into the immobility of conforming to the group.

Under the system of tyranny and deprivation that the Russian people were forced to endure for seven decades, illicit "profiteering" – "think of the worker stealing wheelbarrows and multiply him by a million," one writer says – made it possible for countless Russians to acquire the goods they needed. We might therefore expect the profiteer to emerge as at least vaguely heroic, but the actual effect seems to have been to poison the idea of profit in the minds of many Russians, since they came to assume that anyone making a profit must be engaged in behavior that was somehow illicit or underhanded.

The countless stories in the Soviet press, as late in the socialist experiment as the 1980s, about vandalism and attacks on small shops by those who resented the success of their fellow man "bear witness to the powerful influence of decades of Leninist indoctrination," Smith explained. "For great masses of Soviet people, capitalism is still a dirty word, and the fact that someone earns more, gets more, is a violation of the egalitarian ideal of socialism. Tens of millions of Soviets deeply mistrust the market, fearing they will be cheated and outsmarted. They see the profit motive as immoral."

The Supreme Soviet's Anatoly Sobchak once remarked, "Our people cannot endure seeing someone else earn more than they do.... They are so jealous of other people that they want others to be worse off, if need be, to keep things equal." Sobchak described this attitude as one of the chief obstacles to economic reform. Television personality Dmitri Zakharov put it this way: "In the West, if an American sees someone on TV with a shiny new car, he will think, 'Oh, maybe I can get that someday for myself.' But if a Russian sees that, he will think, 'This bastard with his car. I would like to kill him for living better than I do.'" That is what Marxism-Leninism did to these people.

That system, the polar opposite of the free market, encouraged greed in the ruling class and apathy, envy, and alienation among everyone else. Scarcely anyone defends it any longer. At the same time, we are urged not to let the socialist debacle sour us on the state itself, which we are told is an indispensable instrument in the pursuit of "social justice." But the less predatory state that such critics have in mind carries its own moral and cultural perils, only a few of which we can consider here.

Economists speak of the disutility of labor. Albert Jay Nock referred to the human inclination to seek after wealth with the least possible exertion. In a formulation familiar to libertarians, Franz Oppenheimer described two ways of acquiring wealth: the economic means and the political means. The economic means involves the production of a good or service that is then sold to willing buyers seeking to improve their own well-being. Both parties benefit. The political means, on the other hand, involves the use of force to enrich one party or group at the expense of another – either to acquire someone else's wealth directly or to give oneself an unfair advantage over his competitors through the use or threat of coercion. That is a much easier way of enriching oneself; and since people tend to prefer an easier over a more difficult path to wealth, a society that hopes to foster both justice and prosperity needs to discourage wealth acquisition via the political means and encourage it through the economic means.

But the state, wrote Oppenheimer, was the organization of the political means of wealth acquisition. It was through this channel that people could find paths to their own economic well-being that involved the use of force – carried out on their behalf by the state – rather than their own honest work. For that reason, the baser aspects of human nature can find in the state an irresistible attraction. It is easier to become dependent on welfare than to work; it is easier to accept farm subsidies and thereby to increase food prices than it is to compete honorably and freely; and it is easier to file an antitrust complaint against a competitor than to out-compete him honestly in the marketplace. By making these and countless other predatory options possible, the state fosters unattractive moral attributes and appeals to the worst features of human nature.

In short order, society degenerates into a condition of low-intensity civil war, with each pressure group anxious to secure legislation aimed at enriching itself at the expense of the rest of society. The Hobbesian war of all against all that allegedly characterizes life under the pre-political state of nature creeps into political life itself, as even those who were initially reluctant to seek political favors pursue them with vigor, if only to break even (that is, vis-à-vis groups who are less scrupulous about using the state to secure their ends). All of this looting under cover of law is what Frédéric Bastiat memorably called "legal plunder."

The same phenomena are observable around the world, when misguided development aid programs have strengthened the interventionist state in less-developed nations. Ben Powell makes the important point, echoing Peter Bauer, that the fashionable proposals we hear about nowadays that seek to direct foreign aid to responsible, relatively non-predatory regimes miss the point: these aid programs are inherently bad, no matter how selectively the funds are allocated. Not only do they tend to enlarge the public sector of the recipient country, but competition for a share of the grant money also diverts private resources away from the satisfaction of genuine wants and into a wasteful, anti-social expenditure of time and resources for the purpose of winning government favors.

If the state is the organization of the political means of wealth acquisition, then the market is the embodiment of the economic means. The market all but compels people to be other-regarding, but not by means of intimidation, threats, and propaganda, as in socialist and statist systems. It employs the perfectly normal, morally acceptable desire to improve one's material conditions and station in life, both of which can grow under capitalism only by directing one's efforts to the production of a good or service that improves the well-being of his fellow man. This is why the title of Frédéric Bastiat's book *Economic Harmonies* is such a beautiful encapsulation of the classical liberal message. (The American Anti-Imperialist League's George McNeill made essentially the same observation, if perhaps more vividly, in the late 1890s: "Wealth is not so rapidly gained by killing Filipinos as by making shoes.")

John Rawls famously argued in *A Theory of Justice* that we could judge a society on the basis of the material condition of the least well-off. The market wins according to that moral criterion as well. Professor Robert Lawson has shown that all around the world, the poor are consistently better off in the least interventionist, most market-oriented societies. America's poor are better off than much of the European middle class today, and better off than the American middle class of the 1950s.

This happy outcome follows from the very nature of capitalism. When businesses invest in capital equipment to render the production process more efficient, they make it possible to produce more goods at a lower unit cost. Competition then passes these cost cuts on to the consumer in the form of lower prices (a phenomenon not always so visible in an inflationary economy, but at work all the same). This greater abundance increases the purchasing power of all real incomes, and thereby redounds to the benefit of everyone.

Needless to say, the market possesses a great many virtues in addition to these. But what we might call the Enron objection will at this point be raised:

doesn't that fiasco reflect a serious moral problem at the heart of capitalism? Enron, it is said, was the free market in action, and Ken Lay an apostle of laissez faire. In fact, neither claim is true. Time constraints limit me to recommending the Enron chapter in Tim Carney's helpful book *The Big Ripoff: How Big Business and Big Government Steal Your Money* (2006). To make a long story short, Enron was on the receiving end of countless waves of government subsidies. It also manipulated the bizarre regulatory thicket that was the California energy market in grotesquely anti-social ways that enriched Enron at the expense, quite literally, of everyone else. The Cato Institute's Jerry Taylor correctly described Enron on balance as "an enemy, not an ally of free markets. Enron was more interested in rigging the marketplace with rules and regulations to advantage itself at the expense of competitors and consumers than in making money the old-fashioned way – by earning it honestly from their customers through voluntary trade."

Enron was in fact punished by the market for its behavior, while the American government, awash in Ponzi schemes, accounting irregularities, and unfunded liabilities it can't possibly cover, goes about its business in peace. "Far from an example of a market failure," argues Jacksonville State University's Christopher Westley, "Enron's saga shows that firms which invest too much in politics can easily become complacent in the face of changing market conditions.... If there's a scandal to be found in the Enron debacle, it is this: Enron's faith that its political investments would eventually solve its problems caused it to avoid making necessary changes in its organization until it was too late. Anyone who checks Enron's stock price, now listed on one of the penny stock exchanges, knows that the market has penalized this strategy." Amazon.com and Kmart, on the other hand, were up front with their investors about their financial difficulties, and ended up doing much better – by and large, their investors, no doubt impressed by these firms' honesty and transparency, stuck by them.

The nature of the attacks on capitalism frequently changes: one day it's the corruption of businessmen, as with Enron, the next it's environmental degradation (which is typically the fault of poorly developed property rights and arbitrary regulatory regimes rather than of capitalism itself). Sometimes capitalism will be criticized for one alleged failing one day and exactly the opposite failing the next. Thus socialists once claimed that capitalism was less efficient than socialism, and could not produce in nearly the same abundance. Now that that argument has been silenced, we have begun to hear exactly the opposite claim: capitalism brings about *too much* wealth, and makes people materialistic and fat. As Joseph Schumpeter put it, "Capitalism stands its trial before judges who have the sentence of death in their pockets. They are going to pass it, whatever the defense they may hear; the only success a victorious defense can possibly produce is a change in the indictment." For a system that has brought about such astonishing and unprecedented advances in the well-being of the great mass of mankind, it is surprisingly vulnerable to attack.

Murray Rothbard was fond of citing the arguments of Étienne de La Boétie (as well as those of such later figures as David Hume and Ludwig von Mises) to the effect that governments survive or perish on the basis of public opinion. Since those who rule are of necessity vastly outnumbered by those who are ruled, it is curious that *any* regime – much less the truly oppressive – should get away with it for so long. The only way they can do so, according to these men, is through the voluntary consent of the public. That consent need not take the form of wild enthusiasm, which is rarely forthcoming for any regime; passive resignation is quite enough.

If a critical mass of the population withdraws that consent, on the other hand, regimes collapse. The fall of the communist regimes in eastern Europe was a textbook example of exactly what La Boétie meant: when next to no one obeys commands any longer, how can the ruling elite hold on to power?

It is not only political regimes but also economic systems that must pass a public opinion test if they are to endure. And here we encounter an essential cultural attribute for the maintenance of a free economy: a critical mass of the population must consider market exchange, and the institutional supports that make it possible, to be fundamentally just.

And yet from our major institutions here in the United States we hear something like the opposite. Schoolchildren are given the impression that the private sector is the source of all wickedness and oppression, from which public-spirited government officials, in their selfless commitment to justice, must rescue and protect us. The selection of subject matter itself exhibits a pro-state bias: students leave school knowing all about how a bill becomes a law, for example, but with no idea of how markets work.

All of this applies just as strongly to popular culture and the media, with of course a few noble exceptions like John Stossel. That is why I am surprised not by how much of the market economy has been suppressed in the United States, but by how much has managed to survive in the face of a hostile educational and cultural establishment. Europe's opinion molders, as Olaf Gersemann observes in his book *Cowboy Capitalism*, are utterly contemptuous of American capitalism, a phenomenon they do not understand, and it is not surprising that in such an intellectual milieu those countries find themselves burdened with even more statism than we do.

We are being much too ambitious if we think even the best economic institutions can transform human beings from flawed creatures into saints. The correction of human failings is the business of families, churches, and voluntary organizations of all kinds. The twentieth century served, among other things, as an extended lesson in both the danger and the folly of state-led efforts to transform human nature. We can be more than satisfied if our economic system is content to take human beings as they are, direct their energies into productive rather than anti-social outlets, and reward them for satisfying the needs of their fellow men.

Thomas Jefferson once observed that the mass of mankind was not "born with saddles on their backs, nor a favored few booted and spurred, ready to ride them." That is what the free economy is all about: anyone is free to serve the public in the manner he thinks best, and no one, not even those who have been most successful in the past, can claim exemption from the daily referenda that take place whenever the public decides to buy or to abstain from buying what he has to sell.

To my ear, the term "culture of enterprise" [TW note: the theme of this conference] suggests a society that possesses a conscious appreciation of the distinct virtues of the market economy, some of which I have described here, and why it is morally and materially superior to statist alternatives, as I have also described here. In other words, the points I have made in my remarks today are the kind of arguments that should resonate with and constitute important pillars for a culture of enterprise. Instead of being held up for condemnation and abuse, entrepreneurs in such a society would be respected and honored for the risks they assume with their own property in order to bring improvement to people's lives, from the latest technological innovation to the most mundane of necessities. For a true culture of enterprise to last, people must see in the unhampered market economy not merely the least intolerable system but a positive good, in which living standards consistently rise, human creativity is given free rein, and human interaction proceeds on the civilized basis of respect for others' person and property.

The decades following World War II taught anyone who was paying attention how *not* to encourage prosperity or escape from less-developed status: demonize producers and the successful, nationalize industry, harass foreign investors, make property insecure, institute "import substitution" policies, and suffocate entrepreneurship through regulation. Development aid programs, meanwhile, either expressly endorsed these policies (as in the case of import substitution) or enabled them to continue by masking the true effects of such disastrous measures or propping up the regimes that implemented them. If the less-developed countries are to grow prosperous, they must abandon the destructive and wicked policies of the past, discard the culture of envy their leaders have fostered, and embrace the principles of freedom that have allowed more people than ever before in history to enjoy the material conditions of civilized life.

And at a time when our countrymen are being courted by all manner of interventionist politicians – with one noble exception, I hasten to add – peddling all kinds of grandiose schemes for human betterment, Americans themselves could stand to be reminded of the values that inform a culture of enterprise. There was something disturbing, and yet revealing, in the title of MSNBC's election coverage segment last year – Battleground: America. Every two years, but especially every four, the country becomes in effect a battleground between opposing forces, in which the winner acquires the power to take the country to war unilaterally, to impose a uniform social policy on 310 million Americans, and to implement all manner of policies on his own authority, by means of executive orders and signing statements. Americans typically take for granted that this is normal, and indeed how life must be.

But in fact we don't need Hillary Clinton or John Edwards, Rudy Giuliani or John McCain, to "run the country" (to use an infelicitous if unfortunately common phrase) or to make us prosperous. A free and responsible people can manage its affairs without the platitudes and paternal custodianship of a Great Leader, and exhibits no superstitious reverence toward the occupants of political office. Once a society begins to absorb this revolutionary discovery, it has already embraced the culture of enterprise.

May 18, 2007

12

THE MISPLACED FEAR OF "MONOPOLY"

Those of us who get drawn, often against our better judgment, into Internet debates soon discover that the case against the market economy in the popular mind boils down to a few major claims. Here I intend to dissect one of them: under the unhampered market we'd be at the mercy of vicious monopolists.

This fear can be attributed in part, no doubt, to the cartoon history of the nineteenth century virtually all of us were exposed to in school. There we learned that rapacious "robber barons" gained overwhelming market share in their industries by means of all sorts of underhanded tricks, and then, once secure in their position, turned around and fleeced the helpless consumer, who had no choice but to pay the high prices that these firms' "monopoly" position made possible.

This version of events is so deeply embedded in Americans' brains that it is next to impossible to dislodge it, no matter the avalanche of evidence and argument applied against it.

Historian Burton Folsom made an important distinction, in his book *The Myth of the Robber Barons*, between political entrepreneurs and market entrepreneurs. The political entrepreneur succeeds by using the implicit violence of government to cripple his competitors and harm consumers. The market entrepreneur, on the other hand, makes his fortune by providing consumers with products they need at prices they can afford, and maintains and expands his market share by remaining innovative and responsive to consumer demand.

It is only the political entrepreneur who deserves our censure, but both types are indiscriminately attacked in the popular caricature that has deformed American public opinion on the subject.

Andrew Carnegie almost single-handedly managed to reduce the price of steel rails from $160 per ton in the mid-1870s to $17 per ton in the late 1890s. Given the importance of steel to a modern economy, that massive price reduction yielded greater wealth and a higher standard of living for everyone. Carnegie was so efficient, in fact, that the 4000 people who worked at his Homestead plant in Pittsburgh produced three times more steel than the 15,000 workers at Germany's Krupps steelworks, Europe's most modern and renowned facility.

Likewise, John D. Rockefeller was able to reduce the price of kerosene from one dollar per gallon to ten cents per gallon. People could finally afford to illuminate their homes. Rockefeller also developed 300 products out of the waste that remained after the oil was refined. Claims that Rockefeller was an "unfair" competitor (whatever that means), the usual gripe of those who cannot deliver a product at prices that sufficiently please consumers, were laid to rest half a century ago in John S. McGee's study for the *Journal of Law and Economics*. (John S. McGee, "Predatory Price Cutting: The Standard Oil (N.J.) Case," *Journal of Law and Economics* 1 [October 1958]: 137-69.)

We might also mention James J. Hill, who grew up in poverty but whose entrepreneurial skill helped make the Great Northern Railroad, which extended from St. Paul to Seattle, a major success without any government subsidies at all. In 1893, when the government-subsidized railroads went bankrupt, Hill's line was able both to cut rates and turn a substantial profit.

Still another of the alleged robber barons was Cornelius Vanderbilt. In 1798 the government of New York had granted Robert Livingston and Robert Fulton a monopoly on steamboat traffic for thirty years. Vanderbilt was hired to run a steamboat between New Jersey and Manhattan in defiance of that monopoly. Vanderbilt evaded capture while at the same time charging only one-quarter of the monopolists' fare.

After *Gibbons vs. Ogden* (1824) overturned New York's steamboat monopoly, the fare for a trip from New York City to Albany dropped from seven dollars to three. The trip from New York to Philadelphia, which had been three dollars, fell to one dollar. Travelers going from New Brunswick to Manhattan now paid only six cents, and ate for free. When he moved his steamboat operation to the Hudson River, Vanderbilt charged a fare of ten cents, as opposed to the previous three dollars. Later he dropped the fare entirely, running his operation on the proceeds from concessions aboard the ship.

Even when his competitors had unfair advantages, Vanderbilt came out on top. Edward Collins received a government subsidy for his steamship business to provide mail delivery across the Atlantic – to the tune of $858,000 a year by the 1850s. When Vanderbilt entered the field in 1855, he outperformed Collins in passenger travel and mail delivery with no subsidy at all. Congress did away with Collins' subsidy in 1858, and before long he went bankrupt.

Meanwhile, Vanderbilt was also outperforming two subsidized steamship lines that brought passengers and mail to California. They charged $600 per passenger per trip. The unsubsidized Vanderbilt charged $150 per passenger, and nothing to deliver the mail.

Forgive me, but I am supposed to fear and despise these benefactors of mankind why, exactly?

These men were able to acquire such substantial portions of their industries because they consistently produced goods at low prices. When they stopped innovating, they lost market share. The cartoon version of events notwithstanding, competition was vigorous. It was only after voluntary efforts – pools, secret agreements, mergers, and the like – failed to stabilize this highly competitive environment that some firms began to look to the federal government and its regulatory apparatus as a way to reduce competition coercively. "Ironically, contrary to the consensus of historians," acknowledges New Left historian Gabriel Kolko, "it was not the existence of monopoly that caused the federal government to intervene in the economy, but the lack of it."

Speaking of the situation that faced Standard Oil, Kolko writes:

> In 1899 there were sixty-seven petroleum refiners in the United States, only one of whom was of any consequence. Over the next decade the number increased steadily to 147 refiners. Until 1900 the only significant competitor to Standard was the Pure Oil Company, formed in 1895

by Pennsylvania producers with $10 million capital…. By 1906 it was challenging Standard's control over pipelines by constructing its own. And in 1901 Associated Oil of California was formed with $40 million capital stock, in 1902 the Texas Company was formed with $30 million capital, and in 1907 Gulf Oil was established with $60 million capital. In 1911 the total investment of the Texas Company, Gulf Oil, Tide Water-Associated Oil, Union Oil of California, and Pure Oil was $221 million. From 1911 to 1926 the investment of the Texas Company grew 572 percent, Gulf Oil 1,022 percent, Tide Water-Associated 205 percent, Union Oil 159 percent and Pure Oil 1,534 percent.

Standard Oil's decline preceded the antitrust ruling against it in 1911, and was "primarily of its own doing – the responsibility of its conservative management and lack of initiative." By the time government got around to breaking up Standard Oil, the normal operation of the free market had already reduced its market share from 80 to 25 percent.

As a matter of fact, it was very difficult for top firms to maintain their positions in a great many industries in the United States in the late nineteenth century. This was true of industries as diverse as oil, steel, iron, automobiles, agricultural machinery, copper, meat packing, and telephone services. Competition was extremely vigorous.

To be sure, there are caveats, as there always are in history. For a time, Carnegie did support steel tariffs. Since he substantially reduced the price of steel rails, though, this political position of his did not harm the consumer. Other critics will point to the Carnegie and Rockefeller foundations and the dubious causes those institutions have supported. Their objection is irrelevant to the specific question of whether the men themselves, in their capacity as entrepreneurs, improved the American standard of living. That question is not even debatable.

Mainstream economics identifies monopolists by their behavior: they earn premium profits by restricting output and raising prices. Was that behavior evident in the industries where monopoly was most frequently alleged to have existed? Economist Thomas DiLorenzo, in an important article in the *International Review of Law and Economics,* actually bothered to look. During the 1880s, when real GDP rose 24 percent, output in the industries alleged to have been monopolized for which data were available rose 175 percent in real terms. Prices in those industries, meanwhile, were generally falling, and much faster than the 7 percent decline for the economy as a whole. We've already discussed steel rails, which fell from $68 to $32 per ton during the 1880s; we might also note the price of zinc, which fell from $5.51 to $4.40 per pound (a 20 percent decline) and refined sugar, which fell from 9¢ to 7¢ per pound (22 percent). In fact, this pattern held true for all 17 supposedly monopolized industries, with the trivial exceptions of castor oil and matches.

In other words, the story we thought we knew from our history class was a fake.

Beyond the appeal to specific examples from history, critics of the market propose plausible-sounding scenarios in which firms might be able to harm consumer welfare. Larger firms can afford to lower their prices, even below cost, as long as it takes to drive their smaller competitors out of business, the major argument runs. Once that task is accomplished, the larger firms can raise their prices and take advantage of consumers who no longer have any choice but to buy from them. That strategy on the part of larger firms is known as "predatory pricing."

Dominick Armentano, professor emeritus of economics at the University of Hartford, surveyed scores of important antitrust cases and failed to uncover a single successful example of predatory pricing. Chicago economist George Stigler noted that the theory has fallen into disfavor in professional circles: "Today it would be embarrassing to encounter this argument in professional discourse."

There is a reason for that disfavor. The strategy is suicidal.

For one thing, a large firm attempting predatory pricing must endure losses commensurate with its size. In other words, a firm holding, say, 90 percent of the market competing with a firm holding the remaining 10 percent of the market suffers losses on its 90 percent market share. Economist George Reisman correctly wonders what is supposed to be so brilliant and irresistible about a strategy that involves having a firm – albeit one with nine times the wealth and nine times the business – lose money at a rate nine times as great as the losses suffered by its competitors.

The dominant firm, should it somehow succeed in driving all competitors from the market, must now drive prices back up, to enjoy its windfall, without at the same time encouraging new entrants (who will be attracted by the prospect of charging those high prices themselves) into the field. Then the predatory-pricing strategy must begin all over again, further postponing the moment when the hoped-for premium profits kick in. New entrants into the field will be in a particularly strong position, since they can often acquire the assets of previous firms at fire-sale prices during bankruptcy proceedings.

During the period of the below-cost pricing, meanwhile, consumers tend to stock up on the unusually inexpensive goods. This factor means it will take still longer for the dominant firm to recoup the losses it incurred from the predatory pricing.

A chain-store variant of the predatory-pricing model runs like this: chain stores can draw on the profits they earn in other markets to sustain them while they suffer losses in a new market where they are trying to eliminate competitors by means of predatory pricing.

But imagine a nationwide chain of grocery stores, which we'll call MegaMart. Let's stipulate that MegaMart has a thousand locations across the country and $1 billion of capital invested. That comes out to $1 million per store. Those who warn of "monopoly" contend that MegaMart can bring to bear its entire fortune in order to drive all competitors from one particular market into which it wants to expand.

Now for the sake of argument, we'll leave aside the empirical and theoretical problems with predatory pricing we've already established. Let's assume MegaMart really could use its nationwide resources to drive all competitors from the field in a new market, and could even keep all potential competitors permanently out of the market out of sheer terror at being crushed by MegaMart.

Even if we grant all this, it still makes no sense from the point of view of business strategy and economic judgment for MegaMart to adopt the predatory-pricing strategy. Yes, for a time it would enjoy abnormally high profits, and indeed the prospect of those profits explains why MegaMart would even consider this approach. But would the premium profits be high enough for the whole venture to be a net benefit for the company?

George Reisman insists, correctly, that they would not. "Such a premium profit is surely quite limited – perhaps an additional $100,000 per year, perhaps even an additional $500,000 per year, but certainly nothing remotely approaching the profit that would be required to justify the commitment of [the firm's] total financial resources."

Let's suppose that the premium profit that could be reaped by MegaMart after removing all its competitors amounted to $300,000, the average of those two figures. Assume also that the average rate of return in the economy is 10 percent. That means MegaMart can afford to lose $3 million – the capitalized value of $300,000 per year – in order to seize the market for itself. Spending an amount greater than that would be a poor investment, since the firm would earn a lower-than-average rate of return (lower, that is, than 10 percent). For that reason, MegaMart's $1 billion in capital is simply irrelevant.

What follows from this, according to Reisman, is that

> everyone contemplating an investment in the grocery business who has an additional $5 million or even just $1 million to put up is on as good a footing as [MegaMart] in attempting to achieve such [premium] profits. For it simply does not pay to invest additional capital beyond these sums. In other words, the predatory-pricing game, if it actually could be played in these circumstances, would be open to a fairly substantial number of players – not just the extremely large, very rich firms, but everyone who had an additional capital available equal to the limited capitalized value of the "monopoly gains" that might be derived from an individual location.

Coming back to the more general "predatory pricing" claim, one final argument buries it forever. Economist Don Boudreaux invites us to imagine what would happen if Walmart adopted the predatory-pricing strategy and embarked on a price war over pharmaceutical products, with the aim of driving other drug retailers from the market. Who would be harmed by this? Consumers, to be sure, as well as rival drug suppliers.

But there's a less obvious set of victims, and it's they who hold the key to solving the alleged problem. Companies that distribute the drugs to Walmart also stand to lose. Why? Because if Walmart drives competitors from the field and then raises drug prices, which is the whole point of predatory pricing, then fewer drugs will be sold. It's as simple as the law of demand: at a higher price of a good there is a lower quantity demanded. That means a company like Merck, which distributes a lot of drugs to Walmart, will sell less of its product.

Is Merck going to take that lying down? Of course not. Since a successful predatory-pricing strategy for Walmart would mean lower sales and profits for Merck, it has a strong incentive to block Walmart's move. And it can do so by means of minimum- or maximum-resale-price-maintenance contracts. A minimum-resale-price-maintenance agreement establishes a minimum selling price at which a retailer must sell a company's product. Such a minimum would make it impossible for Walmart to engage in predatory pricing in the first place; they would have to sell the product at the stipulated minimum price, at the very least, and could not go any lower. Maximum-resale-price-maintenance agreements would allow a company, once predatory pricing has succeeded – and again, for the sake of argument we set aside all the reasons we've given for why predatory pricing can't work – to limit the extent of the damage. It would forbid a retailer to sell its product above a stipulated price. Walmart's putative "monopoly profits" could not be realized to any great extent under such an arrangement.

In other words, profits all across the structure of production are threatened when one stage, whether retailing or anything else, attempts to reap so-called monopoly profits. You can bet that firms threatened with a reduction in their own profits will be particularly alert to the various ways in which they can prevent the creation of "monopolies."

What about the DeBeers diamond cartel? Surely that is an example of free-market "monopoly," defying the economists' assurances that cartels on a free market tend to be unstable and short-lived. In fact, there has been no free market in diamonds. The South African government nationalized all diamond mines, even ones it hadn't yet discovered. Thus, a property owner who discovers diamonds on his property finds ownership title instantly transferred to the government. Mine operators, in turn, who lease the mines, must get a license from the government. By an interesting happenstance, the licensees have all wound up being either DeBeers itself or operators willing to distribute their diamonds through the DeBeers Central Selling Organization. Miners trying to distribute diamonds in defiance of government restrictions have faced stiff penalties.

In short, opponents of laissez faire have spooked public opinion with a combination of bad history and worse theory. The average person, although in possession of few if any hard facts in support of his unease at the prospect of laissez faire, is nevertheless sure that such a dreadful state of affairs must be avoided, and that our selfless public servants must protect us against the anti-social behavior of the incorrigible predators in the private sector.

November 1, 2012

PART III

LIBERTARIANISM ATTACKED, AND MY REPLIES

13

PROGRESSIVES: WE OWE EVERYTHING TO GOVERNMENT

Several readers of my blog at TomWoods.com alerted me to an article in the *New York Times* in November 2011 by a Gail Collins, making fun of Ron Paul for not believing in the need for various government agencies and functions. One reader in particular shared with me the kinds of comments that accompanied the article. They were overwhelmingly of the low-self-esteem statist variety: we're too stupid to figure out how to organize society without guys with guns directing everything, so Ron Paul is silly and naive to believe in freedom.

Thus: "It's unlikely that Ron Paul would be here today if he had grown up in the world he wants the rest of us to live in. There's a reason we stopped living like self-sufficient nomads and built civilizations which could provide food, education, health care, defense, and commerce to a large and diverse citizenry."

Let's leave aside that England had achieved practically universal education well before the introduction of "free" schools, or that every single good this person insists we are too stupid and helpless to provide without guys with guns can indeed be and has in fact been so provided.

Let's focus just on commerce.

The person quoted above actually thinks opposition to government power means opposition to commerce, and a retreat into self-sufficiency. I hardly know what to say. One of the key classical liberal (libertarian) criticisms of government is that it *disrupts* commercial activity and *undermines* the international division of labor.

Worse than this elementary mistake is the casual assumption, shared by folks across the ideological spectrum, that we owe the great achievements of mankind, including commerce itself, to guys with guns.

For one thing, what is so impressive about the international division of labor is that it occurs *without* central direction of any kind. Note what happened when designer Thomas Thwaites tried to build a toaster from scratch, entirely on his own. As he explained in a TED talk, it turned out to be an unspeakably difficult thing that took him nearly a year and a pile of dough, and the toaster wound up working for ten seconds.

Yet the production process by which the various inputs that go into toaster production are produced, transported, and assembled, in just the right quantities without any surpluses or shortages, occurs every day without any Global Toaster Production Planning Board. And it isn't just a matter of getting a few pieces together. It isn't even just a matter of understanding mining or wiring. Every stage involves technical knowledge possessed only by a very few, and requires the outlay of capital and the allocation of productive factors to make it a reality. Toaster production requires the manufacture of rubber in order to make the tires that the trucks will need to transport the toaster's component parts. Thus the more closely we look at it, the more mind-bogglingly complex the whole matter becomes. This occurs every day, and hardly anyone appreciates or even notices it.

The extension of commerce, moreover, has in fact involved *striking down state-imposed barriers* to the free interaction of individuals. It's a bit rich for the state to try to take credit for it.

The more sophisticated critic may argue that the legal infrastructure necessary to make commerce work originated with the state. Wrong again. Merchant law developed in medieval Europe without the involvement of the state. This is particularly remarkable given that it sought to provide dispute resolution and basic legal standards across a wide territorial expanse that included peoples who spoke different languages and practiced different customs. You can read a good discussion of it in the classic work of Bruce Benson, *The Enterprise of Law: Justice Without the State.*

For all the commitment to peace and nonviolence that is supposed to define progressivism, there's a tad bit too much admiration for what we might call a military model of social organization for my taste. The casual assumption that all good things come about because of large-scale organization overseen by a leader barking out orders speaks ill of their understanding of how society actually functions.

In such a context, it may be interesting to note the zeal with which progressives (with only a handful of exceptions, so there goes the myth of the progressive peacenik) urged U.S. involvement in World War I. Yes, Germany had to be smashed, they said, but the American economy also needed the kind of regimentation and central organization that the pressures of wartime would surely bring. Once people had become accustomed to government direction of the economy, they would be more prepared in peacetime to abandon or at least modify their backward ideas about the sanctity of private property and all that.

I conclude with these remarks by Harvard's Samuel Huntington, a man of the Establishment if there ever was one:

> On the military reservation…there is ordered serenity. The parts do not exist on their own, but accept their subordination to the whole. Beauty and utility are merged in gray stone…. The post is suffused with rhythm and harmony which comes when the collective will supplants individual whim…. The behavior of men is governed by a code…. The unity of the community incites no man to be more than he is. In order is found peace; discipline, fulfillment; in community, security….

> Is it possible to deny that the military values — loyalty, duty, restraint, dedication — are the ones America most needs today? … America can learn more from West Point than West Point from America…. If the civilians permit the soldiers to adhere to the military standard, the nations themselves may eventually find redemption and security in making that standard their own.

In short: shut up and obey, citizen. It is this principle, and not your vaunted "voluntary social interaction," that makes the world go round.

November 28, 2011

14

"THE QUESTION LIBERTARIANS JUST CAN'T ANSWER"

For some reason, the finger-waggers at Salon think they've got us stumped with this one: "If your approach is so great, why hasn't any country in the world ever tried it?"

So *this* is the unanswerable question? What's supposed to be so hard about it? Ninety percent of what libertarians write about answers it at least implicitly.

Let's reword the question slightly, in order to draw out the answer. You'll note that when stated correctly, the question contains an implicit non sequitur.

(1) "If your approach is so great, why doesn't local law enforcement want to give up the money, supplies, and authority that come from the drug war?"

(2) "If your approach is so great, why don't big financial firms prefer to stand or fall on their merits, and prefer bailouts instead?"

(3) "If your approach is so great, why do people prefer to earn a living by means of special privilege instead of by honest production?"

(4) "If your approach is so great, why does the military-industrial complex prefer its revolving-door arrangement and its present strategy of fleecing the taxpayers via its dual strategy of front-loading and political engineering?"

(5) "If your approach is so great, why do businessmen often prefer subsidies and special privileges?"

(6) "If your approach is so great, why do some people prefer to achieve their ends through war instead?"

(7) "If your approach is so great, why does the political class prefer to live off the labor of others, and exercise vast power over everyone else?"

(8) "Special interests win special benefits for themselves because those benefits are concentrated and significant. The costs, dispersed among the general public, are so insignificant to any particular person, that the general public has no vested interest in organizing against it. An extra 25 cents per gallon of orange juice is hardly worth devoting one's life to opposing, but an extra $100 million per year in profits for the companies involved sure is worth the time to lobby for.

"If your approach is so great, why does this happen?"

(9) "If your approach is so great, why don't people want to try it out, after having been propagandized against it nonstop for 17 years?" (K-12, then four years of college.)

June 4, 2013

15

"THE QUESTION LIBERTARIANS JUST CAN'T ANSWER," PART II

Now E.J. Dionne, inspired by Michael Lind (see chapter 14), has come along to remind everyone why we need our overlords. He thinks Lind's question is a super one, too. I will have plenty to say if I confine myself to this one Dionne paragraph:

> We had something close to a small-government libertarian utopia in the late 19th century, and we decided it didn't work. We realized that many would never be able to save enough for retirement and, later, that most of them would be unable to afford health insurance in old age. Smaller government meant that too many people were poor and that monopolies were formed too easily. And when the Depression engulfed us, government was helpless, largely handcuffed by this antigovernment ideology until Franklin Roosevelt came along.

Every aspect of this statement is false.

In the nineteenth century there was no such thing as "retirement," so no one would have said, "Under this system, people won't be able to save enough for retirement!" Only continued capital accumulation, which occurs when businesses may reinvest their profits in the purchase of capital goods without being expropriated by government, made it possible for the economy to become physically productive enough for something like "retirement" even to become conceivable. Even when Social Security was established, the retirement age was higher than the average life expectancy, meaning most people would be dead before they could get any of their money back.

As for health insurance in old age, this too is belied by the facts. "Most of the government's medical payments on behalf of the poor compensated doctors and hospitals for services once rendered free of charge or at reduced prices," writes historian Allen Matusow. "Medicare-Medicaid, then, primarily transferred income from middle-class taxpayers to middle-class health-care professionals."

And what made health care so costly in the first place? Not the "free market," which Dionne himself would admit hasn't been anywhere near health care in anyone's lifetime. (Vijay Boyapati, formerly of Google, provides a big chunk of the answer at bit.ly/Boyapati.)

Dionne then says, "Smaller government meant too many people were poor." This is flat-out idiocy. The greatest gains against poverty in the United States occurred when government was least involved. In 1900, the poverty rate by today's standards was 95 percent. By the time the federal government got involved in poverty relief in a non-trivial way, in the late 1960s, that figure had already plummeted to between 12 and 14 percent, where it has remained to this day. There's a good discussion of all this in *Back on the Road to Serfdom*, a collection of essays I edited for the Intercollegiate Studies Institute.

Since government got involved, the poverty rate has stagnated. Trillions of dollars have been spent, yet the figures won't budge.

So the truth is *exactly the opposite* of what Dionne claims. Government has done a rotten job of alleviating poverty. The natural operation of the market is what has come as close as any institution can to conquering it.

In the same sentence, Dionne says: "Smaller government meant that...monopolies were formed too easily." Dionne is here relying more on his recollections from eighth grade than he is on specialized studies and actual data. For the truth of the matter, see chapter 12 of this book.

Finally, we read this: "And when the Depression engulfed us, government was helpless, largely handcuffed by this antigovernment ideology until Franklin Roosevelt came along."

So Dionne repeats the "Hoover believed in laissez faire" myth that historians rejected decades ago. In case E.J. doesn't believe me, here's a scholar being interviewed at pbs.org: "Historians now acknowledge [Hoover's] progressive inclinations, and his commitment to counter-cyclical planning and the belief that the nation ought to have a reservoir of big projects in the planning stages that could be executed when the time was right. Programs begun during the Hoover years, such as the Reconstruction Finance Corporation, were forerunners of the New Deal, and years later New Dealer Rexford Tugwell acknowledged that – even though no one would say so at the time – 'practically the whole New Deal was extrapolated from programs that Hoover started.'"

Hoover expressly said that laissez-faire was a thing of the past. He had said so all through the 1920s. He launched public works projects, raised taxes, extended emergency loans to failing firms, hobbled international trade, and lent money to the states for relief programs. He sought to prop up wages as prices were falling. His deficits, as a percentage of GDP, rivaled FDR's.

Dionne evidently thinks there are lots of things government can do to fix depressions if they're not "handcuffed" by ideology. This is incorrect, as I've explained in many places. But the U.S. government was not handcuffed, under either Hoover or FDR, and yet the Great Depression persisted longer than any economic downturn in U.S. history.

Naturally, Dionne speaks of the Depression as if it just "came along," without a cause. But it did have a cause: the interventions of the Federal Reserve into the economy throughout the 1920s. Murray Rothbard tells the story in *America's Great Depression*.

As for the welfare states Dionne seems to like, their effect is everywhere the same: the number of births shrinks (because of the incentives of the programs themselves), and the shrinking youth population eventually becomes unable to support the overwhelming burden of old-age transfer programs. It is beginning to happen all over the world.

In short, Dionne himself, who has a huge audience from his perch at the *Washington Post*, repeated half a dozen preposterous pro-government myths *in just one paragraph*. Then he presents the question of why people aren't more sympathetic to libertarianism as if it were some kind of puzzle. If it's a puzzle, then E.J. Dionne and his friends are a big piece.

June 11, 2013

16

GROW UP, LIBERTARIANS

That's what Michael Lind is saying now.

You see, we're not "experimental" like he is. He's willing to try out lots of things: freedom, semi-freedom, and full-on coercion. And we keep sticking to our whole freedom thing, and our view that the same moral code ought to govern all individuals, whether they belong to that mystical thing called "the state" or not.

In case you missed it, you might enjoy my first reply to Lind (which appears in this book as chapter 14), and then my reply to the *Washington Post*'s poor E.J. Dionne, who tried to help out the hapless, ill-read Lind (see chapter 15).

Here's a passage from Lind's latest:

> And what exactly does the libertarian movement contribute to con-
> temporary American debate? Here are a few of the ideas that the
> rest of us, from center-left to center-right, are supposed to treat with
> respectful attention: calls for a return to the gold standard; the abo-
> lition of the Federal Reserve; the abolition of the Internal Revenue
> Service; and the replacement of all taxes by a single regressive flat
> tax that would fall on low-income workers while slashing taxation
> of the rich.

My critic in *The Economist*, Will Wilkinson, writes:

"The ideal of anti-theoretical experimentalism leads me to a preference for policies that promote the sort of cosmopolitan pluralism in which cultural synthesis and invention thrives. It leads me to favour decentralised authority over monumental central administration. It leads me to suspect that it would be better if America were twelve separate countries, or had 200 states. It leads me to think seasteads are a great idea."

Ron Paul, who merely wants to abolish the Federal Reserve, looks like a boring centrist compared to Will Wilkinson, who thinks it might be worthwhile to abolish the United States, subdividing it into a dozen separate countries. (My Southern ancestors who supported the Confederacy would have been satisfied with two.)

Will Wilkinson, in turn, looks like a boring centrist compared to me, but I'll leave Wilkinson out of this.

So let's review the positions that are just too juvenile and unreasonable for us to ask others to entertain. According to Lind:

(1) *We can't return to the gold standard.* It is vastly preferable for money creation to be untethered to anything but political will. There is no chance such a system will undermine money's purchasing power, interfere with economic calculation, cause resource misallocation, be used to bail out influential firms, etc. Also, the creation of money can lift us out of recessions – which, in turn, are of course not caused by misallocations or entrepreneurial errors brought on by the fiat money itself.

(2) *We can't abolish the Federal Reserve.* Why, we need the experts in charge of the money supply! Sure, they gave us the Great Depression, the stagflation of the 1970s, and the current disaster, but nobody's perfect! We need monopoly provision of the medium of exchange, and we need government-granted privileges for the Fed as the supplier of that medium of exchange. The Fed has been super-awesome: it's given us fewer and shallower recessions than we had before!

(3) *We can't abolish the Internal Revenue Service.* That's right: it's unthinkable for us to live the way the vast majority of mankind lived for 99 percent of its history, and how Americans lived a mere 100 years ago. It is essential that the federal government be able to decide what percentage of the fruits of people's labor they are allowed to keep, and what percentage will be seized by means of threats of violence. Libertarians are childish and moronic to think civilization could survive without institutionalized expropriation.

(4) *We can't substitute the current income tax with a flat tax.* On this, libertarians agree. There's little point in substituting one kind of institutionalized expropriation for another.

(5) *The United States cannot be one square inch smaller than it is now.* It is inconceivable to Lind to imagine the division of the United States into 12 or more political units. The United States as it exists today occupies the precise, heaven-sent amount of square mileage – namely, three million, seven hundred ninety-four thousand, one hundred – that God and destiny demand she hold.

The U.S., for Lind, is not a practical arrangement to be evaluated according to objective criteria. It is a mystical, self-justifying entity. It is metaphysically impossible that it should ever grow so large as to be dysfunctional. Other countries may split into smaller units by mutual consent, but being the awesomest of the awesome, our political unit is not subject to such considerations. We are to treat it with reverence and devotion.

(By the way, there is absolutely nothing cultish about treating a political unit as sacred and inviolable. It's only the libertarians who are cultish.)

Now sure, if the U.S. were 12 units, maybe all 12 wouldn't be the basket cases that our giant fiefdom now is, and probably not all 12 would have engaged in the counterproductive foreign policy of the past century, which has yielded the American public nothing but grief. But I have forgotten myself, citizen! I am speaking of the United States as if her dismemberment were conceivable! Those libertarians have driven me to the very edge of blasphemy.

I realize Michael Lind is a Serious Person whose time must be spent contemplating various ways in which he might experiment on the American public, but I think he is perhaps too dismissive of views that happen to fall outside the 3×5 card of approved opinion from which he insists we draw our views. Here's how I'd reply to his objections:

(1) A return to the gold standard is still a statist solution – the complete separation of money and state would be the best approach – but it's better than nothing, and eminently defensible. (For how the separation of money and state would work, see TomWoods.com/money.)

What about all those panics we had under the gold standard? I cover that at TomWoods.com/panics.

But there isn't enough gold! Gold causes deflation! For replies to the standard objections, see my resource page on sound money: LibertyClassroom.com/soundmoney.

(2) The abolition of the Fed would be a major economic step forward. For a reply to the customary pro-Fed claims, see, for starters, chapter 31 of this book, as well as *The Fed at One Hundred: A Critical View on the Federal Reserve System*, eds. David Howden and Joseph T. Salerno (New York: Springer, 2014).

(3) and (4). Yes, we can live without institutionalized expropriation. E.J. Dionne, in his effort to help out Lind, listed a whole bunch of things we need government intervention for: why, we'd have poverty, monopolies, no stimulus to help us through recessions, etc. I answered him in chapter 15. And yes, there is a moral point as well:

(5) Why are decentralization and secession unthinkable? Lind's religious reverence for the present size and makeup of the United States, which is a mere human contrivance, is a little creepy. The twentieth century showed us what nationalism and megastates can do, and it wasn't really super fun.

June 13, 2013

17

THANKS FOR PROVING OUR POINT

Shortly after the death of former British Prime Minister Margaret Thatcher, a meme appeared that read as follows:

On Wednesday, 17th April 2013, I will be kind.

I will give money to charity, and my time to someone who needs my help.

I will smile at strangers (not in a scary way) and hold the door open for others.

I will make a donation to my local food bank.

I will make an appointment to give blood.

I will even forgive drivers who cut me up.

I will do this because I believe in Society, and I can think of no better way to overcome the legacy of a leader who did not.

I invite you to join me. (Yes, we should be kind every day, but let's make a special effort this Wednesday.)

Because the best protest against Margaret Thatcher's funeral is to prove her wrong.

This is in response to Thatcher's statement that "there's no such thing as society." So these progressives are going to show her!

Naturally, they interpret her perfectly defensible statement in the most inane and uncharitable way possible. Why, we'll show her there really is society, by helping our fellow man!

But that was exactly her point. There is no such thing as an abstract, disembodied blob called "society." All that exists are individuals, and it is up to those individuals – not "society" – to perform the great works of charity and civilization.

Her actual words: "There is no such thing as society. There is living tapestry of men and women and people and the beauty of that tapestry and the quality of our lives will depend upon how much each of us is prepared to take responsibility for ourselves and each of us prepared to turn round and help by our own efforts those who are unfortunate."

Now go back and read the juvenile statement above. *Every one of those statements is in perfect harmony with what Thatcher actually said*, yet the progressives who drafted it seriously think they are letting her have it. They apparently think Thatcher opposed helping the poor, or donating blood, or smiling at people. In my experience, this is all too typical among progressives: not one moment is expended on trying to understand the people they oppose. They actually seem to think Thatcher meant, "It's every man 4 himself!! Don't help anyone!!! KEEP ALL UR STUFF FOR URSELF!!!!"

Just beneath the surface here, and the source of much "progressive" confusion, is the failure to distinguish between society (a shorthand term for the individuals of whom the polity is composed) and the state. No, we don't think people should be exploited by guys with guns, even if ten percent of the exploitation is laughingly portrayed as helping the poor. That doesn't mean we're "atomistic individuals" who despise mankind. We support society, which is precisely why we oppose the state.

May 10, 2013

18

SOME AMERICANS DISTRUST AUTHORITY

According to Slate editor-in-chief Jacob Weisberg (in "The Right's New Left: The Tea Party Movement Has Two Defining Traits: Status Anxiety and Anarchism," September 2010), a specter is haunting America: the specter of anarchism. Not real anarchism – that's Weisberg's emotional hypochondria at work – but merely a growing skepticism of authority.

This won't do at all. Americans were born to be ruled by people and ideas of which Jacob Weisberg approves, and they are supposed to like it, or at least shut up about it. If they absolutely must complain, their complaints and modes of resistance must be kept within bounds approved of by Slate, a division of the Washington Post Company.

In other words, if these uppity peons would just stick to ideas and strategies chosen for them by their enemies, it would be easier for our betters to tolerate them.

Let's hear from Weisberg himself. "The Tea Party movement has two defining traits: status anxiety and anarchism.… [It's] a movement predominated by middle-class, middle-aged white men angry about the expansion of government and hostile to societal change." I like Lew Rockwell's reply: "Weisberg, need I mention, is a middle-class, middle-aged white man angry about any opposition to the expansion of government, and hostile to societal change not directed from the top. Oh, and no intellectual important in the current order is anxious about losing his status."

The "Tea Party" designation refers to a diverse lot, and Weisberg is exaggerating its anti-establishment features. Some Tea Partiers speak of "taking our country back" while looking forward to pulling the lever for Mitt Romney in 2012, or think Sarah Palin, a complete nonentity, is a "maverick" despite being in Bill Kristol's hip pocket. This branch of the Tea Party poses no threat to any established interest, and in fact strengthens the regime by misdirecting justifiable anger into officially approved channels.

But there is a sliver of genuine rebelliousness to be found here and there in the Tea Party, and it is this that Weisberg finds so awful and scary. "What's new and most distinctive about the Tea Party," he writes, "is its streak of anarchism – its antagonism toward any authority, its belligerent style of self-expression, and its lack of any coherent program or alternative to the policies it condemns." Perhaps worst of all, Weisberg huffs, the peons don't trust the experts, a designation they insist on preceding with the adjective "so-called"!

They *don't trust the experts*? I can't imagine why. Could it be that the experts told us the economy was fine in 2006? (James Galbraith admits this: only about a dozen economists predicted the financial crisis, according to him, though – natch – he pretends the Austrian economists do not exist.) Or maybe it's because economist Paul Krugman said in 2001 that what the economy needed was low interest rates to spur housing – the very thing that gave rise to the housing bubble. Or maybe because Ben Bernanke denied there was a housing bubble, said lending standards were sound, denied that the subprime problem would spill over into the rest of the economy – there's no real need to go on, since one of those uppity anarchists has collected these and other whoppers into one of those authority-undermining YouTubes that are destroying America. (See bit.ly/BenIsWrong.)

I can't resist one more example: Just two months before Fannie and Freddie collapsed and were taken over by the government, then-Treasury Secretary Hank Paulson told reporters not to worry: after all, he said, their regulator reported that they are adequately capitalized. When called on this two months later, Paulson denied having misled anyone: "I *never said* the company was well capitalized.

What I said is *the regulator said* they are adequately capitalized." See, Jake, people don't trust someone like that.

And the masses are losing confidence in the experts. Imagine that.

You know what also might be turning people off, Jake? The implication that they may adopt only those views that have been vetted in advance by people who despise them, and that they must be deranged losers if they choose not to avail themselves of this kind solicitude from their betters.

I happen to be the author of *Nullification*, a book that makes the historical and moral case for state nullification of unconstitutional federal laws and urging that it be resuscitated as a live option, given the complete failure of all other efforts to limit the federal government. Weisberg will have none of this crazy talk, of course. No one consulted him before advocating this, and since none of his friends at *Newsweek* or the *New York Times* have given nullification the seal of approval as an officially permitted position, we are breaking all codes of gentlemanly conduct by speaking about it anyway.

In any case, says Weisberg, we all know nullification was "settled" in 1819, with *McCulloch v. Maryland*. *McCulloch* held that when the federal government exercised a constitutional power the states could not interfere with it. That of course begs rather than settles the question, since a nullifying state contends precisely that the federal government is *not* exercising a constitutional power. But in Weisberg's world, everyone at the time leaped to accept John Marshall's ridiculous and unsupportable nationalist rendering of American history, a rendering completely at odds with what people had been told about the nature of the Union at many of the state ratifying conventions, and indeed at odds with the most obvious facts of American history.

On this planet, on the other hand, states continued to resist the national bank for years afterward, "settled law" to the contrary notwithstanding, until its charter went unrenewed in the 1830s. Spencer Roane, the chief judge of Virginia's Supreme Court, completely dismantled Marshall and his reasoning in a series of unrelenting critiques. James Madison said Virginia would never have ratified the Constitution had anyone thought the federal government's powers to be as expansive as John Marshall was proposing, given that exactly the opposite view of the new government was expressly promised to the people at the Richmond ratifying convention (where Marshall himself sat mute instead of correcting this impression). Thomas Jefferson wrote the following year: "The judiciary of the United States is the subtle corps of sappers and miners constantly working under ground to undermine the foundations of our confederated republic. They are construing our constitution from a co-ordination of a general and special government to a general and supreme one alone."

And I suppose someone forgot to tell Wisconsin it was violating "settled law" when it declared the Fugitive Slave Act of 1850 unconstitutional in 1859 and acted accordingly.

For Slate, a "settled" issue is one they don't want discussed. Normal people consider an issue "settled" when the arguments for both sides have been exhaustively heard, and with reason as the arbiter one side emerges triumphant. That has not occurred in this case. Contrary to popular belief, Daniel Webster was judged the loser of the Webster-Hayne debate at the time. Littleton Waller Tazewell crushed Andrew Jackson's convoluted proclamation on nullification, as I note in my book, but no one hears or knows about this exchange today. Nationalism is the best way to organize human society, students are told, and that's that. Anyone who thinks otherwise is too perverse to be worth mentioning.

"The tricorn hats and powder horns carried by Revolutionary re-enactors," Weisberg continues, "point to the most extreme libertarian view: a Constitutional fundamentalism that would limit the federal government to the exercise of enumerated powers." That's not even close to "the most extreme libertarian view," of course, not that Weisberg actually knows anything about libertarianism, but it does happen to be what one state ratifying convention after another was told would be the guiding rule of constitutional interpretation. This is now "wacko," fashionable opinion at Slate having supplanted the state ratifying conventions as the arbiters of matters constitutional. This would also make Thomas Jefferson "wacko," but Weisberg prefers (surprise!) not to mention Jefferson.

I had a bit of fun at Weisberg's expense in my book *Meltdown*, where I quoted his impatient lecture to libertarians – why, don't these people realize that their stupid commitment to the free market is what got us into this mess in the first place? Libertarians should just shut up and let the grownups put things right. Not a word about central banking and the teensy-weensy role it might have played in the financial implosion. He need not deign to acknowledge this line of argument. Criticism of central banking didn't make it onto the three-by-five card on which Weisberg has written out all allowable opinions, so that view doesn't really exist in any sense that matters.

What makes nullification so much fun is (1) that opponents of the idea almost invariably know none of the relevant history, so they find themselves reduced to stomping their feet and shouting, or trying to win arguments by low-IQ smears; and (2) the sheer horror of the political and media classes when confronted by people who refuse to be force-fed the two feckless alternatives that Slate and the rest of the establishment want them to choose from.

Weisberg then speculates that people whose political views do not fall along that compendious spectrum from Hillary Clinton to Mitch McConnell may be mentally deranged – these people's views are "nutball." But the main problem with the people Weisberg identifies is that they refuse to be told what to think, and they shun media outlets that insult them. They're not interested in debating what Slate wants them to debate – e.g., whether the top marginal income tax rate should be 39 percent or 39.8 percent. They want to discuss matters a smidge more significant than that. They refuse to read from the script Slate keeps trying to hand them. That is what makes them so troublesome.

Of course, the people Weisberg has in mind do not read Slate in the first place, so they won't even see his funny article. Even worse, how do you insult people who don't care what authority says about them? It's enough to drive a commissar crazy.

Weisberg thinks the problem with the Tea Party is that it's too unpredictable. That sure isn't Weisberg's problem: his first book was called *In Defense of Government*.

September 24, 2010

19

MEET AN ENFORCER OF APPROVED OPINION

To be attacked by a Gore Vidal, or an H.L. Mencken, one of the great word-smiths of American criticism, while surely unpleasant, must have been oddly exhilarating for the poor souls on the receiving end. I, on the other hand, have the more dubious and prosaic distinction of being a regular target of Ian Millhiser.

So you've never heard of Ian Millhiser. You've never seen him. But you only think you haven't. You have.

Ever met someone who's dying to let you and the rest of the world know he holds all the approved opinions? Then you have met Ian Millhiser.

In every hysterical reaction to dissident voices – i.e., voices that (gasp!) differ from both Barack Obama *and* Mitt Romney! – you have seen him.

You have seen Ian in every social climber who would die a thousand deaths before entertaining an unconventional thought.

In literature and television we have the *stock character*: the absent-minded professor, the stuck-up cheerleader, the backwoods yokel. Millhiser, too, is a stock character. He is the thought controller: impatient with diversity, predictable, establishment, banal, humorless.

Millhiser typically insinuates that people who disagree with him strongly, like me, are probably indifferent to or even privately supportive of slavery. *Slavery.* But consider this: abolitionist political parties were lucky to receive two percent of the vote. How likely is it that someone desperate to hold approved, establishment-friendly opinions would have been – of all things! – an abolitionist?

Ian has no scholarly accomplishments I can uncover – no peer-reviewed articles, no books from major scholarly publishers, indeed no books from any publisher at all. That in itself doesn't make Ian a bad guy, of course. But it's kind of funny that the entire Millhiser corpus of panicked articles about the takeover of the United States by unlettered rubes is composed by someone of no scholarly distinction whatever.

Once or twice a year I reply to another one of Ian's pieces. They're all pretty much the same: uncomprehending analysis, stern rebukes of dissidents, and stolid, sledgehammer prose without elegance or nuance. He is a self-parody, the epitome of the hectoring, p.c. automaton.

Millhiser pretends my replies to him do not exist. He continues to make the same inane arguments, in the full confidence – alas, probably justified – that his limited audience has not read my refutations. In fact, he refuses to quote anything I have written in the past 15 years.

That's about what one can expect from ThinkProgress and the other left-wing thought-control sites that monitor and censure unapproved thoughts.

My Nullification FAQ (reprinted here as chapter 40) was largely inspired by Millhiser, who raises the same long-exploded arguments again and again, no matter how many times I refute them. I finally decided to write up a FAQ and leave it at that. You will not be surprised to learn that Millhiser pretends the FAQ does not exist.

I have written a whole book about nullification of unconstitutional federal laws. Millhiser has attacked and smeared me for years without once quoting from that book, or from anything I have written on the topic. In my book I included many primary documents, in part so readers wouldn't have to take my word for things, and in part to make it harder for the world's Millhisers to erase them from history.

His latest is an interview at AlterNet, with editor Joshua Holland, called "American Right-Wingers Are No Longer Conservative – They're Extremists." Oooh! Well, we can't have that!

Extremist is one of the commissar's favorite words. Nothing gets under the thought controller's skin more than an uppity peon who thinks there might be more to political philosophy than John Kerry and Mitch McConnell. Be satisfied with the range of debate we allow you, citizen. Any opinion a reasonable person might want to hold can be found in that yawning chasm that separates these two men. You have an opinion that differs from both of them, you say? Why, you're an *extremist*.

Millhiser and Holland are appalled at conservatives' lack of respect for "long-standing precedent" and "venerable tradition." (These would make excellent rebukes of Socrates and Copernicus, I note in passing.)

Falsehoods and abuses, we are to believe, become truths and virtues if perpetrated long enough. And for heaven's sake, *venerable tradition*? Is this what AlterNet, which advocates social policy that would have horrified even the left-liberals of two generations ago, is now pretending to favor?

Of course, Millhiser does not care one whit about "precedent" and "tradition," else he would be writing articles about the risible jurisprudence of the New Deal Court and its transparently political departures from longstanding precedent. What Millhiser cares about are nationalism and government power, just like the neoconservatives he pretends to oppose. Law school taught him the nationalist theory of the Union, and he is going to defend this preposterous notion come what may.

So in the interview we are treated to the following analysis. Some Tea Party groups are attempting to resist government power in unapproved ways. Some of them even think the states can nullify unconstitutional laws. This makes them *reactionaries*. If they were real conservatives, they would roll over and die like the good losers left-liberals expect them to be.

According to Millhiser, these conservatives supposedly have a faulty understanding of the Tenth Amendment:

> About four years ago, you started to hear these weird noises about how things violate the 10th Amendment. And not just, you know, the Affordable Care Act – that's when they made this argument over and over again – but it was also people claiming that Medicare violates the 10th Amendment. Social Security violates the 10th Amendment. And what I started to hear at these Tea Party rallies that were popping up is speakers got up and they were saying things that very closely resembled

this discredited constitutional theory that existed about 100 years ago. At the time, it led to child-labor laws getting struck down, it allowed pretty much any law protecting unions getting struck down, that led to minimum wage getting struck down – all of these essential worker protections getting struck down…. And while we were asleep at the switch, they were writing books and they were educating their partisans about how awesome it would be if we had this crazy theory of the 10th Amendment, and then I guess we wouldn't have to be stuck with these terrible child-labor laws anymore.

As usual with Millhiser, it is enough for him simply to point out his opponents' view; he need not trouble himself to refute it.[1] So we never actually learn why these people are wrong to read the Tenth Amendment the way they do, apart from the fact that this reading makes Ian Millhiser unhappy. Theirs is a "discredited constitutional theory." Discredited by what? By anything relevant?

The modern consensus of law professors, to which Millhiser would undoubtedly point, does not count. There is no room in republican theory for it. The ratifying conventions, according to James Madison, are where we look for our understanding of the Constitution. Even before the Tenth Amendment

---

[1] For the real story about child labor – which was not a matter of selfless crusaders for justice heroically rescuing oppressed children from factories and mines, contrary to what Millhiser learned in third grade – see Bill Kauffman, "The Child Labor Amendment Debate of the 1920s," *Journal of Libertarian Studies* 10 (Fall 1992): 139-169. For the economics of child labor, see Thomas E. Woods, Jr., *The Church and the Market: A Catholic Defense of the Free Economy* (Lanham, MD: Rowman & Littlefield, 2005), 66-67.

On working conditions and the free market, the best analysis is George Reisman, "The Free Market and Job Safety," https://mises.org/daily/1143/The-Free-Market-and-Job-Safety (January 20, 2003). On wages – and contrary to Millhiser's view that wages are arbitrary and can without harm be raised by the political authority – see Woods, *The Church and the Market*, 59-63.

On labor unions, American law has always protected them as long as they have not been using coercion. The assault on labor law that Millhiser refers to exists only in his imagination. With few exceptions (and those exceptions strengthened rather than weakened unions), exactly the same legal principles governed labor from the time of *People v. Fisher* (1835) through the 1920s. I tell the whole story in question 30 of my book *33 Questions About American History You're Not Supposed to Ask* (New York: Random House/Crown Forum, 2007).

Social Security and Medicare are a longer story, but it's interesting that Millhiser doesn't think it worth mentioning that the present value of the underfunding of these programs – in other words, the amount of money that would be necessary to invest today, right now, to make it possible for everyone to receive what he is owed – is more than $200 trillion.

codified the principle, we find one ratifying convention after another saying that the federal government would have only the powers "expressly delegated" to it. This was the basis on which the Constitution was ratified. At Virginia's ratifying convention, skeptics of the Constitution were even told that if the federal government took one step beyond the expressly delegated powers to impose "any supplementary condition" upon the states, Virginia would be "exonerated."

So it turns out that the crazy reactionaries Millhiser is at pains to demonize have some pretty good arguments on their side. I have never – as in not even once – seen Millhiser acknowledge these, or even so much as hint that he might understand or be aware of them.

Millhiser's interviewer then says:

> Reactionaries have really floated this idea that the states can just nullify any federal law that they don't like, based on the 10th Amendment.
>
> Um, wasn't that something that we settled with the Civil War?

The doctrine of nullification deals with unconstitutional laws, not "any federal law that [the states] don't like," though I see nothing wrong with the latter idea, either. But I love the "Um" that begins the next sentence, don't you? As in, "These rubes are so stupid, I can't believe I have to tell them that this is like, you know, 2013! (For a reply to the morally grotesque "wasn't this settled by the Civil War" argument, see chapter 40.)

To my surprise, though, Millhiser makes the following concession – a pretty lame one, but a big step for a thought controller:

> So there's one group of sheriffs that has said that they will actively thwart the enforcement of federal law [on issues related to guns]. So if the FBI agent shows up trying to enforce federal law, they will stand in that agent's way and try to prevent them from enforcing federal law, and that's unconstitutional. That's a form of Nullification.
>
> There are other sheriffs who are saying that they will not enforce the federal law themselves, but if the feds show up, they won't stop them.

And that second thing is wrong, because in many cases these are good laws. And in the case of Colorado, where it's a Colorado state law, they probably have an obligation to enforce the state law, and I think it's a mistake if you tell your sheriffs that they're allowed to decide, on their own, which state laws they want to comply with.

But, you know, I think that there is a broader principal [sic], you know, with respect to these sheriffs who are just saying, "You know, if the feds want to show up and enforce federal law, that's cool. We just won't help them." I don't agree with their decision. But I think that's less troubling, and I think that part of the reason why I take that position that there's a similar battle going on right now over marijuana laws, where in states like Washington and Colorado, where marijuana is legal, I don't want to see state officials enforcing the federal marijuana laws. If the federal government wants to send DEA agents in there to enforce these laws, they have the right to do that. But, you know, at least as a constitutional matter, that is an area where the state and the federal governments are separate.

Can you make sense of that? "I don't agree with their decision," Millhiser says about sheriffs who won't assist federal agents in enforcing new gun regulations. But then he says, "I don't want to see state officials enforcing the federal marijuana laws." And then he says the federal government has the right to send DEA agents into Colorado and Washington to enforce the federal drug laws.

And he thinks *nullification* is incoherent?

Yes, I'm sure he could explain himself. He likes the gun laws but not the drug laws, so I guess the new rule would be that state officials should enforce only the federal laws Ian Millhiser likes, although all these laws – just or un-just, constitutional or not – may in Millhiser's view be enforced by federal goons, who "have the right to do that." Until our great, final arbiter, the glori-ous Supreme Court of the United States, says otherwise, we are to sit around and wait.

Well, not just wait. We can write articles about how nice it would be if federal agents would stop enforcing bad laws, and in these same articles make clear that they have every right to enforce those bad laws. Meanwhile, we can demonize people who might not want to wait 200 years to see results.

I am unconvinced.

April 23, 2013

20

SMASHED YGLESIAS

I have gone and upset Respectable Blogger Matt Yglesias more than once with my uppity, I'm-allowed-to-think-outside-the-Biden-to-Romney-spectrum nature. He first became annoyed with me in 2008:

> Bored by the proceedings at the Republican National Convention in St. Paul one day in 2008, I decided to try to gather some color down the road in Minneapolis, where Ron Paul and fellow dissident conservatives and libertarians were holding a counter-convention at the Target Center. At one point a speaker thundered that Barack Obama and John McCain "both have a lot to learn about Austrian business-cycle theory." The crowd went delirious with cheers, and soon chants of "end the Fed" echoed throughout the arena.

He is referring to my speech, which appears in this book as chapter 32. He doesn't get the quotation quite right; I certainly wouldn't have said anything as wooden as "have a lot to learn about Austrian business-cycle theory." What I did say, having been taken by surprise by the loud cheers for Austrian business cycle theory, was that it would be interesting to ask John McCain what he knew about the subject. We may as well be speaking Chinese, I said.

So appalled is Yglesias at unapproved thought that he doesn't even notice or care about the shot I was taking at McCain. Yglesias, like the fake progressives who follow him, will take McCain over Ron Paul any day. (The rest of his article is devoted to a "progressive" defense of the Federal Reserve, an institution we all know is deeply committed to the welfare of the common man.)

Instead of being impressed that thousands of people were economically literate enough to know something about the Mises-Hayek theory of the business cycle, which won the Nobel Prize in 1974, Yglesias is beside himself that so many people had adopted a view that neither he nor his friends had approved for them in advance. He evidently prefers the crowds at the Democratic and Republican conventions, which – whatever else we may say about them – were probably not composed of people who could tell you a whole lot about business-cycle theory.

Here's how Yglesias describes his reaction to the scene:

> It was funny at the time. A bunch of cranks talking about their crank monetary theories and espousing a crank prescription.

> Today, Paul is the chairman of the House Subcommittee on Monetary Policy.

Ron Paul is so scary that Yglesias resorts to the single-sentence paragraph to dramatize for us just how scary he is. Today, Paul is the chairman of the House Subcommittee on Monetary Policy. The earth may break free of its axis!

Since Austrian business cycle theory is not discussed by anyone along the officially approved Biden/Romney axis, for Yglesias it is crankish by definition. For who but an incorrigible crank would look for economic truths outside the glorious reservoir of wisdom that is the American political establishment? (The vast majority of the economics profession was completely blindsided by the recent crisis, yet Yglesias still thinks it's a strike against the Austrians that they happen to be out of favor with the economics mainstream.)

The Austrian School argues that interest rates are not arbitrary things, and that interfering with them leads the economy down an unsustainable path that does not correspond to existing resource availability or the pattern of real consumer demand. There are plenty of good reasons, both theoretical and empirical, to subscribe to this eminently reasonable theory. It was the centerpiece of *Meltdown*, my *New York Times* bestseller from 2009, and you can learn all about it online at LearnAustrianEconomics.com.

The non-crankish view, evidently, is that interest rates perform no essential coordinating function, and may be second-guessed by wise central planners who know better than the sum total of millions of economic actors, who give rise to market interest rates, what they should be. And if we want prosperity, why, we simply force those suckers lower. For no so-called economic law is any match for the iron will of our great leaders!

Yglesias, if he had his way, would impose on us, as chairman of the Monetary Policy Subcommittee, still another of the interchangeable drones committed to the idea that there's nothing wrong with our monetary system that couldn't be fixed with a one percent change, give or take. Ron Paul's recent hearing with witnesses James Grant, Lew Lehrman, and Joseph Salerno would be out of the question. Dissident opinion would be studiously excluded, the former progressive slogan "question authority" long since abandoned. Do not question your overlords, citizen. Imbibe the new progressive slogan: shut up and obey!

Incidentally, James Grant has ten times the writing ability, 100 times the wit, and ten thousand times the knowledge of a nonentity like Yglesias. According to Matt's *ex cathedra* pronouncement, Grant – whose *Grant's Interest Rate Observer* is widely consulted and sought after, which is why the thing is so expensive – must be a crank, since he questions the existing system. Go ahead and read Grant for yourself (the very thing Yglesias is obviously trying to discourage, by disparaging as "cranks" people orders of magnitude more intelligent than he is) and decide who possesses a true mastery of the situation, and who is the poser.

Yglesias, in typically Orwellian form, refers to a system that once existed, and yielded the world extraordinary prosperity and stability, as a "crankish" idea. As I have shown elsewhere, the crises and panics of the nineteenth century had precisely zero to do with the gold standard, and occurred more or less in direct proportion to derogation from the gold standard. By the time of the 1920s, the so-called gold standard was a pale imitation of the real thing, being in fact a mere gold-exchange standard in much of the world and a fractional-reserve system in the United States, but that hasn't stopped the likes of Yglesias, who is evidently incapable of making or even understanding these distinctions, from blaming gold for the Great Depression.

We could ask Yglesias about time preference, the heterogeneity of capital, or the Hayekian triangle – all of which are fairly central to an understanding of Austrian theory – and we may as well be asking him to explain the Copenhagen interpretation of quantum physics. He knows none of this. All he knows is that if the Austrian theory is correct, his cherished overlords are part of the problem rather than the solution. Human beings can arrange their affairs without the violent intervention of the state? That's a world our blogger refuses even to consider.

Now who is Matt Yglesias, anyway, such that he is even entitled to an opinion about a theory that his idols – Paul Krugman, most notoriously – can't even state correctly? He holds a degree in philosophy from Harvard, then he worked for some magazines, and now he's a blogger. And here I was thinking he might not know what he's talking about.

Yglesias' wave-of-the-hand dismissal of a theory he knows only in caricature, along with all those who advance it, as "cranks," calls to mind one of my favorite columns by Glenn Greenwald. Greenwald – unlike Yglesias a genuine progressive whom Robert La Follette would have been proud of – notes how terms like "crankish" or "crazy" are used as weapons in our political culture, and how selectively people like Yglesias deploy them:

> Those who support countless insane policies and/or who support politicians in their own party who do – from the Iraq War to the Drug War, from warrantless eavesdropping and denial of habeas corpus to presidential assassinations and endless war in the Muslim world – love to spit the "crazy" label at anyone who falls outside of the two-party establishment.

> This behavior is partially driven by the adolescent/high-school version of authoritarianism (anyone who deviates from the popular cliques – standard Democrats and Republicans – is a fringe loser who must be castigated by all those who wish to be perceived as normal), and is partially driven by the desire to preserve the power of the two

political parties to monopolize all political debates and define the exclusive venues for Sanity and Mainstream Acceptability. But regardless of what drives this behavior, it's irrational and nonsensical in the extreme.

I've been writing for several years about this destructive dynamic: whereby people who embrace clearly crazy ideas and crazy politicians anoint themselves the Arbiters of Sanity simply because they're good mainstream Democrats and Republicans and because the objects of their scorn are not. For me, the issue has nothing to do with Ron Paul and everything to do with how the "crazy" smear is defined and applied as a weapon in our political culture. Perhaps the clearest and most harmful example was the way in which the anti-war view was marginalized, even suppressed, in the run-up to the attack on Iraq because the leadership of both parties supported the war, and the anti-war position was thus inherently the province of the Crazies. That's what happens to any views not endorsed by either of the two parties.

Greenwald then quotes Conor Friedersdorf:

Forced to name the "craziest" policy favored by American politicians, I'd say the multibillion-dollar war on drugs, which no one thinks is winnable. Asked about the most "extreme," I'd cite the invasion of Iraq, a war of choice that has cost many billions of dollars and countless innocent lives. The "kookiest" policy is arguably farm subsidies for corn, sugar, and tobacco -- products that people ought to consume less, not more....

If returning to the gold standard is unthinkable, is it not just as extreme that President Obama claims an unchecked power to assassinate, without due process, any American living abroad whom he designates as an enemy combatant? Or that Joe Lieberman wants to strip Americans of their citizenship not when they are convicted of terrorist activities, but upon their being accused and designated as enemy combatants?

...These disparaging descriptors are never applied to America's policy establishment, even when it is proved ruinously wrong, whereas politicians who don't fit the mainstream Democratic or Republican mode, such as libertarians, are mocked almost reflexively in these terms, if they are covered at all.

It so happens that my 2011 book *Rollback* contains a chapter on the Fed that smashes to smithereens pretty much everything Yglesias has ever written about central banking. For example, the claim that the Fed has, after all, made the economy more stable and given us fewer and shallower recessions is proposed as if it were so obvious that only a blind ideologue – or a "crank" – would challenge it. But it turns out that this familiar claim relies on statistics that have been exploded over the past two decades. Even Christina Romer, former chair of Barack Obama's Council of Economic Advisers, has noted that these faulty figures overstate the instability that existed before the Fed and understate the instability since. The instability of output that did exist before the Fed was due almost entirely to the kind of natural output swings, as from harvest failures, that plague an agricultural society, while the instability we have seen since the Fed's creation is attributable far more to monetary policy itself.

We can be fairly certain, I think, that Matt Yglesias knows not a blessed thing about nineteenth-century bank panics, pre-Fed business cycles, or the scholarly revisions, to be found throughout the professional journals, to the previously accepted economic statistics that were once used to prove the relative success of the Fed. For that matter, neither do the vast majority of those who would condemn us as cranks for thinking there might be something dangerous and destabilizing about a central planning agency tinkering with interest rates and exercising a money monopoly. They bluff their way through snarky blog posts, knowing they'll never have to debate a knowledgeable opponent face to face. It's enough, they think, to call us cranks and leave it at that. We who are so perverse as to reject the glorious Biden/Romney spectrum deserve no better.

But meanwhile, hordes of brilliant young kids are mastering and building upon the edifice of Austrian thought. That an uncredentialed blogger who has made precisely zero scholarly contributions to anything at all wishes to lecture them for adopting something other than the reigning paradigm in economics – wherever did they get the idea that they ought to question authority? – is unlikely to give them much pause.

That's bad news for poor Matt Yglesias, who is the worst kind of progressive – the left-shill for the regime. Not only are we not going away, but we're actually getting stronger and more numerous. The rising generation of Austrians, I can testify, is full of geniuses – I might mention off the top of my head David Howden, Philipp Bagus, Mateusz Machaj, G.P. Manish, Malavika Nair, Per Bylund, Xavier Méra, Matt McCaffrey, and many more – who have mastered both the mainstream stuff to which Yglesias ritually genuflects as well as the Austrian alternative about which he knows only the cartoon version he encounters in the *New York Times*.

Good luck, buddy. You'll need it.

March 8, 2011

21

BE HAPPY WITH YOUR CABBAGE AND NAVY BEANS, CITIZEN

A quotation from Benjamin Franklin is being passed around by leftists these days:

> All the Property that is necessary to a man, for the conservation of the individual and the propagation of the species, is his natural right, which none can justly deprive him of: But all property superfluous to such purposes is the property of the publick, who, by their laws, have created it, and who may therefore by other laws dispose of it, whenever the welfare of the publick shall demand such disposition. He that does not like civil society on these terms, let him retire and live among savages.

This is supposed to shut me up, because it's Ben Franklin speaking. Why should it? Franklin was a mere mortal, and his arguments are only as strong as the logic behind them.

(A brief digression: my favorite Franklin story comes from 1729, when debate arose in Pennsylvania over whether the colonial government should engage in yet another round of paper money inflation. Franklin came to the assistance of the inflationists in government by writing *A Modest Inquiry into the Nature and Necessity of a Paper Currency*, which helped get the inflationary policy through the

Assembly. In return, guess whose print shop got the contract to print the money? Franklin noted that his "friends" in the Assembly, "who conceived I had been of some service, thought fit to reward me by employing me in printing the money, a very profitable job.")

There are quite a few problems with Franklin's argument – which is actually more assertion than argument – but a key issue is the distinction between property that is "necessary to a man, for the conservation of the individual and the propagation of the species" on the one hand, and property that is merely "superfluous" on the other. How does Franklin propose to make that distinction?

Economist George Stigler noted decades ago that in order to meet the nutritional standards of the U.S. government in 1943 least expensively, a man of 154 pounds could consume, in a year, 370 pounds of wheat flour, 57 cans of evaporated milk, 111 pounds of cabbage, 23 pounds of spinach, and 285 pounds of dried navy beans.

Is that all I'd be allowed under the Franklin scheme? Strictly speaking, all else is "superfluous." Yet Franklin leaves no record of having been quite so abstemious himself.

How about theater tickets? Are those "superfluous"? If not, how many theater tickets would Ben Franklin consider essential for a satisfying life?

You see how arbitrary and inane this becomes.

And who's going to decide what part of my property is necessary (and therefore all right for me to keep) and what part is "superfluous"? Government, of course – the very institution that will be able to grab the allegedly superfluous part for itself. Seems like the institution charged with making the decision about my property might – *might*, I say – have a vested interest in the outcome.

August 14, 2012

22

LEFT AND RIGHT: PEAS IN A POD

Whatever other problems mainstream conservatives have these days, the most pronounced is what we might call their readiness to hysteria.

To wit: just launch a military offensive, justifying it however you like – on behalf of national security, the liberation of an oppressed people, simple revenge, whatever – and they'll promptly leap to its defense. Everyone who supports the mission will be a great patriot, while opponents should be censored, jailed, or even executed. (Those people are probably in league with the terrorists anyway.) Certainly anyone who believes in alternatives to large-scale violence will be dismissed as a deluded idealist who lacks the realism that our dangerous world demands. All too many conservatives will readily believe and defend the stupidest, crudest propaganda and sloganeering, and launch crazed attacks on people telling what later (and inevitably) turns out to be the truth.

Yet so-called progressives aren't much better. Except with them you simply need to say something is in the public interest, and that it helps restrain all the bad guys who would otherwise prey upon the public. Everyone who supports the government's regulatory mission will be a great citizen – civic-minded, responsible, unselfish. Anyone who doesn't buy the official propaganda will be marginalized and ignored. (Those people are probably in league with big business anyway.) Certainly anyone who thinks alternatives exist to large-scale violence – after all, the state gets what it wants thanks to its power to threaten imprisonment and expropriation – will be dismissed as a deluded idealist who lacks the realism that our dangerous world demands. They'll readily believe the dumbest sloganeering about the public sector and all its alleged contributions to our standard of living.

What they think they know, since they learned it in school, is that life was unbearably awful before the days of multi-trillion dollar federal budgets. People were poor, worked long hours, and had much less living space than they do today. "Monopolies" dominated the economy and exploited worker and consumer alike. Without the modern regulatory apparatus, everything was poisonous and unsafe. You don't need me to continue, since this is what all of us got in school.

That people might have been impoverished because no other outcome was technically or even logically possible in a capital-starved economy is not even considered, if indeed it is even understood. That it is an unusual group of "monopolies" whose prices fell several times faster than did prices elsewhere in the economy is unknown and thus not mentioned. That the private-sector alternative to the 80,000 pages of government regulation in the Federal Register might be something other than *caveat emptor* and every man for himself is simply never entertained.

The state only wishes all its citizens could be this servile. In weaving their apologias on the state's behalf, so-called progressives – how that misleading term grates on me – are playing exactly the role the state seeks from them: legitimizing state behavior in the minds of the public. Their lack of curiosity about non-statist solutions and approaches – they show little interest in finding out how people managed their affairs in the days before the New Deal, for instance – is also a plus. All the easier to portray the past as unbearable, and the state as savior.

Of course, American history affords us no examples of pre-New Deal Americans climbing over the corpses of children and the elderly on their way to work, so presumably something was being done to care for people, but there seems to be relatively little interest in finding out exactly what that was. (David Beito explores this question in his important book *From Mutual Aid to the Welfare State.*)

Now what is the state, anyway? Forget all the romanticizing nonsense about social contract theories, the consent of the people, whatever. What *is* this institution? Here's Murray Rothbard:

The State is a group of people who have managed to acquire a virtual monopoly of the use of violence throughout a given territorial area. In particular, it has acquired a monopoly of aggressive violence, for States generally recognize the right of individuals to use violence (though not against States, of course) in self-defense. The State then uses this monopoly to wield power over the inhabitants of the area and to enjoy the material fruits of that power. The State, then, is the only organization in society that regularly and openly obtains its monetary revenues by the use of *aggressive* violence; all other individuals and organizations (except if delegated that right by the State) can obtain wealth only by peaceful production and by voluntary exchange of their respective products. This use of violence to obtain its revenue (called "taxation") is the keystone of State power. Upon this base the State erects a further structure of power over the individuals in its territory, regulating them, penalizing critics, subsidizing favorites, etc. The State also takes care to arrogate to itself the compulsory monopoly of various critical services needed by society, thus keeping the people in dependence upon the State for key services, keeping control of the vital command posts in society and also fostering among the public the myth that *only* the State can supply these goods and services. Thus the State is careful to monopolize police and judicial service, the ownership of roads and streets, the supply of money, and the postal service, and effectively to monopolize or control education, public utilities, transportation, and radio and television.

That single paragraph does more than a lifetime of social studies classes to clarify the true nature of the state and its activities. There's your great vehicle for progress, stripped to its essentials.

Albert Jay Nock, as we noted in chapter 11, discussed the human inclination to seek after wealth with the least possible exertion. This is why employing the state for one's private benefit is so tempting for so many people. Franz Oppenheimer described two ways of acquiring wealth: the economic means and the political means. The economic means involves the production of a good or service that is then sold to willing buyers seeking to improve their own well-being. Both parties benefit. The political means, on the other hand, involves the use of force to enrich one party or group at the expense of another – either to acquire someone else's wealth directly or to give oneself an unfair advantage over his competitors through the use or threat of coercion. That is a much easier way of enriching oneself; and since people tend to prefer an easier over a more difficult path to wealth, a society that hopes to foster both justice and prosperity needs to discourage wealth acquisition via the political means and encourage it through the economic means.

Progressives are confident, however, that when the smoke clears, the net effect of all this looting, all these coerced exchanges, and the massive increase in state power it brings about, will be to benefit the least among us, even though these happen to be the people with the least spare time to engage in political lobbying, have the fewest resources to use for the purposes of bribery and corruption, and are connected to by far the fewest old boys' networks.

So here's what we have: a right-wing cheering gallery and excuse factory for the state's behavior abroad, and a left-wing cheering gallery for its aggression and looting at home. (The political "center" cheers both the foreign and the domestic aggression, of course, as evidence of its wise moderation.) Both of them duly accept and defend the state's official motivations, and demonize anyone who dares to be skeptical either of the purity of its intentions or the potential effectiveness of its actions. Meanwhile, the politicos running the show toast themselves and enjoy a good laugh over the amazing racket they have going, and what a bunch of gullible automatons it is their good fortune to rule.

May 8, 2007

23

MY SUBVERSIVE BOOK

Nearly two years after its release I continue to get emails about, and to observe praise and condemnations of, my *Politically Incorrect Guide to American History*. Although the book received plenty of kind reviews by a great many people – especially memorable was being named Most Original Thinker of the Year by Pat Buchanan on the year-end episode of PBS's long-running news program *The McLaughlin Group* – it's more interesting to say a few words about the negative ones.

The most important ran on the *New York Times* editorial page, and for the most part consisted of listing the forbidden things I'd said without troubling to inform us why they were wrong. Why, these things just shouldn't be said, that's all! It's probably not necessary to point out that my sales rank shot up again following the *Times*'s condemnation.

Incidentally, not long after the *New York Times* hit piece (which I believe is now available online only for a fee; my reply is on the Articles page at TomWoods. com, under "Replies to Critics"), the *Times* actually let me give my part of the story in the form of a favorable profile by writer Natalie Canavor, who interviewed me in my office for 90 minutes. Complete with a picture of me smiling at my desk, the resulting article "Revisionist History? A Professor Hopes So," was on balance favorable toward the very person they'd condemned as an enemy of society not a month earlier.

Reason magazine contributing editor Cathy Young took to the pages of the *Boston Globe* to portray me as — wait for it — a "neo-Confederate" with disreputable motives. She's a libertarian and everything, she assured the world, but I was taking the whole libertarian thing much too far: didn't I know that some of those American wars just had to be fought, and that only some kind of extremist would dissent from the regime's portrayal of Abraham Lincoln? Just after September 11, by the way, Young lectured libertarians that "a free society is not a suicide pact," and explained that we would just have to accept new forms of government surveillance. No wonder she didn't like my book.

About ten days before her article appeared, Young wrote to ask a few questions about my "background." I gave lengthy and detailed answers to all of them. They created a problem for her, though, since they made me sound intelligent and reasonable. In addition, I constructed the sentences so that she would not be able to take a few words out of context; the entire sentence would have to be quoted in order for my remarks to make sense. That wouldn't do at all for Cathy Young, who solved that little problem by not quoting a single word that I wrote to her.

The nefarious Tom Woods has friends and allies everywhere, however — even, as it turns out, in the upper echelons of the *Reason* world. One such ally made clear to all concerned that Young's attack was unacceptable and that I was to be left alone. They never said a word about me again.

What has amazed me most is the longevity of Max Boot's review, published on the website of the *Weekly Standard*. Boot personifies every horrifying and jingoistic feature of what we laughingly call conservatism today. Boot famously observed in late 2001 that the United States had not suffered enough casualties in its War on Terror, and later called for a "Freedom Legion" of foreign soldiers who could serve in that war. With the U.S. military increasingly strapped, Boot explained, we need to realize that there is "a pretty big pool of manpower that's not being tapped: everyone on the planet who is not a U.S. citizen or permanent resident." This is a good idea, according to Boot, because (among other things) congressmen would have fewer scruples about sending non-Americans into battle than they would about sending their own constituents.

Here's what historian Juan Cole has had to say about Boot:

Boot never saw a war he didn't love, never saw a conquest he didn't find exhilarating, never saw an occupied land he didn't think could be handled. He wrote an op-ed for the *New York Times* in which he monstrously expressed approval of the way the US killed 200,000 Filipinos to make the occupation of the Philippines stick. July 6, 2003 NYT: "The United States eventually won, but it was a long, hard, bloody slog that cost the lives of more than 4,200 American soldiers, 16,000 rebels and some 200,000 civilians. Even after the formal end of hostilities on July 4, 1902, sporadic resistance dragged on for years. There is no reason to think that the current struggle in Iraq will be remotely as difficult. But the Philippine war is a useful reminder that Americans have a long history of fighting guerrillas – and usually prevailing, though seldom quickly or easily."

Yet leftist bloggers happily linked to Boot's angry review of my book – they could overlook all that immigrants-as-cannon-fodder stuff in order to go after an iconoclastic historian who strays from allowable opinion. Likewise, every neoconservative who dislikes me solemnly refers to the Boot review. (The print edition of the *Weekly Standard* ran a surprisingly favorable review, which my neocon critics pass over in silence.) But the Boot review is probably the most foolish one of all.

For instance, Boot dismisses my criticism of Harry Truman – the neoconservatives' favorite Democrat, after Woodrow Wilson – for going to war in Korea without a congressional declaration of war; don't I know that "previous presidents had sent U.S. troops into battle hundreds of times without any declaration of war"? This laughable hundreds-of-times claim originated as a piece of official propaganda during the Korean and Vietnam Wars. For the truth, see TomWoods.com/warpowers.

Again in typical neocon fashion, Boot distills important questions into bumper-sticker slogans, with failure to endorse the U.S. government's position indicating "sympathy" for the other side. Thus my "sympathy extends not only to slave-owning rebels but also to German militarists." Yes, that's a fair and sensible summary of my views: I favor private property, individual rights, and peace – except when slaveowners or German militarists violate those things, in which case I abandon all my principles and stand up and cheer.

I sympathize with German militarists, you see, because I think it was a bad idea for Woodrow Wilson to send armed merchant ships, ordered to fire on surfacing submarines, into a war zone, at a time when the country was overwhelmingly in favor of peace. I also have this crazy idea that Britain's starvation of 750,000 German civilians – 150 times as many people as the Germans are estimated to have killed in Belgium – was kind of bad.

Boot's discussion of my position on the Fourteenth Amendment – he'd apparently never heard the view, most recently advanced by historian Forrest McDonald, that it was not constitutionally ratified – takes a single sentence out of context in order to make it seem that I opposed the Amendment because it disqualified ex-Confederates from holding political office. (As if who's allowed to run for government positions is a subject that would keep me, of all people, up at night.) I actually argued, correctly, that that was one of the reasons that *nineteenth-century Southerners* opposed the Amendment.

The real reason to be concerned about the Amendment – not that anyone reading Boot's review would know it – is its utility to the federal government as an entering wedge into local concerns, a phenomenon well documented by the Cato Institute's Gene Healy. Boot, a nationalist to the core, has more interest in figuring out how to recruit Togolese nationals into the U.S. Army than in the centralizing implications of the Fourteenth Amendment, but he should probably mention them all the same.

Boot's objections to my book were pretty much the same as the ones advanced by the *New York Times*, which tells you something about neoconservatism. The neocons, in my experience, don't have all that much of a quarrel with the standard narrative of U.S. history. The conservatives of the old *National Review* certainly did, but when it comes to major episodes of the American past, I don't see where a neoconservative truly dissents. In fact, after reading Boot's *Times*-like attack, Pat Buchanan wrote to tell me that Boot "takes the establishment line on American history – one the old *National Review* rejected – and swallows it in one gulp."

Ronald Radosh, New Leftist-turned-neoconservative, referred in his own review to what he called the "tough-minded and accurate blast by Boot." To this day I still shake my head at that phrase. Radosh, himself a professional historian, is so committed to neoconservatism that he can bring himself to endorse this tissue of nonsense? Is Boot's discussion of presidential war powers "accurate," Professor Radosh? Is his summary of the Principles of '98 "accurate"? Was U.S. entry into World War I such an act of genius that criticizing it is necessarily perverse?

The occasional leftist review reflected sheer horror at my temerity in pulling down the icons of Lincoln, FDR, and the rest of the "great presidents" before whose august visages we are supposed to wave incense as we meditate upon our own unworthiness. Several early Amazon reviewers actually called the book "jingoistic." Could they even have read it? What is "jingoistic" about a book that celebrates no American war other than the War for Independence? In the Age of Bush you might think the left, while not necessarily starting up a Tom Woods fan club, might at least be satisfied that a bestselling book being read by many conservatives denounced modern presidential war powers and glorified not a single American war – and therefore didn't feed into the worst and most despicable aspects of modern conservatism.

Instead, left-wing law professors linked to Max Boot's review, indicating that rather than just staying out of the dispute – or, heaven forbid, siding with me – they preferred to direct their readers to someone who 1) believes the president may send as many troops as he likes anywhere he likes without needing anyone's consent; 2) wants to recruit foreigners into the U.S. Army because congressmen would be more likely to send them than native-born Americans into harm's way; and 3) thinks the U.S. government's suppression of Filipino nationalists was just the right thing to do. I'd love to hear an explanation of how these positions are preferable to the conclusions of my book, or why I, an antiwar antistatist, am a more dangerous person than Boot.

You can perhaps understand, incidentally, why I am therefore skeptical when fellow libertarians tell me we need to "reach out to the left." There was no reason for leftists to treat me as they did, particularly if they are consistently antiwar, which I am now inclined to doubt. I have had vastly more success turning conservatives antiwar than I have to getting leftists to read a single sentence I write, though I have had a little success even here, without really trying. (Having had my hand bitten off by every allegedly antiwar leftist who responded to my book, I think I was a pretty good sport to go ahead and extend my other hand to them by writing the book *We Who Dared to Say No to War* with my leftist friend Murray Polner.)

Once in a while, incidentally, I hear from a libertarian who criticizes the book's occasional arguments from the Constitution – i.e., its claims that this or that government measure violated that document. Who cares about the Constitution, demand these critics, since what matters are natural rights rather than positive law – and Lysander Spooner already showed that the Constitution isn't truly binding anyway.

Whatever their merits, though, these arguments are beside the point. It is not to make a fetish of the Constitution to observe that the federal government has systematically denigrated and ignored it, or interpreted it in tendentious ways. A rather good proselytizing point for our side, it seems to me, involves calling attention to the federal government's contempt for the Constitution, the very rules it agreed to observe. I know of a number of people who abandoned their fairly conventional conservatism once it finally hit them that a "return to the Constitution" would be unstable and impermanent even if it were possible, since a piece of paper that the government alone interprets is unlikely to keep that same government restrained.

October 9, 2006

PART IV

RON PAUL AND FORBIDDEN TRUTHS

24

RON PAUL AND THE REMNANT

Few people in public life ever stray from what I often call the three-by-five card of approved opinion. On those rare occasions when they do, a macabre ritual of clarifications, retractions, and apologies – a veritable liturgy of expiation – invariably follows. Forgive me, for I have contradicted the holy mainstream. Never again shall I stray from the Biden-to-Romney spectrum.

The world changed on May 15, 2007. Someone strayed from Establishment opinion, and then not only declined to do penance, but actually stood his ground and refused to be intimidated into silence.

That day, in a Republican presidential debate, Ron Paul said things Americans were not supposed to hear about their government's foreign policy. When former New York mayor Rudy Giuliani demanded a retraction, Dr. Paul wouldn't give him the satisfaction. He instead pressed his point even harder.

Jon Arden, a regular American who happened to be watching, was instantly converted to the Paul cause: "Ron Paul, without a friend in the world, nothing but hostility aimed at him from all directions, stood his ground and did not back down. Just reiterated his points even stronger. I was blown away. I felt at that moment that the world changed forever, that there had been this massive shift in reality and what could happen."

It wouldn't be the last such moment. In a GOP debate – in Florida, of all places – Ron Paul said the U.S. government should normalize trade relations with Cuba. In a South Carolina debate he stuck by his guns on the drug war. At a meeting of an Arab-American association, he was asked if he had a special speech tailored to their group. No, he said. It would be the same speech he gives everywhere.

That's who Ron Paul is.

Why did he do these things? Why didn't he take the path of least resistance by speaking in slogans and taking no political risks? One reason is obvious: he's an honest man.

The other reason may not be so obvious: he was seeking out the Remnant.

Once in a while we hear Ron Paul speak of the Remnant – how he's been trying to find it, speak to it, build it up. What does he mean by it?

He's referring to "Isaiah's Job," a famous essay by Albert Jay Nock. In that essay, Nock borrowed the example of the prophet Isaiah to describe the task of the honest man in public life. (I think the example of Elijah is a bit closer to what Nock had in mind, but that's not the point.)

Listen as Nock adapts the Lord's instructions to Isaiah into a modern vernacular:

> "Tell them what is wrong, and why and what is going to happen unless they have a change of heart and straighten up. Don't mince matters. Make it clear that they are positively down to their last chance. Give it to them good and strong and keep on giving it to them. I suppose perhaps I ought to tell you," He added, "that it won't do any good. The official class and their intelligentsia will turn up their noses at you and the masses will not even listen. They will all keep on in their own ways until they carry everything down to destruction, and you will probably be lucky if you get out with your life."

Isaiah had not been reluctant to take on his divinely appointed task, but when it was put to him like that, it seemed like a fruitless task indeed. What was the point of embarking on a mission that was doomed to failure?

"Ah," the Lord said, "you do not get the point. There is a Remnant there that you know nothing about. They are obscure, unorganized, inarticulate, each one rubbing along as best he can. They need to be encouraged and braced up because when everything has gone completely to the dogs, they are the ones who will come back and build up a new society; and meanwhile, your preaching will reassure them and keep them hanging on. Your job is to take care of the Remnant, so be off now and set about it."

And that's what Dr. Paul has been doing. He's been looking for this heretofore invisible Remnant, giving them comfort, making them aware of themselves, providing them a rallying point. Selling out for the sake of mainstream respectability would defeat his purpose entirely. Those approaches repel the Remnant, Nock said. On the other hand, the truth-teller who appeals to the Remnant will find them.

To be sure, Ron Paul has wanted to make his message as appealing to as many people as possible. He never gratuitously drives anyone away. But he has accomplished this task not by the usual method, which is to water down the message according to focus-group results. He has simply explained himself, boldly and without retreat.

And thus Nock:

> [Isaiah] preached to the masses only in the sense that he preached publicly. Anyone who liked might listen; anyone who liked might pass by. He knew that the Remnant would listen; and knowing also that nothing was to be expected of the masses under any circumstances, he made no specific appeal to them, did not accommodate his message to their measure in any way, and did not care two straws whether they heeded it or not. As a modern publisher might put it, he was not worrying about circulation or about advertising. Hence, with all such obsessions quite out of the way, he was in a position to do his level best, without fear or favor, and answerable only to his august Boss.

A lot of people, possibly even the majority, don't want their worldviews challenged. They want endless goodies. They want checks with their names on them. They want to be flattered. As I've said before, they want: "You are the awesomest of the awesome, and that's why your government is hated around the world: because of your awesomeness."

Someone at this level of moral and intellectual development is not going to understand Ron Paul, much less support him.

It is frustrating and fruitless to appeal to such people, says Nock.

> They ask you to give them what they want, they insist upon it, and will take nothing else; and following their whims, their irrational changes of fancy, their hot and cold fits, is a tedious business, to say nothing of the fact that what they want at any time makes very little call on one's resources of prophesy. The Remnant, on the other hand, want only the best you have, whatever that may be. Give them that, and they are satisfied; you have nothing more to worry about.

Ron Paul had so much fundraising success because the Remnant had rarely if ever been sought out by a presidential candidate before. Here was a man of intelligence who defied all political convention, taught the public about things they didn't even realize they should be interested in, and could boast a record of consistency that impressed even the most hardened cynic. That got their attention.

Nock had things mostly right, but I would amend his presentation just a bit. He appeared to speak as if the Remnant were a fixed number of people. They might be sought out, but that's it. Dr. Paul has shown that the Remnant can be increased, not just found and inspired. Dr. Paul's commitment to the truth, even when it seemed to yield him only grief, seized the attention of a great many apathetic Americans, and added them to the ranks of the Remnant.

Nock further described the task of finding the Remnant as a largely thankless one, a job for which one would search in vain for tangible results.

> In any given society the Remnant are always so largely an unknown quantity.... You do not know, and will never know, who the Remnant are, nor what they are doing or will do. Two things you do know, and no more: First, that they exist; second, that they will find you. Except for these two certainties, working for the Remnant means working in impenetrable darkness.

Nock lived before the Internet. Ron Paul now knows who the Remnant are. He has a sense of their numbers. He knows some of the things they're doing. He knows he has had an impact. Nock didn't think this was possible. In his day, it wasn't.

Today we live at a moment of opportunity none of us could have imagined a generation ago. A revolution in information transmission is under way. Anyone can express his ideas before the whole world. All of a sudden, ideas, books, and people shunned by the Biden-to-Romney spectrum can get a worldwide hearing. Next to this, Gutenberg looks like a lazy bum.

Ron Paul did his job. He found and built up the Remnant. And there, rather than in the fleeting passage of legislation, is where genuine, long-term change will emerge.

June 22, 2012

25

RON PAUL DOES NOT HAVE A "CULT" FOLLOWING

We hear this claim all the time: Ron Paul has a "cult-like" following. I guess because people are so devoted to him, flocking to straw polls in droves while supporters of other candidates can't be bothered to get off the couch to vote for their guy, people assume there must be some kind of cult of personality at work. Instead of asking what's so wrong with the other candidates that they generate so little enthusiasm, critics instead assail Paul's supporters.

Yet the Paul movement, as should be obvious, is the very opposite of a cult. For one thing, their leader hardly ever uses the word "I." For another, they have substantive reasons for supporting him. Speak to a Ron Paul supporter and you'll find someone who knows much more than the average person about topics like monetary policy, the Constitution, U.S. history, economics, and much else. That person can give as many solid, substantive reasons for supporting Ron Paul as you have time to listen to.

Contrast this to what we often see from supporters of other candidates. They like theirs because the candidate "looks presidential," "seems like a leader" (isn't *that* kind of cultish?), was a businessman, gives a nice speech, and so on. In other words, the reasons tend to be based on the person as opposed to the ideas that person champions.

I am not trying to turn the accusation around and say supporters of other candidates are the real cultists, though you can see the sense in which the shoe fits. Their support for their candidates is much too fickle, as the poll fluctuations we've seen make clear, for the "cult" designation to work.

But for heaven's sake, what explanation is there for the support for businessman Herman Cain? Is it his stance on the issues? The Tea Party people supporting him are supposed to be against bank bailouts, which Cain supported. They're supposed to be against Mitt Romney, whom Cain supported. They're supposed to care about the debt, and Cain is criticizing Ron Paul for being too extreme in wanting to balance the budget in three years! They're supposed to care about the economy, but Cain gave the economy a clean bill of health on September 1, 2008, on the eve of the collapse.

So Cain directly *defies* the principles his supporters claim in the abstract to stand for, yet they support him anyway. And people say Ron Paul's supporters are cultish?

Cain's poll numbers began a substantial decline thanks to accusations of marital infidelity, an issue the very same voters are prepared to overlook in Newt Gingrich, whose numbers were simultaneously rising. What did not manage to bring Cain's poll numbers down, oddly enough, was his actual record on issues his supporters pretended to care about. Cain would have been brought down months earlier by his stated views, if people cared more about principles and less about whether a guy stands up straight, gives a good speech, or ran a business.

Newt Gingrich, who has been rising in the polls, is another candidate perfectly suited for what the average GOP voter appears to want: an Establishment candidate offering insignificant changes.

A Suffolk University poll of Florida Republicans in October 2011 found 25 percent in support of Mitt Romney and 24 percent supporting Herman Cain. In other words, these voters believe the country is about 4 percent off track but basically all right. For all their talk about how bad Obama is, apparently things aren't *that* bad if they want to replace him with a safe establishment man like Romney or Cain (former head of the Kansas City Federal Reserve).

Under Romney it's obvious nothing will change. Under Cain it's only slightly less obvious. His big proposal is a revenue-neutral tax shifting. He has no plans to cut anything. He supported Romney in 2008. He supported TARP – he had *no idea* it would be used to "pick winners and losers"! – which means that on the key economic issue of our time, which Reagan budget director David Stockman calls "the single greatest economic-policy abomination since the 1930s, or perhaps ever," Cain chose the Establishment over the people. He lectured "free-market purists" for opposing it.

You can imagine how much "change" we can expect from someone like that — the whole establishment lines up on one side (the *New York Times*, the *Washington Post*, the cable news commentators, John McCain, Barack Obama) and the American people on the other, and Cain goes with the establishment. But he'll be a maverick next time that happens, right?

Not to mention he thought there was nothing wrong with the economy as late as September 1, 2008. It was an "imaginary recession," he said, cooked up by a hostile media that hates Republicans.

Over the following two weeks, (1) Fannie Mae and Freddie Mac were taken over by the U.S. government (Sept. 7); (2) Merrill Lynch was sold to Bank of America; (3) Lehman Brothers declared bankruptcy; (4) the Fed bailed out AIG; (5) Washington Mutual was sold to JP MorganChase; (6) Treasury Secretary Hank Paulson said the economy was so bad that $700 billion must be spent on bailouts immediately; otherwise, warned Ben Bernanke, "we may not have an economy on Monday."

How could Cain be expected to fix something he couldn't perceive, and actually ridiculed other people for pointing out? Worse still, he is such a lightweight on the economy that he calls his economic adviser onto the stage to answer even simple questions.

His foreign policy is indistinguishable from Hillary Clinton's. Both subscribe to the entirely conventional bipartisan foreign-policy consensus, which has yielded Americans one budget-busting boondoggle after another.

Meanwhile, Ron Paul specifically warned in 2001 that Alan Greenspan and the Federal Reserve, whose NASDAQ bubble had just burst, were in the process of creating a housing bubble. He made comparably prescient statements over the next several years, while every single other Republican candidate in the running was either mute on the economy or actually thrilled with it. Thus Joe Scarborough asked him: "How could it be that you knew this on the Banking Committee in 2003, and nobody else did until after the collapse?"

So Florida voters are telling us this: we don't want a truth-teller who in 2001 explained precisely what was happening to the economy. We don't want any deviation from the trillion-dollar bipartisan foreign policy, even though we don't support any other bipartisan program. We want someone as oblivious as we can find who will more or less keep things the way they are.

We are facing a serious, long-term and systemic problem, and all the Cains, Gingrichs, Romneys, and Perrys of the world can come up with is a little regulatory tinkering and some tax reform. This is completely irrelevant to the problems we face right now. We need sweeping, systemic changes, carried out by a real supporter of the free market who sees the whole picture, not trivial tinkering by some empty suit.

Yes, I know, we are not supposed to like Ron Paul because of his foreign policy. The presumption seems to be that anyone who dissents from a foreign policy cooked up and supported by Hillary Clinton, Mitt Romney, Joe Biden, Mitch McConnell, the *New York Times*, and the *Washington Post* is probably crazy. But in the end, it may not really be all that conservative to blow trillions of dollars, supposedly to fight Islamic radicalism, on a war against the two-bit nobody who ran a secular Iraq, while our own country is drowning in red ink.

The misnamed "Defense" Department (misnamed because after 9/11 the federal government created an entirely new department, Homeland Security, whose stated purpose was to in fact defend the country) is the one government program conservatives may never question. This one is run by omniscient angels who don't even need to be audited. This one has no entrenched interests of its own that it might pursue at the expense of the common good. That's true only of the farm lobby and the education bureaucracies. This is the Department of Defense, citizen. Trust them! USA! USA!

Can conservatives for once realize that their "limited government" slogan means limited government, not limited government plus a far-flung military presence at odds with every shred of advice from the Founding Fathers about the incompatibility of permanent war with the health of a republic? Might they consider the slight – *slight* –possibility that the federal government is not just deceiving them about health care but about foreign affairs as well?

Can we do this just long enough to let Ron Paul, armed with more economic knowledge than the rest of the Republican field combined (I realize this is the faintest praise known to man), steer the country back in the right direction?

November 14, 2011

26

26 THINGS NON-PAUL VOTERS WERE BASICALLY SAYING

During the 2008 and 2012 presidential campaigns, Ron Paul spoke forbidden truths, didn't measure his every word according to the promptings of political consultants, stuck to his principles through thick and thin, and refused to speak to the American public in slogans. Yet millions of Republican voters insisted on being talked down to by plastic men straight out of central casting.

What could they have been thinking? I came up with these 26 possibilities.

(1) The American political establishment has done a super job keeping our country prosperous and our liberties protected, so I'm sure whatever candidate they push on me is probably a good one.

(2) Our country is basically bankrupt. Unfunded entitlement liabilities are in excess of $200 trillion. Therefore, it's a good idea to vote for someone who offers no specific spending cuts of any kind.

(3) Vague promises to cut spending are good enough for me, even though they have always resulted in higher spending in the past.

(4) I prefer a candidate who plays to the crowd, instead of having the courage to tell his audience things they may not want to hear.

(5) I am deeply concerned about spending. Therefore, I would like to vote for someone who supported Medicare Part D, thereby adding $7 trillion to Medicare's unfunded liabilities.

(6) I am opposed to bailouts. Therefore, I will vote for a candidate who supported TARP.

(7) The federal government is much too involved in education, where it has no constitutional role. Therefore, I will vote for a candidate who supported expanding the Department of Education and favored the No Child Left Behind Act.

(8) Even though practically everyone was caught by surprise in the 2008 financial crisis, which we are still reeling from, it's a good idea not to vote for the one man in politics who predicted exactly what was bound to unfold, all the way back in 2001.

(9) I am not impressed by a candidate who inspires people, especially young ones, to read the great economists and political philosophers.

(10) I am concerned about taxes. Therefore, I will not vote for the one candidate who has never supported a tax increase.

(11) I believe it is conservative to support bringing the Enlightenment to Afghanistan via military intervention.

(12) Even though I lost half my retirement portfolio when the economy crashed from the sugar high the Federal Reserve's artificially low interest rates put it on, I would like to vote for someone who is not really interested in the Federal Reserve.

(13) Even though 50 years of the embargo on Cuba did nothing to undermine Fidel Castro, and in fact handed him a perfect excuse for all the failures of socialism, I favor continuing this policy.

(14) If someone has a drug problem, prison rape is the best solution I can think of.

(15) Even though the Constitution had to be amended to allow for alcohol prohibition, and even though I claim to care about the Constitution, I don't mind that there's no constitutional authorization for the war on drugs, and I will punish at the polls anyone who favors the constitutional solution of returning the issue to the states.

(16) I believe only a "liberal" would think it was inhumane to keep essential items out of Iraq in the 1990s, even though one of the first people to protest this policy was Pat Buchanan.

(17) The Brookings Institution says Newt Gingrich's 1994 Contract with America was an insignificant nibbling around the edges. I favor people who support insignificant nibbling around the edges, as long as they occasionally trick me with a nice speech.

(18) I am deeply concerned about radical Islam, so it was a good idea to depose the secular Saddam Hussein – who was so despised by Islamists that Osama bin Laden himself offered to fight against him in the 1991 Persian Gulf War – and replace him with a Shiite regime friendly with Iran, while also bringing about a new Iraqi constitution that makes Islam the state religion and forbids any law that contradicts its teachings.

(19) Indefinite detention for U.S. citizens seems like nothing to be worried about, especially since our political class is so trustworthy that it could never abuse such a power.

(20) Following up on (19), I believe Thomas Jefferson was just being paranoid when he said, "In questions of power, then, let no more be heard of confidence in man, but bind him down from mischief by the chains of the Constitution."

(21) Even though the war in Iraq was based on crude propaganda I would have laughed at if the Soviet Union had peddled it, and even though the result has been hundreds of thousands of dead Iraqis, four million people displaced, trillions of dollars down the drain, tens of thousands of serious injuries among American servicemen and an epidemic of suicide throughout the military, not to mention the ruination of America's reputation in the world, I see no reason to be skeptical when the same people who peddled that fiasco urge me to support yet another war as my country is going bankrupt.

(22) I have not been exploited enough by the cozy relationship between large financial firms and the U.S. government, and I would like to see it continue.

(23) I know the media will smear or marginalize anyone who would really fix this country. But when the media smears and marginalizes Ron Paul, I will draw no conclusion from this.

(24) I want to be spoken to like this: "My fellow Americans, you are the awesomest of the awesome, and the only reason anyone in the world might be unhappy with your government is because of your sheer awesomeness."

(25) I think it's a good idea to vote for Mitt Romney, whose top three donors are Goldman Sachs, Credit Suisse, and Morgan Stanley, and a bad idea to vote for Ron Paul, whose top three donors are the U.S. Army, the U.S. Navy, and the U.S. Air Force.

(26) I do not trust the media. But when the media tells me I am not to support Ron Paul, who says things he is not allowed to say, I will comply.

February 8, 2012

27

WARNING: FORBIDDEN TRUTH UTTERED

Ron Paul violated one of the most consistently observed rules of American political life in the GOP debate in South Carolina the other night: government officials are never, ever to level with the American population. The people are to be endlessly flattered, spoken to in bumper-sticker slogans, and in general treated like seven-year-olds.

Congressman Paul crossed another, more specific forbidden line when he contradicted one of the major working assumptions of nearly all mainstream American pundits: foreigners never, ever get angry at the U.S. government's foreign policy, and would never for any reason want to avenge themselves against it. You can go out of your way to prevent water treatment facilities from being repaired, you can starve and bomb without compunction, and you can bring about half a million deaths, and the people will quietly take it. In fact, they probably spend their time reproaching themselves for having so displeased the U.S. government.

A man of principle and in possession of an IQ above 80, Paul naturally refused to play along. He explained that foreign policy has consequences, and that political and military interference around the world has a tendency to stir up whole peoples against us. If we ignore this simple and obvious fact, we do so at our peril. His implicit conclusion was that the shenanigans of our government have made our people more hated and more vulnerable than ever. In sum, if you want to play empire, you cannot pretend that doing so will be costless.

To the automatons of 2007 America, this is called "blaming America" for 9/11. Detectives should bear that in mind the next time they seek the motive behind a murder. "You're looking for *motive*? Are you saying the dead man had it coming?"

Reports from all over the intelligence community have repeatedly confirmed Paul's point, as if we needed express confirmation of what in normal times would be a matter of simple common sense. The CIA's Michael Scheuer told CNN: "We're being attacked for what we do in the Islamic world, not for who we are or what we believe in or how we live. And there's a huge burden of guilt to be laid at Mr. Bush, Mr. Clinton, both parties for simply lying to the American people."

Now I can already hear the other objection: Islamic history and theology provide ample pretext for jihad violence for anyone who wants to find it. Supposing the truth of that claim for the sake of argument, what exactly is it that makes them seem to want to find it? Are we to ignore the countless reports showing how the dumb belligerence of the current administration has increased the ranks of the radicals? And why does Osama bin Laden bother producing recruitment tapes detailing atrocities against Muslims if all he really has to do is point to the Koran and send the suicide bombers on their way to America?

The rest of the world, hearing Paul's remarks, will doubtless be relieved to know that there are still at least a few Americans in public life who are able to process information at higher than a sixth-grade level, and whose understanding of international affairs isn't cartoonish and delusional. But being a conservative today, of course, means that on principle you don't care what the rest of the world thinks — what are you, some kind of commie? God bless America!

It's a good thing for him that Russell Kirk didn't have to live to see the deranged caricature of itself that American conservatism has now become. Kirk, one of the key architects of that movement, spent the last years of his life opposing every military adventure of the U.S. government. The average conservative today, on the other hand, who knows only what the government and its neocon shills tell him, would be at an utter loss to account for that.

(On the domestic front, one brief observation: only Ron Paul spoke forthrightly of scaling back the scope of the federal government. Poor Tommy Thompson couldn't think of a single thing he'd want to cut – oh, except paragraph 17b, line 32, from some health program whose purpose would take fifteen minutes to describe. He wasn't alone: the rest of the candidates droned on about cutting waste and abuse – code for business as usual. As Lew Rockwell put it, "The others couldn't name one federal typewriter they would sell off." No wonder they hate having Ron Paul there.)

There are still some Americans who don't enjoy being propagandized, talked down to, or treated like imbeciles, and it is they in particular who appreciate Ron Paul. Long after the self-promoting phonies on that stage are gone and forgotten, Ron will still be admired.

May 17, 2007

28

WHY DO THEY HATE US?

Days after the fateful South Carolina debate in which Ron Paul refused to flatter and patronize the American people, instead explaining to them the concept of "blowback" –that foreign intervention can lead to unintended, undesirable consequences, the Texas congressman held a special press conference with Michael Scheuer, the former head of the CIA's bin Laden unit. (Scheuer, incidentally, is a conservative who has never voted for a non-Republican candidate.)

The event should have received more attention than it did – since Scheuer was there to say that Dr. Paul had been exactly right in his exchange with Rudy Giuliani:

> There are now ten Republican candidates in the field and there are eight Democrats. Seventeen of them are not at all a worry to Osama bin Laden and what he represents.... Dr. Paul has hit on exactly the only indispensable ally that al Qaeda, Osama bin Laden, and their allies have, and that's U.S. foreign policy.

> It is a patent absurdity on the part of the governing establishment in the United States to believe that the war we are engaged in at the moment has anything to do with our freedoms, our democracy, gender equality, or my having a Budweiser after work.... This war has to do with our

foreign policy and its impact in the Islamic world. That has nothing to do with judging the moral or monetary or political worth of our policies. It's simply to understand what motivates our enemy.

Scheuer went on to recount the Ayatollah Khomeini's abject failure over the course of a decade to instigate a jihad against America on account of our debauchery, our entertainment, our women in the workplace, and the like. It was a complete flop. No one blew himself up because of R-rated movies.

What made Osama bin Laden's message attractive, on the other hand, was precisely that it was defensive in nature, focusing on specific grievances that resonated with his Muslim audience. That, and not a war against the West over its decadence, is what won recruits. In other words, we may in fact be dealing not with comic-book villains but with actual human beings.

"It's very common for the slurs to be thrown when you say something like this," Scheuer hastened to add. "You're an appeaser, you're an anti-American. I think it's a shame, but the governing establishment wants to protect itself. It does not want to talk about these issues.... I think Dr. Paul has done a tremendous service to the American people." It is important to debate American foreign policy for a change, he said. "At the end of the debate, Americans may decide that the foreign policy status quo that exists at the moment is what they want. But if they do, they will at least go into it with their eyes open, and know that they are in for an extended period of war, a tremendously bloody and costly war."

In an interview with Antiwar Radio several days before the press conference, Scheuer said: "I thought Mr. Paul captured it the other night exactly correctly. This war is dangerous to America because it's based, not on gender equality, as Mr. Giuliani suggested, or any other kind of freedom, but simply because of what we do in the Islamic world – because 'we're over there,' basically, as Mr. Paul said in the debate."

To be sure, Scheuer observed, Muhammad described the end state of Islam on earth as a caliphate in which the whole world would be Muslim. But "there's as much chance of that happening in any kind of foreseeable future as the application of the Golden Rule, and 'turn the other cheek' and 'love thy neighbor' in the Christian world. There's no chance. Bin Laden is popular and his message resonates because it is a defensive message. It is very much a message of 'get out and leave us to our own problems.'"

He continued:

> About the only thing that can hold together the very loose coalition that Osama bin Laden has assembled is a common Muslim hatred for the impact of U.S. foreign policy…. They all agree they hate U.S. foreign policy. To the degree we change that policy in the interests of the United States, they become more and more focused on their local problems: attacking the Philippine government, attacking the Saudi government or the Egyptian government….
>
> Mr. Paul spoke not only the truth, but he spoke in the interests of the American people. And from the right and from the left he got chopped up. And at the end of the day you admire Mr. Paul's courage but what you fear for is the security of America, because the people who attacked Mr. Paul are much more concerned with staying in power than they are with protecting my family and yours.
>
> Unfortunately, what Mr. Paul is saying…will become so clear to the American people the next time Osama bin Laden attacks inside the United States and we have a disaster bigger than 9/11. And then the talk of "they hate us for primary elections" and "they hate us for gender equality" – that will go out the window, and maybe we can get down to brass tacks after we have multiple tens of thousands of dead Americans.

Antiwar Radio's Scott Horton also interviewed former CIA counter-terrorism officer Philip Giraldi, who largely shared Scheuer's assessment:

> I think anybody who knows anything about what's been going on for the last ten years would realize that cause and effect are operating here – that, essentially, al Qaeda has an agenda which very specifically says what its grievances are. And its grievances are basically that "we're over there."

So all Ron Paul was basically saying was that – as even the 9/11 Commission report indicated – there were consequences for our presence in the Middle East and if we seriously want to address the terrorism problem we have to be serious about that issue. Giuliani indicated that he was not only not serious about that issue, but seemed to be ignorant of both the 9/11 [Commission] report and political realities in the Middle East.

Ray McGovern, a 27-year veteran of the CIA, said largely the same thing, telling Horton: "I'm really edified by Ron Paul stepping up and stating what he believes to be the case. If you believe that they hate us for our democracy or for our freedoms, well I've got a bridge in Brooklyn that I'd really like to sell you at a cut rate. They hate us for our policies and that's what Ron Paul was saying.... Giuliani...really showed his true colors there as a demagogue."

If you want to be talked down to and spoken to in slogans, there is no shortage of opportunities in today's America. Ron Paul, on the other hand, on this as on everything else, refuses to pander to anyone, and tells the truth as he sees it. (He once told an audience filled with NASA employees that he had consistently voted against their programs – a typical and unremarkable episode for an honest man like Paul.) Which kind of candidate we wind up with will tell us a lot about the state of our country.

July 19, 2007

29

RON PAUL NOT ALLOWED HERE

This episode from Ron's 2008 campaign is trivial enough, to be sure, but just for the record, I want to reproduce what I wrote at the time. This is the kind of sleaze the good Ron Paul folks had to deal with day in and day out. In the end, Ron held his own event across the hall, and he attracted twice as many attendees as did the competing event featuring half a dozen candidates. It was the first time the strength of the Ron Paul Revolution made itself felt.

The Iowa Christian Alliance and Iowans for Tax Relief are co-sponsoring a Republican candidates' forum for June 30 [2007]. The event will feature Mitt Romney, Tommy Thompson, Sam Brownback, Jim Gilmore, Mike Huckabee, and Tom Tancredo.

Ron Paul, however, is to be excluded.

In fact, that's what Paul's campaign was expressly told when they inquired. Campaign manager Kent Snyder tells the story:

> We heard about this forum from numerous supporters in Iowa who asked why Dr. Paul was not going to participate. Those supporters assumed that Dr. Paul was invited.

> The campaign office had not received an invitation so we called this morning; thinking we might have misplaced the invitation or simply

overlooked it. Lew Moore, our campaign manager, called Mr. Edward Failor, an officer of Iowans for Tax Relief, to ask about it. To our shock, Mr. Failor told us Dr. Paul was not invited; he was not going to be invited; and he would not be allowed to participate. And when asked why, Mr. Failor refused to explain. The call ended.

Lew then called Mr. Steve Scheffler, president of the Iowa Christian Alliance, to talk with him. Mr. Scheffler did not answer so Lew left a message. He has yet to respond.

After reading this, I called Edward Failor myself. I said I was calling about the exclusion of Ron Paul from his candidates' forum, particularly in light of Paul's extraordinary record on taxes.

"Is there a question in there you want me to answer?" came the annoyed reply.

"Well, yes. Are you excluding Ron Paul, and if so, why?"

Failor explained that the event had been scheduled months ago, and that at that time they had made a decision about who the most "credible" candidates would be.

I didn't quite understand his answer, though it was apparently more than he'd bothered to provide the Paul campaign. "You thought Tommy Thompson was a more credible candidate than Ron Paul?" I asked. (Can you imagine people gleefully sharing YouTube clips of Thompson with their friends, or holding up "Tommy Thompson Revolution" signs?)

Failor refused to answer that or any other question I posed to him, and closed with, "That is the only statement I am willing to make."

This explanation is not believable at all. We'll leave aside his organization's mixed record when it comes to picking out the "credible" candidates. Had this really been a mere logistical question, why would Failor not simply have said so to the Paul campaign when they initially inquired? (Not that that would have been a good explanation, but it would have been something.) A non-hostile person with good manners might have said something like, "We're very sorry about the way things turned out; we arranged this event a long time ago, and of course we'd have been delighted to have your campaign participate if we'd been able to feature more people on the stage."

The answer I got was pretty obviously one Failor had devised on the fly, not having expected anyone to call him on his decision to exclude Paul.

But the answer I got is also an obvious lie. I tracked down the schedule of the event as of a June 8 press release. Then I found the schedule just the other day. This one replaces Jim Gilmore with Duncan Hunter.

I wonder why Hunter hadn't been told that the arrangements had been made months in advance, that he'd been determined not to be credible – the whole story.

Failor, you're busted.

After our call, I got to thinking about this Failor character: what kind of person running a "tax relief" organization would exclude the presidential candidate with – and this is no exaggeration – possibly the best record on taxation in all of American history, someone who favors the abolition of the income tax and the drastic reduction or elimination of nearly all other federal taxes? Should this be the Iowans For a Little Tax Relief, But Not *Too* Much?

I did a little poking around, and it turns out that our Edward Failor was initially a supporter of...George Pataki. *George Pataki*! And here I was thinking Failor had a hard time pinpointing credible candidates.

I remember seeing Pataki and Rudy Giuliani opening a Saturday Night Live episode years ago. Pataki was reading off his cue card so badly and awkwardly you just had to change the channel. Slightly less intelligent than George W. Bush: who will dispute this description of Mr. Failor's credible candidate?

The New York Sun, writing about Pataki's record, observed in 2006: "Mr. Pataki could be a hard sell to small-government conservatives, given that state spending in New York has grown to a projected $75 billion in the coming fiscal year from $43 billion in 1995." No problem for Edward Failor. According to the *Sun*, "Mr. Failor said the increases were the necessary result of growth brought on by aggressive tax cuts." Oh.

Maybe this is Iowans Who Are Only Marginally Unhappy With the Status Quo, or Iowans for Shell Games That Look Like Tax Cuts. Maybe it's Iowans Who Want Guarantees that Nothing Will Change.

Excluding Ron Paul from a "tax relief" candidates' forum is like excluding Batman from an Anti-Riddler forum. Even funnier is that these two organizations, in blacklisting Paul, reveal themselves to be even worse than the mainstream media they always criticize: the very day the Paul campaign discovered it had been barred from this Iowa event, they got a call from ABC News confirming Ron Paul's participation in the August 5 debate in Des Moines, Iowa.

We shouldn't be surprised at all this; such treatment is exactly what a truly anti-establishment candidate can expect in a world of phonies and hacks. But Ron Paul's supporters are legion, and growing all the time. I rather suspect they will have something to say about their candidate's exclusion.

Here's my follow-up report.

I've received emails from people telling me that the folks at the Iowa Christian Alliance (ICA) insist that they had nothing to do with excluding Dr. Paul, and that the blame rests with Ed Failor of Iowans for Tax Relief. (Ed's not too popular with a lot of people these days, apparently.)

Now I have no doubt that there may be some decent people at the ICA, and that they may really believe what they are saying. But that organization cannot be believed when it innocently claims it has nothing against Ron Paul. The ICA has a page on its site that lists all the announced candidates for president. Until yesterday, when I pointed it out on Lew Rockwell's blog and embarrassed them a bit, there was no Ron Paul.

Ever heard of Hugh Cort? John Cox? Mark Klein? The people at the ICA evidently have, since there they are on the list. But they apparently hadn't heard of Ron Paul until just yesterday.

Actually, though, they did know who Ron Paul was. They even used to have him on their list, as a cached page reveals. But then he disappeared.

They also used to have a link to Paul's YouTube site, along with those of the other candidates, at the bottom of the page, but that's also been suppressed. So if they thought they could claim that deleting the link to Ron Paul's campaign site was some kind of innocent mistake, that isn't going to work.

Heck, they even include a list of "potential" candidates. That list includes Al Sharpton.

So Al Sharpton merits inclusion, but Ron Paul does not. There is the faith of the apostles, according to the Iowa Christian Alliance.

Now let's return to my other favorite Iowa organization, the Iowans (Allegedly) for Tax Relief. Its executive vice president, Ed Failor, wasn't happy about my published remarks on Wednesday. Not happy at all.

In fact, he called me on Wednesday and insisted that I correct something I'd said – that by replacing Jim Gilmore with Duncan Hunter at the last minute (a fact I discovered by comparing press releases from earlier this month), Iowans for Tax Relief implicitly revealed that the reason they were excluding Ron Paul – that the event had supposedly been organized months ago and was now cast in stone – was bogus, and a lie.

Here is the earth-shattering change Failor wanted me to make. Hunter, he said, *had* been one of the original invitees – man, these guys are just *great* at picking out the credible candidates, aren't they? – but failed to respond by the deadline. So when Gilmore dropped out, they went back to Hunter, who accepted.

But if they really wanted "credible" candidates, why would they do such a thing? By now even the zombie population can see that Ron Paul is far more credible than Hunter by any measure. The comparison is almost laughable. And since Hunter had his chance to participate but elected not to respond, why not give Paul a chance, since his initial exclusion – on the ludicrous grounds that he was not a "credible" candidate – has subsequently been shown to be a gross misjudgment? Paul seems particularly "credible" given that he came in second behind Fred Thompson in a straw poll that Iowans for Tax Relief itself co-sponsored!

Meanwhile, with Failor's technicality off his chest, he had absolutely nothing to say about 99 percent of what I wrote: he never denied his support for the execrable George Pataki (what non-hack ever supported Pataki for anything, much less for president?), his support for Pataki's spending increases, or his donations to the McCain campaign, for which Failor is a senior advisor....

June 20, 2007

30

THANK YOU, RON

In the days and weeks leading up to the Iowa caucuses in early January 2012, it looked as if Ron Paul might win outright, or at least be a strong second. He came in third with a solid 22 percent of the vote, an outcome that would have been thrilling had our hopes not been raised so much. Here's what I wrote the next morning.

Certainly it's a disappointment. At the same time, 22 percent in a state that is not ideologically in Ron's camp, with all the media hate and ridicule so intense for two solid weeks – and heck, with Ron's opposition to ethanol subsidies thrown in – is nothing to sniff at.

So many people worked so hard in Iowa for this strong showing – particularly A.J. Spiker, David Fischer, and Drew Ivers, all friends of mine – and we owe them our thanks.

As a knowledgeable friend explained to me in 2008, it is extremely difficult to reach many traditional voters, who decide on which candidate to choose on the basis of how much he sounds like the typical GOP product they've come to expect. So they listen for a speech that says, "I love America, Americans are the awesomest of the awesome, we need jobs, Obama is bad, war war war – and did I say Americans were the most awesome people ever, in the most awesome country, and the only reason anyone might not be thrilled with our government is because of our sheer awesomeness?"

At the same time, the race is still up in the air in the sense that voters have not settled on the preferred anti-Romney. This morning, while involuntarily subjected to FOX News, I heard a newscaster say, "You can't get more anti-Mitt than Rick Santorum." You know what? I'm pretty sure you can.

What lifted my spirits last night was Ron Paul's speech. The man is as genuine as can be, as we already knew, so his enthusiasm last night wasn't a put on. He is thrilled that issues once neglected are now being discussed everywhere. He is delighted to see young people flocking to something other than the standard GOP talking points from 1983, which appear to satisfy older voters too set in their ways to have an original thought. He crushed everyone in the under-40 vote. That means his ideas are the future.

He has every reason to be proud right now – of his supporters, and of himself.

Not one of us would have begrudged Ron Paul a quiet retirement had he chosen not to run this year. He had already awakened more Americans to the real American tradition of liberty, along with the Austrian School of economics, than any living person, and he had stared down the Ministry of Information and its war-propaganda politicians more consistently than anyone I can think of.

Yet he chose to impose on himself the unthinkable physical and mental toll of a rigorous presidential campaign. He opened himself up to ceaseless, vicious attack by intellectual and moral pygmies who enjoy nothing more than dragging the name of the one honest man in politics through the mud.

I'm sure Ron could have lived without the exhausting travel, the nonstop attacks from left and right, all of it. But he's enduring it for us, because – corny as this may sound – he knows these ideas are the key to a better world.

January 4, 2012

PART V

END THE FED

31

LIFE WITHOUT THE FED?

We have heard the objection a thousand times: Why, before we had a Federal Reserve System – which can create legal-tender money out of thin air, and which both serves as a "lender of last resort" and an alleged stabilizer of the American economy – the United States endured a regular series of financial panics. Abolishing the Fed is an unthinkable, absurd suggestion, for without the wise custodianship of our central bankers we would be thrown back into a horrific financial maelstrom, deliverance from which should have made us grateful, not uppity.

The argument is superficially plausible, to be sure, but it is wrong in every particular. We heard it quite a bit in the financial press several months ago when it was learned that Congressman Ron Paul, a well-known opponent of the Fed, would chair the House Financial Services Subcommittee on Domestic Monetary Policy. Fed apologists were beside themselves – a man who rejects the cartoon version of the history of the Fed will hold such an influential position? He must be made into an object of derision and ridicule.

My favorite example comes from columnist Joseph N. DiStefano, whose article on the subject is so defiantly at odds with the historical record, so ludicrously at variance with easily verified facts, that I thought for pedagogical purposes we ought to make an example of him.

DiStefano spends most of his article on the current crisis, but, having written quite a bit about that already, I prefer to spend most of mine on the cartoonish version of American monetary and banking history that seems to inform every outraged pro-Fed reply to Fed critics, this one being no exception. They read like fourth-grade book reports. Except DiStefano didn't even read the book.

The premise is familiar enough: Why, without a central bank or its lesser cousin, a national bank, we had nothing but boom, bust, and sorrow – but since the creation of the Federal Reserve System, it's been nothing but sunshine and lollipops. It really is that simple. People who believe in a free market in banking, as opposed to these cartel arrangements, are evidently so uninformed or so blinded by ideology that they have never heard or internalized this one-sentence encapsulation of 19th- and 20th-century monetary history.

The 19th-century boom-bust cycles DiStefano mentions in drive-by fashion are consistently attributable to artificial credit expansion, a practice government either connived at or actually participated in, through the various privileges it granted to the banking industry.

First, let's consider DiStefano's 19th century. We are to believe that national banks were indispensable sources of stability, while their absence yielded terrible business cycles. How does DiStefano account for the Panic of 1819, which contemporaries attributed to the inflationary and then rapidly contractionary policies of the Second Bank of the United States, the great stabilizer? That's easy – he leaves it out. (He likewise leaves out the Great Depression from his discussion of the 20th century, an episode one might think would count against the Fed, and which was likewise set in motion by central-bank inflation; Benjamin Strong, who headed the New York Fed, told other central bankers in 1927 that he planned to "give a coup de whiskey to the stock market.") The standard account is Murray Rothbard's *The Panic of 1819: Reactions and Policies* (Columbia University Press, 1962).

DiStefano does mention the Panic of 1837, and for that episode we are urged to blame President Andrew Jackson for having dissolved the Second Bank of the United States. DiStefano does not deign to reveal what the causal mechanism might have been. The strong implication, based on the rest of his article, is that we need institutions with monopoly privileges to oversee our money, and if they should ever be forced to close because the stupid rubes don't understand how indispensable they are, the economy will crash. That's not much of an explanation, but it's all DiStefano chooses to share with us.

Funny, the economy hadn't crashed when the First Bank of the United States was shut down more than two decades earlier. When the charter of the original Bank of the United States expired in 1811, and the institution set about calling in its loans and closing its doors, the DiStefanos of the world made wild predictions of bankruptcy and economic collapse. Nothing of the sort occurred. A contemporary noted in 1816: "Many persons viewed a dissolution of the late Bank of the United States as a national calamity; it was asserted that a general bankruptcy must follow that event. The fact was otherwise: every branch of industry continued uninterrupted – no failures in the mercantile community were attributable to that occurrence."

DiStefano fails to mention any causal link between the closing of the Second Bank and the Panic of 1837, so I'll provide him with one. The most common argument is this: without a national bank to discipline the state banks, the state banks that received the federal deposits after the closure of the Second Bank went on an inflationary binge that culminated in the Panic of 1837 and another downturn in 1839. This standard diagnosis is partly Austrian, surprisingly, in that it blames artificial credit expansion for giving rise to unsustainable booms that end in busts. But the alleged solution to this problem, according to modern commentators, is a robust central bank with implicit regulatory powers over smaller institutions.

Senator William Wells, a hard-money Federalist from Delaware, had been unconvinced from the start that the best way to encourage sound practices among smaller unsound banks was to establish a giant unsound bank. "This bill," he said in 1816,

> came out of the hands of the administration ostensibly for the purpose of curtailing the over-issue of Bank paper: and yet it came prepared to inflict on us the same evil, being itself nothing more than a simple paper making machine; and constituting, in this respect, a scheme of policy about as wise, in point of precaution, as the contrivance of one of Rabelais's heroes, who hid himself in the water for fear of the rain.

> The disease, it is said, is the Banking fever of the States; and this is to be cured by giving them the Banking fever of the United States.

Another hard-money U.S. senator, New York's Samuel Tilden, likewise wondered, "How could a large bank, constituted on essentially the same principles, be expected to regulate beneficially the lesser banks? Has enlarged power been found to be less liable to abuse than limited power? Has concentrated power been found less liable to abuse than distributed power?"

A much better solution recommended by hard-money advocates at the time is what became known as the "Independent Treasury," in which the federal deposits, instead of being distributed to privileged state banks and used as the basis for additional rounds of credit creation there, were retained by the Treasury and kept out of the banking system entirely. Hard-money supporters believed that the federal government was propping up (and lending artificial legitimacy to) an unsound system of fractional-reserve state banks by (1) distributing the federal deposits to them, (2) accepting their paper money in payment of taxes and (3) paying it back out again. As William Gouge put it,

> If the operations of Government could be completely separated from those of the Banks, the system would be shorn of half its evils. If Government would neither deposit the public funds in the Banks, nor borrow money from the Banks; and if it would in no case either receive Bank notes or pay away Bank notes, the Banks would become mere commercial institutions, and their credit and their power be brought nearer to a level with those of private merchants.

DiStefano is convinced that the movement against the Bank was led by antimarket, antiproperty populists. "Last time we had a central bank," he writes, "its advocates were conservative, hard-money businessmen, and its opponents were subprime borrowers and lenders who convinced President Jackson the bank was holding back the nation." That is as wrong as wrong can be, as we'll see in a moment. DiStefano proceeds from this error to the false conclusion that supporters of the market economy then as now should be supporters of the central bank.

To be sure, opponents of the Second Bank of the United States were no monolith, and even today the central bank is criticized both by those who condemn its money creation as well as by those who criticize its alleged stinginess. On balance, though, the fight against the Second Bank was a free-market, hard-money campaign against a government-privileged paper-money producer. "The attack on the Bank," concluded Professor Jeff Hummel in his review of the literature, "was a fully rational and highly enlightened step toward the achievement of a laissez-faire metallic monetary system."

We have already cited hard-money senators against the Bank. But for DiStefano to claim that the movement against the Second Bank was a movement of propertyless boobs who didn't understand banking, he would also have to be unaware of the most important monetary theorist of the entire period, William Gouge (mentioned above). Gouge was a champion of hard money who opposed the Bank; he considered these two positions logically coordinate, indeed inseparable.

"Why should ingenuity exert itself in devising new modifications of paper Banking?" he asked. "The economy which prefers fictitious money to real, is, at best, like that which prefers a leaky ship to a sound one." He assured Americans that "the sun would shine, the streams would flow, and the earth would yield her increase, if the Bank of the United States was not in existence." The conservative *Bankers' Magazine*, upon Gouge's death, said that his hard-money book *A Short History of Paper Money and Banking* was "a very able and clear exposition of the principles of banking and of the mistakes made by our American banking institutions."

DiStefano might also look into the work of William Leggett, the influential Jacksonian editorial writer in New York who memorably called for "separation of bank and state." Economist Larry White, who compiled many of Leggett's most important writings, calls him "the intellectual leader of the laissez-faire wing of Jacksonian democracy." He denounced the Bank for its repeated expansions and contractions, and for the economic turmoil that such manipulation left in its wake.

The Panic of 1819 was likewise due to such behavior on the part of the Bank, said Leggett, with a repeat performance in the mid-1820s. "For the two or three years preceding the extensive and heavy calamities of 1819, the United States

Bank, instead of regulating the currency, poured out its issues at such a lavish rate that trade and speculation were excited in a preternatural manner." Leggett continues,

> But not to dwell upon events the recollection of which time may have begun to efface from many minds, let us but cast a glance at the manner in which the United States Bank regulated the currency in 1830, when, in the short period of a twelve-month it extended its accommodations from forty to seventy millions of dollars. This enormous expansion, entirely uncalled for by any peculiar circumstance in the business condition of the country, was followed by the invariable consequences of an inflation of the currency. Goods and stocks rose, speculation was excited, a great number of extensive enterprises were undertaken, canals were laid out, rail-roads projected, and the whole business of the country was stimulated into unnatural and unsalutary activity.

But maybe the 19th century shows we need an institution capable of monetary "stimulus" to restore the economy to health following a crash. If so, the evidence isn't obvious. President James Buchanan engaged in no vain effort to reflate the economy in the wake of the stock-market crisis and bank run that constituted the relatively mild, six-month Panic of 1857 – which DiStefano, who is in a bit over his head when it comes to 19th-century economic history, calls a "howling depression." (That relatively mild downturn, incidentally, is attributable to the system of inflationary paper money, not the "gold standard"; as Buchanan said in his first annual message, "It is apparent that our existing misfortunes have proceeded solely from our extravagant and vicious system of paper currency and bank credits.")

Fashionable modern advice did not exist in Buchanan's day, and it showed. The economy recovered within six months, even though the money supply fell, interest rates rose, government spending was not increased, and businesses and banks were not bailed out. But Buchanan cautioned Americans that "the periodical revulsions which have existed in our past history must continue to return at intervals so long as our present unbounded system of bank credits shall prevail."

Buchanan envisioned a federal bankruptcy law for banks that, instead of giving legal sanction to their suspension of specie payments (that is, their failure to honor their depositors' demands for withdrawal), would in fact shut them down if they failed to make good on their promises. "The instinct of self-preservation might produce a wholesome restraint upon their banking business if they knew in advance that a suspension of specie payments would inevitably produce their civil death," Buchanan said.

DiStefano makes specific mention of the 1870s, which once again reveals the superficiality of his knowledge. Unknown to DiStefano, the modern consensus holds that there was no "Long Depression" of the 1870s after all. Even the *New York Times*, which admits nothing, admits this:

> Recent detailed reconstructions of nineteenth-century data by economic historians show that there was no 1870s depression: aside from a short recession in 1873, in fact, the decade saw possibly the fastest sustained growth in American history. Employment grew strongly, faster than the rate of immigration; consumption of food and other goods rose across the board. On a per capita basis, almost all output measures were up spectacularly. By the end of the decade, people were better housed, better clothed and lived on bigger farms. Department stores were popping up even in medium-sized cities. America was transforming into the world's first mass consumer society.

Perhaps DiStefano may concede in a candid moment that he unthinkingly accepted a caricature of the 19th century, but he'll still have his strong feeling that at least the Fed did away with financial panics. Not quite. Andrew Jalil of the University of California, Berkeley, concluded in a 2009 study that "contrary to the conventional wisdom, there is no evidence of a decline in the frequency of panics during the first fifteen years of the existence of the Federal Reserve." Elmus Wicker, in *Banking Panics of the Gilded Age* (2000), observes that

> there were no more than three major banking panics between 1873 and 1907 [inclusive], and two incipient banking panics in 1884 and 1890. Twelve years elapsed between the panic of 1861 and the panic of 1873,

twenty years between the panics of 1873 and 1893, and fourteen years between 1893 and 1907: three banking panics in half a century! And in only one of the three, 1893, did the number of bank suspensions match those of the Great Depression.

By contrast, there were five separate bank panics in the first three years of the Great Depression alone. (For these sources, see the Cato Institute Working Paper "Has the Fed Been a Failure?" by George Selgin, William D. Lastrapes, and Lawrence H. White, available online.)

Even during the pre-Fed panics, from the Civil War to 1907, the bank failure rate was small, as were the losses depositors suffered. Depositor losses amounted to only 0.1 percent of GDP during the Panic of 1893, which was the worst of them all with respect to bank failures and depositor losses. By contrast, in just the past 30 years of the central-bank era, the world has seen 20 banking crises that led to depositor losses in excess of 10 percent of GDP. Half of those saw losses in excess of 20 percent of GDP.

Moreover, the post-Civil War panics in the United States were due in large part to the unit-banking regulations in many states that forbade branch banking of any sort. Confined to a single office, each bank was necessarily fragile and undiversified. Canada experienced none of these panics even though it did not establish a central bank, DiStefano's trusted panacea, until 1934.

With regard to fluctuations both past and present, DiStefano implicitly gives us the classic pro-Fed position: business cycles occur spontaneously, and the Fed fixes them. We might call this the Fed as Innocent Bystander/ Good Samaritan (IB/GS). DiStefano does not consider – not even to refute it, like an honest opponent – the Austrian argument that the Fed's manipulation of money and interest rates is what gives rise to the cycle in the first place. The Fed's palliative measures, in turn, amount to more of what caused the original problem. This was one of the points of my book *Meltdown*, the *New York Times* bestseller that the *New York Times* pretended did not exist, which gave a free-market overview of the economic crisis as a counter to DiStefanism.

(My reply is already longer than I'd prefer, so for the Austrian theory of the business cycle I refer readers to my Austrian resource page at LearnAustrianEconomics.com, and for the "TARP was a great idea" argument to the work of David Stockman, particularly his book *The Great Deformation: The Corruption of Capitalism in America.*)

What would we do in such situations without the Fed? Under a more sound monetary system these fluctuations would be far less violent in the first place. And unsound firms would go bankrupt, as a former CEO of AIG later admitted would have been the best course of action after all. The world would not come to an end. If the market is freely allowed to re-price assets, which was the phenomenon we were terrified into not wanting to occur, that doesn't change the amount of physical stuff in existence. The assets themselves may be redistributed to new owners in bankruptcy proceedings, but the world has just as much stuff as it did before. Ownership titles are transferred, and a leaner outfit with more competent leadership moves the economy forward. An important lesson is learned for the future. Or we could be satisfied with DiStefano's solution, which is to keep Wall Street just as it is, without this salutary purge of leadership and capital, and without the corresponding change in entrepreneurial character that might yield a less debt-based and more equity-based business model and hence more stability in the future.

But the key problem with the DiStefano analysis is that it is no analysis at all. It takes the crisis as an irreducible given, and then launches into the IB/GS routine. The Austrian School argues that manipulation of interest rates causes discoordination across the structure of production, that this disfigured structure is unsustainable, and that the inevitable result is the bust. DiStefano gives us no reason to believe otherwise, or even to have confidence that he understands or even knows about the argument, an argument that won F.A. Hayek the Nobel Prize in 1974.

All these issues are covered in greater detail in the Fed chapter of my book *Rollback*, which confronts the standard claims not just for the Fed but also for all the major areas of life we are told could not be managed without institutionalized coercion.

As with the Fed, so with these other things: critics of the status quo are reflexively condemned as cranks, and alternatives to the status quo are dismissed as unthinkable. But they are only unthinkable because we have allowed fashionable opinion to keep us from thinking them. We have been forced into a box that confines our choices to various forms of statism. The movement to end the Fed is an astonishing and most welcome first step toward clawing our way out.

April 5, 2011

32

THE LIFEBLOOD OF THE EMPIRE

I delivered these remarks at Ron Paul's Rally for the Republic on September 3, 2008. I had strongly advocated that Dr. Paul hold such a rally – near the Republican National Convention, and held at the same time – and it was one of the great moments of my life to speak there. He asked me to draw a link between the Fed and war, and I obliged.

About fifteen years ago a conservative columnist wrote that Americans are faced with a choice between the Stupid Party and the Evil Party. And that once in a while the two parties get together and do something that's both stupid and evil, and that's called bipartisanship.

If anything, that view was too optimistic. On so many issues that matter, we may as well have a one-party system.

Some people on the left are finally discovering to their chagrin that the so-called change Barack Obama would make to American foreign policy is just cosmetic. What did they expect? His foreign-policy panel, a who's-who of the establishment, includes Madeleine Albright, the former Secretary of State who said "the price has been worth it" when asked on *60 Minutes* what she thought of the fact that the Bush/Clinton sanctions on Iraq had led to half a million dead children.

So that's the "change" candidate. Well, how very refreshing.

On taxes, the Democrat favors a top income tax rate of 39.5 percent, and the Republican favors a top rate of 35 percent. Well, ain't democracy grand! We get to debate a whole four and a half percentage points.

Forget about spending. The Democrat spends his time devising new ways to throw away money we don't have. Who knows what additional billions the Republican nominee's foreign-policy bellicosity will saddle us with. But *he* pledges to balance the budget without a tax increase by 2013, while also strengthening the dollar and closing the $70 trillion entitlement shortfall. And we're expected to believe this.

Been there, done that.

And by the way, if I may be forgiven for stating the obvious, you are not a fiscal conservative – or any other kind of conservative, for that matter – if you think it's a-okay to stay in Iraq for one hundred years. [TW note: John McCain had recently said that a one-hundred-year occupation would be fine by him.]

The subject I've been asked to address here, though, is yet another one that finds the two major candidates – let's call them McBama – in agreement: namely, money and the Federal Reserve System.

Since the Fed was established in 1913 the dollar has lost 95 percent of its value. The Fed has given us more financial bubbles than we can count. When it inflates the money supply it lowers the value of the dollars in Americans' pockets and hurts society's most vulnerable. It redistributes wealth from the middle class and the poor to the politically well connected, by means of what economists call distribution or Cantillon effects.

What's more, F.A. Hayek won the Nobel Prize in economics for showing how central banks like the Fed create the boom-bust business cycle in our economy. When the central bank manipulates interest rates, it causes massive discoordination. The interest rate is supposed to coordinate production across time, but it can do so only when it reflects an aggregate of voluntary choices, not the whim of the Fed chairman. Entrepreneurs are misled into making investments that make no sense in light of current resource availability. The Fed's intervention starts the economy on an artificial boom that ends in an inevitable bust.

More and more financial analysts are coming to accept Hayek's view, known as the Austrian theory of the business cycle, because it corresponds so closely to what's happening all around us. Let's go ask John McCain what he knows about the Austrian theory. We may as well be speaking Chinese.

In the 1920s, when so-called mainstream economists were foolishly assuring us that permanent prosperity had arrived, economists of what's known as the Austrian School of economic thought, to which Ron Paul also belongs, stood alone in predicting the Great Depression.

Yet in spite of all this, we've had no serious discussion of the Federal Reserve System for nearly 100 years. It has been fantastically successful in depoliticizing itself. No politician ever mentions it. And although he is too genuinely humble to acknowledge it, one man is responsible for finally blasting open this forbidden question: Ron Paul.

Look at how members of Congress treat the Fed chairman when he appears before them. He gets asked only the most inane, sycophantic questions. Members of the Banking Committee, decked out in their "I Heart Bernanke" T-shirts, wave incense before him.

Ron Paul, on the other hand, looks him in the eye and says, "You are stealing from the poor!"

The economic and historical arguments against sound money (that is, money that government can't just print up at will) are surprisingly weak – really just a string of fallacies. For now I refer you all to the education page at CampaignForLiberty.org for plenty of resources in defense of sound money. [TW note: Campaign for Liberty has since chosen to remove the substantial resource pages on foreign policy, economics, sound money, and civil liberties that were featured on the original website.]

But Joseph Schumpeter, one of the great economists of the twentieth century, said that even if you accepted all the bogus economic arguments against gold, it still made perfect sense to favor it. Why? Because it is the only system compatible with freedom.

If "fiscal responsibility" is your issue, you'll never get anywhere as long as the government can create out of thin air all the money it wants. If the federal government is an addict, then the Federal Reserve System is its enabler.

Or suppose you're concerned about war and what Ron Paul calls our government's "bull-in-a-china-shop foreign policy." (By the way, that's a concern shared by the genuine left – people like Kirkpatrick Sale and Gore Vidal – and the genuine right, by which I mean traditional conservatives like Russell Kirk and Robert Taft, not today's neoconservative death cult.) Well, you, too, should care about the Fed, since the central bank is the lifeblood of the empire. If you want to stop the war machine, you'll have to go after the money machine.

How did Lyndon Johnson get away with his war spending in Vietnam? By a deliberate policy of concealing the cost through inflation — a cost the American people bore only later, in the stagflation of the 1970s. Just the cost overruns on two Pentagon projects added up to more than the combined GDPs of North and South Vietnam. By silently looting the American population, the government was able to get away with much more spending than would otherwise have been possible.

Then there's the disastrous war in Iraq, the propaganda for which was fed to us by America's *Pravda*, the *New York Times*. How has that war been funded? By borrowing from foreigners, and creating new money out of thin air.

As for our current economic mess, McBama agree with the president, who summed up his own business cycle theory in these words: "Wall Street got drunk." Their solution? For starters, hundreds of billions of dollars in bailouts to the alleged drunkards. Bailouts and scapegoating – anything other than pointing the finger where it belongs – are all McBama can think to do. To hear them speak, you'd never know the Fed's mad money creation spree and its resulting economic distortions had even occurred.

And no, the free market doesn't cause housing bubbles and mortgage crises. The federal government has been pushing unsound loans on banks for years, both through legislation and by a Federal Reserve policy of flooding the economy with cheap credit. This new money went overwhelmingly into the housing market, the result being the housing bubble that is now bursting. Fannie Mae and Freddie Mac are Government Supported Enterprises (GSEs) that get special tax and regulatory breaks, and that everyone knows will be bailed out if it should come to that. So there's nothing to stop them from buying up risky mortgages from banks. And banks in turn are more likely to make risky loans in the first place if they know Fannie and Freddie will be happy to buy them up.

This crazy system is a layer cake of moral hazard, not the free market. But as usual, the free market is being blamed for the stupidity and recklessness of the blockheads who rule us.

Every four years we're subjected to a pair of empty suits whose only real argument is over exactly how and through what channels they plan to squander Americans' wealth. It's enough to make the non-comatose segment of the population despair. What can we do?

For starters, you can do what Ron Paul does, which is to start your day by reading LewRockwell.com. You can go to TheAmericanConservative.com and read and subscribe to *The American Conservative* magazine.

But above all, today we have a special suggestion. If you're tired of having to choose between two wings of the same bird of prey, then help us change America: go to CampaignForLiberty.org and join Ron Paul's Campaign for Liberty! [TW note: Ron asked me to write the mission statement and statement of principles for Campaign for Liberty, which I did, and which can still be found on the organization's website as of this writing. He also asked me to move to Texas to lead the organization, but, needing stability for my young family, I had to decline.]

H.L. Mencken put it this way: "The most dangerous man, to any government, is the man who is able to think things out for himself, without regard to the prevailing superstitions and taboos. Almost inevitably he comes to the conclusion that the government he lives under is dishonest, insane and intolerable, and so, if he is romantic, he tries to change it."

Publishers Weekly says Dr. Paul "gives new life to old debates." But you know what? Without him, we wouldn't be having these debates in the first place.

Ron Paul reminds us that our future is not cast in stone, and that if we as a people so choose, we do not have to live in the kind of America the two major parties have in store for us.

Thanks to all of you for the sacrifices you've made on behalf of this great American cause – and above all, thank you, Ron Paul.

September 3, 2008

33

KILL THE MONSTER

This was my five-minute opening statement in a debate in Las Vegas (FreedomFest, 2009) on the Federal Reserve. Gene Epstein (of Barron's*) was on my side; we debated John Fund of the* Wall Street Journal *and economist Warren Coates.*

A lot of people seem to believe that although the market economy is a swell system, it requires the equivalent of a Soviet commissar to be in charge of money and interest rates. This belief is altogether misplaced. The Federal Reserve System, or simply "the Fed," is both harmful and unnecessary.

Since the Fed was created in 1913 the dollar has lost at least 95 percent of its value. If the much-maligned gold standard had produced such a result we'd never hear the end of it, but in our system the Fed is, for whatever reason, curiously exempt from criticism. Under the Fed, therefore, people have lost an option they once had: accumulating savings in cash. Under a commodity standard, people could save for the future simply by accumulating precious-metal coins – which, back when they functioned as money, held or even increased their value. No one has that option any longer. In other words, only a fool would try to save by piling up dollar bills. Instead, everyone is forced to become a speculator, and to invest in securities markets they know little about and that can wipe them out entirely if times turn bad.

As early as the eighteenth century, Richard Cantillon identified distribution effects as another way inflation harmed the general public. The newly created money is injected at particular points. Whoever receives it first – that is, people who happen to be politically well connected – get to spend it before prices have commensurately risen, and these fortunate few thereby receive a windfall. By the time it trickles through to ordinary people, on the other hand, the general public has in the meantime been forced to pay the higher prices to which the new money gives rise.

Private and public debt have exploded under this system, especially since the collapse of Bretton Woods in 1971. No one has a right to be surprised when indebtedness skyrockets under a system in which credit can be created out of thin air.

The very existence of the central bank institutionalizes the problem of moral hazard. Moral hazard involves an actor's willingness to behave with an artificially elevated level of risk tolerance because he believes any losses he incurs will be borne by someone else. Since there is no physical limitation on paper money creation, market actors know the paper money producer can bail them out if things go terribly wrong. They have been vindicated in this belief time and again. They will, therefore, be more reckless in their investment activity and speculation than they would in the absence of such a system.

We were once told that boom-bust business cycles were a thing of the past because, thanks to the Fed, we now had scientific management of the money supply. If anyone believes that today, I'd like to meet him. Artificially low interest rates courtesy of the Fed do not yield us a utopia of sunshine and kittens. To the contrary, they artificially stimulate capital-goods production and long-term investment. They thereby deform the structure of production into a configuration that the public's freely expressed pattern of saving and consumption will be unable to sustain. When this phony boom inevitably collapses, it is "capitalism" that takes the blame – when in fact the Fed, a non-market institution, is the culprit.

I am interested in neither the saccharine promises nor the technical details of the alleged superiority of a monopoly fiat-money system. The Fed is the life-blood of the empire, the great enabler of the perversion of the original American republic into the world's largest and most powerful government. Even if the central bank did confer a net economic benefit, a contention the great Austrian economists F.A. Hayek and Ludwig von Mises strenuously denied (and indeed Hayek won the Nobel Prize in the process of denying), the alleged benefit could not possibly be worth the destruction of the American soul.

As it turns out, we don't have to make that choice. When it comes to the Fed, justice, economic prosperity, and the values of the original American republic are joined together.

The Fed, its academic apologists, and the drones in our supposedly free press who demonize all dissent from the monetary status quo, have done our economy enough damage. For the sake of American freedom and prosperity, it is long past time that, in the spirit of Andrew Jackson, we killed the monster.

July 10, 2009

34

THE PRESIDENT WILL PROTECT YOU FROM BUBBLES

In case you've ever wondered what it must have been like to read *Pravda*, the American media's treatment of the financial crisis and our wise leaders' expert management of it all has given everyone a wonderful opportunity. For instance, check out this 2010 article from Politico: bit.ly/ObamaBubbles.

If you can't bring yourself to visit the link, I'll give you the headline: "Obama Would Regulate New 'Bubbles.'"

Yes, you read that right. "Bubbles" just occur spontaneously. They have no cause or explanation. We just need government to identify and destroy them.

Sometimes I wish our overlords would get their stories straight. First, Alan Greenspan – whom the *New York Times* once described, in its typical toadying, totalitarian fashion, as "the infallible maestro of our financial system" – told us it was impossible to tell if a bubble existed at any given time. Now we have Barack Obama insisting that not only *can* we detect bubbles, but we can also deflate them with sufficient dispatch to prevent them from causing any serious economic disturbances.

How are we peons to decide between the competing views of our *infallible maestro* on the one hand and the man who would be FDR on the other?

I shouldn't be so cynical. It is not for us to question how our overlords intend to distinguish between genuine growth in some industry on the one hand and bubble conditions on the other. Just to be safe they may have to quash all rapid growth wherever it occurs. Perhaps they can cut off credit to an entire sector of the economy, or levy industry-specific taxation. (Anyone who thinks this type of discretion and micromanagement might be exercised with political motivations in mind, or for any purpose other than the common good, is almost surely a good candidate for surveillance in our progressive commonwealth.)

In their quest to free us from economic instability, our betters may find it necessary to institute new rules. It is our job to accept these new rules with docility and thanks. These rules might have to be kind of sweeping, perhaps on the order of *nobody may do anything*. In liberal times that could perhaps be modified to *nobody may do anything without asking permission*. True, we could then wind up with a lengthy debate about whether asking permission itself counted as doing something, such that we'd need to ask permission in order to ask permission, in an endless regress. We'd then be back to the original *nobody may do anything*, which is probably the safest place to be anyway.

Or perhaps our rulers could shut down the electrical grid from time to time. I'd like to see those greedy fat cats inflate a bubble without any electricity!

Now the possibility that the government itself could be the primary culprit in the generation of asset bubbles is of course not merely rejected; the very idea cannot even be entertained. The great progressive institutions of government and central banking the causes rather than the solutions to our problems? Impossible!

Everyone knows Bad Things happen in the economy because of wicked speculators and grasping businessmen. If someone were to ask whether the Federal Reserve's creation of $8 billion out of thin air every week on average for four solid years might have had a tiny bit to do with the housing bubble, well, we'd have to remind such a cynic that the Fed was created in order to give us macroeconomic stability. Our present crisis was caused by excessive "leverage," you see – though we won't bother asking where major economic actors managed to get all this credit in the first place. That might lead people to ask hard questions about the Fed yet again, and as we've seen, the Fed is our Wonderful, Stabilizing Friend.

It is true that Anna Schwartz, the famous monetarist (and not an Austrian economist), recently observed that asset bubbles cannot form without loose monetary policy by the central bank to fund them. "If you investigate individually the manias that the market has so dubbed over the years," she says, "in every case it was expansive monetary policy that generated the boom in an asset. The particular asset varied from one boom to another. But the basic underlying propagator was too-easy monetary policy and too-low interest rates that induced ordinary people to say, well, it's so cheap to acquire whatever is the object of desire in an asset boom, and go ahead and acquire that object. And then of course if monetary policy tightens, the boom collapses."

(Schwartz also rejects former Fed chairman Alan Greenspan's "attempt to exculpate himself" for the housing bubble.)

Schwartz is here echoing what Austrian economist Ludwig von Mises said decades earlier. A sudden drive for a particular kind of investment will raise the prices of complementary factors of production as well as the interest rate itself. In order for a mania-driven boom to persist, there would have to be an increasing supply of credit in order to fund it, since investments in that sector would grow steadily more costly over time. That could not occur in the absence of credit expansion. The dot-com and housing bubbles can both be explained by artificial credit expansion, say such economists.

If we are to believe these economists, the best way to prevent future asset bubbles would be to stop the Fed from creating so much money out of thin air in the first place. Better still, we should abolish the Fed altogether, since in the view of these economists it is entirely superfluous to a market economy.

Again, though, our trust should be in princes. After all, Austan Goolsbee, an economic adviser to the president, assures us that Obama will be on the lookout for both bubbles and busts.

The president, Politico notes, is "prepared to intervene to make sure that kind of red-hot growth doesn't occur. And he's willing to do it with added government regulation if needed to prevent any one sector of the economy from getting out of balance – the way the dot-com boom did in the 1990s and the real-estate market did earlier this decade."

See, those things *just happened*! No cause. They just happened. And government will protect us from them.

Mark Zandi, a former economic adviser to John McCain, adds that "policymakers always intervene in a downturn. So it is necessary for policymakers to take action against bubbles. You've got to be symmetrical in your policy." What we need, says Zandi, is a "systemic regulator" who will decide whether or not bubbles exist and then take appropriate action.

Naysayers may point out that the Fed's own economists denied that a housing bubble existed, and that, as we observed earlier, Greenspan himself believes it's impossible to detect bubbles at all. But surely one more regulator, a big, giant, super-duper regulator, should be able to get things right.

Some people say the market is the best regulator. After all, they say, the free market doesn't pump up the money supply and push interest rates down to levels that promote unsustainable bubbles. The free market punishes reckless risk takers, this argument goes, while it is government that bails them out (and thereby encourages them to take greater risks in the future). It was the Fed, not the free market, from which the "Greenspan put" – the implicit promise to bail out major Wall Street players – emerged. The *Financial Times* warned that these guarantees were encouraging dangerously risky investments. The free market makes no such guarantees, and thereby cultivates a more cautious class of entrepreneur.

But enough with these naysayers. I for one welcome our new overlords. Every American citizen could stand to learn from that model of filial piety, Britney Spears, who urged, "I think we should just trust our president in every decision he makes and should just support that, you know, and be faithful in what happens."

Amen.

May 18, 2009

35

WHY DO THEY LOVE THE FED?

Once in a while during Ron Paul's presidential campaigns a progressive blogger here and there would have some good things to say about the Republican congressman. Some even noted that Paul had been more antiwar than any Democrat and that his record on civil liberties was second to none.

Naturally, though, many progressives were hostile: so what if he's better on the crucial issue of our time, they essentially said. He's anti-government! One even said the neocons were much better than Paul, since at least they wouldn't try to scale government back. (It was limited government, you know, that caused the Katrina fiasco.) That kind of candor is refreshing: when presented with a small-government, local-control libertarian who will resolutely keep the country out of war, some progressives prefer perpetual war.

One took Paul to task for favoring the gold standard. Now we can't have that, of course, since it would be unthinkable to call for something that isn't even on the radar screen of the *New York Times*, the *Washington Post*, or Chris Matthews. And doesn't Ron Paul know that our betters can do a much better job running our money for us? Doesn't Paul know the Federal Reserve is a wonderful institution designed by the government to prevent economic downturns?

So there you have it: when push comes to shove, this vaunted progressive, for all his claims to independent thought, merely repeats a stream of platitudes that may as well have come from a Federal Reserve press release.

Now if this alleged progressive could, for seven seconds, turn off the voice in his head that forces him to give all existing government institutions the benefit of the doubt – and yes, an institution created by act of Congress, whose board is appointed by the president, which could not survive without special monopoly privileges, and which does the government's bidding, is for all intents and purposes a government institution – he might actually be able to ask some useful questions. What exactly is self-evidently "progressive" about the Federal Reserve? Why is it obviously a step forward when we make it far easier for the federal government to wage war and prey upon the public?

In the progressive la-la land, the Federal Reserve was founded when the American people demanded reform of the banking industry, and their elected representatives, eager to contribute to the public good, complied with their wishes. The resulting Federal Reserve smooths out the business cycle and keeps our economy strong.

Anyone interested in living on *this* planet, on the other hand, might be interested to know a fact that almost sounds too spooky and conspiratorial to be true: bankers in fact drafted the legislation that created the Fed themselves, in a private meeting in Jekyll Island, Georgia, in 1910. And – can you believe it? – it was not designed to benefit the public at bankers' expense; oddly enough, bankers drew up legislation that benefited themselves.

Now this is not how bills are drawn up according to your tenth-grade social-studies class, which gives you the government line: bills are drawn up by the people's public-spirited representatives in order to benefit and protect them. That's a nice way to think about it if you're in the business of keeping the racket going, but not especially useful if you actually want to know how the world works.

It's sadly amusing to observe progressives functioning as shills for well-connected banks and businesses, but that's precisely what they're doing by mindlessly supporting the Fed and assuming all its critics to be cranks and fools. The Federal Reserve System makes it possible for the banks to profit from all manner of financial shenanigans that they could never get away with under a gold standard — for more on this, see my reading suggestions below — and it stands ready to serve as a lender of last resort in case the banks' reckless behavior gets them in trouble. How many other industries benefit from such overt grants of special privilege?

The Fed doesn't just benefit the well connected; it also *harms* those who aren't so well connected. We know inflation hurts people on fixed incomes (since their incomes stay the same while the prices for the goods they buy go up), but what people usually overlook are the distribution effects of inflation. More money in the economy normally means higher prices. But when the government spends billions of dollars created out of thin air (yes, the Fed can do this) on the defense industry, for example, defense firms get the money at the very beginning of this process, *before* prices have commensurately risen. In effect the economy doesn't yet know how much the money supply has increased, and prices have not yet adjusted accordingly. By the time the new money makes its way through the whole economy, prices will have risen throughout most if not all sectors.

But *while* this process is taking place, the privileged firms that are lucky enough to get the new money early benefit from being able to make their purchases at the previously existing price level — thereby silently looting those from whom they buy. By the time the new money finally makes its way to the average Joe, prices have already been rising for quite a while, and he's been paying those prices all this time on his existing income.

What exactly is so "progressive" about that? Why do progressives not condemn this expropriation of the poorest that goes on day after day? Surely their commitment to government management of all sectors of society, money included, cannot be so strong that they have lost the ability to ask fundamental questions.

Here is another way to think about it. Money in your possession amounts to compensation for some good or service you have provided in the past. When you buy a dozen apples, you do so with the proceeds from a good or service that *you yourself provided in the past*. So you are able to buy the apples because in the past you gave someone else something he needed.

Now imagine a situation in which business firms or banks connected to the government receive a new round of paper money courtesy of Fed credit expansion. That money comes out of thin air, not from the sale of some previous good or service. Thus when these favored firms spend this money, they are in effect taking goods out of the economy *without providing anything themselves*. Here we see very clearly how they benefit at the expense of the rest of society: they take from the stock of goods without giving anything in return. The money they pay for their goods didn't originate in a good or service that they themselves had previously provided; it came from nowhere. The analogous case under a system of barter would be one in which I come and take your apples, period.

This is "progressive" why, exactly?

The Federal Reserve can prevent massive contractions of the money supply, our critic tells us, and that's how it can avoid things like the Great Depression (an event it mysteriously failed to prevent, I might add). Whether the Fed should have engaged in expansions of the money supply in the first place, whether these expansions themselves might not deform the economy, or whether we're really expected to believe that the power to print up green paper tickets out of thin air can make society wealthier and the economy more stable – well, none of these questions are asked. They're not listed on that Federal Reserve press release, after all.

The dollar has lost over 95 percent of its value since the Fed was created. Now had the value of our money declined by 95 percent under the gold standard, the progressive would cite that as evidence against gold. When the government is responsible for debasing the currency to that extent, on the other hand, the matter is passed over in silence. This is example number 5,271 of Westley's Law, which I've sometimes rendered this way: the public sector is always held to lower standards than the private sector.

Now it's bad enough that the federal government loots rich and poor alike. Much worse is when its victims, too bamboozled by state propaganda to know any better, cheer on the looting, and solemnly warn their fellow citizens about how frightening and perilous life would be without it.

These are the same people who wouldn't dream of taking a Pentagon press release at face value, and who attribute the basest motives to the architects of American foreign policy. But apply the same standard of criticism and skepticism to the motivations behind, say, the Federal Reserve? What are you, some kind of extremist?

May 9, 2007

36

CONSERVATIVES AND THE ELEPHANT IN THE LIVING ROOM

One of my pet peeves is the conservative who lectures us on the "limits" of markets and looks with a self-satisfied and condescending shake of the head upon the stupid rubes he must endure who persist in supporting the market all the same. Why, haven't these dopes read Wilhelm Roepke, whose views are to be considered definitive?

In "Wilhelm Roepke and the Limits of Markets," over at the website of *The American Conservative* (a publication for which I am a contributing editor), Scott Galupo treats us to the usual laments about what "capitalism" has done to the public. If only banking had stayed local we wouldn't have had all these problems, the financial crisis, and so on.

Absent as always from these critiques is any discussion of the Federal Reserve, the elephant in the living room, which is a friend neither of localism nor the free market. Likewise absent is any acknowledgment that to call the banking system of today a "free market" is at best an expression of one's sense of humor. The current system is rather far from the Misesian ideal. It includes:

(1) a coercively imposed monopoly on the production of money;

(2) monopolistic legal tender laws, which artificially privilege the money issued by the government-established central bank;

(3) a central bank with the monopoly power to create legal-tender money out of thin air, a power granted to it by the government, and with a mandate to manipulate the money supply in the purported service of maximizing output and minimizing unemployment and price inflation;

(4) interest rates influenced by a monopoly monetary authority instead of by the free market;

(5) implicit and explicit bailout guarantees for large financial institutions;

(6) artificially low borrowing costs for large institutions, since the public knows these institutions will be bailed out;

(7) artificial protection of the banks, in the form of government deposit insurance and various Federal Reserve mechanisms, thereby keeping afloat a fractional-reserve system that would be radically different under a free market; under the existing system the banks will therefore create more money out of thin air than they otherwise would.

This is just off the top of my head. A free-market banking system would have no central bank and no "monetary policy." It would not rely on politicians to print up "interest-free money." It would not require any guns or badges. It would preserve the purchasing power of people's money, as it did even under the classical gold standard. It would make entrepreneurial profit-and-loss calculation far easier, without the white noise introduced by the monetary manipulations of the government or its privileged central bank.

The idea that if only "capitalism" hadn't created mortgage-backed securities, we wouldn't have had the problems we did, amounts to an especially defiant refusal to consider the role of the Fed. Consider this description of events:

Rising prices affected both banks and their customers with an optimism which swept aside the conservative standards of experience and promoted extravagance and speculation. Whatever the customers purchased, whether merchandise or land, they were able to sell at an extraordinary profit; whatever was produced on their farms brought unusual returns. Some few persons, uncertain of what disposition should be made of the unexpected harvest, began reducing their fixed indebtedness. It was not long, however, until the continuously rising prices, the encouragement of the bankers, and the methods used by the government in selling war securities, had convinced the majority that debt was a blessing in disguise, as it became progressively easier to liquidate and offered a means of extending profit-making activities. Under the urge of these influences, industry expanded and thrived, promoters of all types came into their own, and thrift gave way to extravagance. Bankers found their accustomed standards of credit analysis growing obsolete, for values increased automatically with the passage of time. Hence it was that, as the speculative fever gained a foothold and grew and the demands for bank funds enlarged, credit was extended to all manner of persons on – or without – all kinds of security, excess lines became commonplace, customers' notes given to promoters of questionable and fraudulent enterprises were discounted for rich rewards, and large sums were advanced to land speculators. Borrowing for the purpose of relending became an established practice. Time and time again the banks were saved from the effects of their ill-advised acts by the continued growth of deposits.

This must be a commentary on the recent economic boom that came to an end in 2007-08, right? Actually, this passage appeared in the *Journal of Land & Public Utility Economics* in 1926, and it's a description of how the credit expansion of 1914 to 1920 affected Iowa.

Finally, there presumably ought to be some admission that any "limits" on the market necessarily strengthen the political class. This is usually not acknowledged. I see no reason to consider it self-evidently desirable, *especially* for a conservative.

July 27, 2012

PART VI:

HISTORY AND LIBERTY

37

HISTORICAL DISTORTION

Walter LaFeber is a pretty good historian of American foreign policy of the late nineteenth and early twentieth centuries. The other day I was flipping through *The American Search for Opportunity, 1865-1913*, the volume he contributed to *The Cambridge History of American Foreign Relations*. In setting the stage for explaining American foreign policy in the late nineteenth century he paints a picture of life on the domestic front. That picture turns out to be more like a cartoon. Thanks to the Internet, I can rectify this outrage immediately.

(1) LaFeber notes that between 1897 and 1904 (but really 1899 and 1902) "the greatest corporate merger movement in the nation's history occurred." He chooses to omit the central point that most of these mergers failed. By leaving that out, LaFeber leaves us to imagine these great behemoths growing without limit, suffocating the poor consumer until the wise hand of government brings relief.

(2) Along the same lines, LaFeber notes almost in passing that competitors sought to "cut competition by merging." (We can leave aside the definitional question of what constitutes competition; LaFeber clearly holds the conventional view that competition is a matter of the number of firms competing with each other, when a better definition involves the state of affairs that ensues when no

violent barriers are placed in the way of entrants into an industry.) Thus we are to believe that a merger is an anti-social act, or at the very least highly suspect.

But this is an arbitrary assertion. The proper size of firms in an industry cannot be determined in advance. Who is to say that the previous array of firms was not suboptimal, and the post-merger state of affairs the better one? Suppose the widget industry requires each firm to own a gigantic amount of capital equipment, and that 15 firms exist in that industry. Is it necessarily best for 15 sets of this expensive equipment, one for each firm, to be purchased and maintained? Maybe so, but only the market test of profit and loss can determine for sure whether these resources might not have been better put to another use. (In other words, if these firms make losses, those losses are the public's verdict on the way these firms chose to employ the economy's scarce resources.) It could well be that the state of demand for widgets is such that no one firm enjoys enough demand for its product to make its large capital investment profitable.

What if one of these firms merged with, say, two other firms, and (assuming each firm produces the same output) now can triple their production – but now need only one set of expensive capital equipment between them? Now the arrangement may well be profitable, and the allocation of resources is now superior from the point of view of consumers.

(3) Andrew Carnegie, LaFeber tells us, "later admitted that he used the 1873 to 1875 depression years to buy cheaply and save 25 percent of his costs." Note the choice of the word "admitted," as if buying cheaply and keeping costs low were some kind of conspiracy against the public. "Again, Carnegie exploited the economic downturn of the 1880s to expand," LaFeber tells us further. "Exploited"! Would it have been better if Carnegie had done nothing and the goods he purchased had instead gone unsold?

(4) And this is not to mention that there was no "economic downturn of the 1880s," a prosperous decade in which prices fell and real wages rose by 20 percent. LaFeber believes in the "twenty-five-year depression" that allegedly ensued after 1873, a view that finds little favor among economic historians today, and which Murray Rothbard – as usual – knew to be false long before conventional

historians figured it out. (See the relevant section in his book *The History of Money and Banking in the United States: The Colonial Period to World War II*.)

(5) But it is LaFeber's coverage of the Homestead Strike of 1892 that stands out the most. Here, in brief, is what actually happened. In 1889 workers had asked for a contract by which their pay would vary with the price of steel. As steel prices increased, so did their wages. And as steel prices fell, so did their wages – except after steel went below $25 per ton, at which point their wages would not be allowed to decline any further.

By the early 1890s, though, steel prices had fallen substantially, all the way down to $22.50 per ton. In 1892 the company offered a new contract, stipulating that the new floor below which wages would not be permitted to fall would be $22 per ton. Of the company's workforce of 3800, only the 800 members of the Amalgamated Iron and Steel Association failed to come to an agreement with the company. The company's further offer of a $23 floor was rejected, and the strike began.

Since nearly all 3800 workers struck even though only a minority of them had failed to reach an agreement with the company, officials at Carnegie's Homestead plant wondered if the union had employed intimidation. This suspicion, combined with local law enforcement's inability to protect company property during a labor dispute years earlier, prompted Homestead to have recourse to the Pinkerton Detective Agency. The Pinkertons were to protect those workers who chose to work, including replacements for strikers, and to get a sense of what really was going on.

LaFeber's summary of all this runs as follows: "In 1892 the members demanded wages that matched their increased productivity." Well, that isn't quite correct. The issue in question was the price of steel that would correspond to the wage floor along the workers' sliding scale. Steel prices were falling precipitously, so the new contract called for the floor to be lowered as well. LaFeber makes no mention of steel prices.

So then what happened? According to LaFeber, "In mid-1892 warfare erupted." Notice the word choice. Warfare simply "erupted." What actually happened is that the strikers surrounded Homestead to prevent nonunion workers from gaining access to the plant. When 300 Pinkerton guards approached the plant on two barges via a river that bordered the plant, strikers opened fire on them, killing one and wounding four others. Only then did the Pinkertons return fire. Then the strikers fired cannons to sink the barges, followed by the use of dynamite and an attempt to set them on fire.

Had the Pinkerton guards or representatives of the company initially fired on the workers, we can be fairly certain LaFeber would not have used the passive construction – with "warfare" simply "erupting," without any human actor being named – he did.

Thankfully, LaFeber devotes only a small portion of his book to this kind of material. The rest is a fairly useful study.

July 14, 2011

38

MY CHALLENGE TO MARK LEVIN

Not long ago I posted "The Phony Case for Presidential War Powers," an essay that examines and then refutes all the major claims advanced on behalf of the U.S. president's alleged right to commit troops to battle without congressional authorization. (See TomWoods.com/warpowers.) Shortly thereafter, radio host Mark Levin launched into an attack on Congressman Ron Paul's views – identical to mine, as far as I can see – on presidential war powers. (On FOX Business he referred to Congressman Paul as "RuPaul," an example of disrespect the gentlemanly and civilized Dr. Paul would never even consider returning in kind.) I in turn replied to Levin.

To my surprise, Levin replied to me – sort of. He refutes nothing I said, and then declares himself the winner. (To see our back-and-forth for yourself, visit TomWoods.com/Levin. I linked my readers to his replies, but he wouldn't let his listeners see mine. I leave the reader to guess why that might be.)

I see nothing in what Levin thinks is a reply that should make any of his supporters proud, or that should cause me to abandon my constitutional views. I am accused of misusing the Philadelphia Convention, the *Federalist*, etc., but Levin does not condescend to share any specific examples of this alleged misuse. We are to be satisfied with his *ex cathedra* pronouncements alone.

Nowhere does he address my refutations of his arguments, whether regarding the real eighteenth-century meaning of "declaration of war," the intentions of the Framers, or the cases of unilateral presidential warmaking Levin wants to cite that I have shown were nothing of the kind.

And no wonder: there is no evidence for his position at all. People coming to a discussion of war powers and the Constitution for the first time may assume, understandably, that Levin can probably cite some sources, I can cite some sources, and the whole thing is probably a stalemate. But Levin can cite nothing.

Wait, I take that back. He can cite Pierce Butler's view at the Philadelphia Convention in support of "vesting the power in the President, who will have all the requisite qualities, and will not make war but when the nation will support it." Unfortunately for Levin, Butler's motion did not even receive a second.

The very fact that Levin thinks this issue is even debatable, in light of how abundant are the citations against his made-up position, indicates how far in over his head he is. He has evidently read John Yoo (whose positions Kevin Gutzman and I dismantled in our book *Who Killed the Constitution?*) and little else.

Now it's true that Levin cites unnamed "scholarly links" that support his position, though he does not share them with me. Were my position so easily refuted, you'd think he'd just go ahead and do it, instead of handing me an unspecified reading assignment.

But you know what? To heck with the scholarly links. They're probably to John Yoo, whose work on war powers is of exactly zero value. Then I'll link to the work of Louis Fisher, and Levin will dismiss him, and we will have made no progress.

So forget the secondary sources. Let's get to the primary sources. Mark Levin, here is my challenge to you. I want you to find me one Federalist, during the entire period in which the Constitution was pending, who argued that the president could launch non-defensive wars without consulting Congress. To make it easy on you, you may cite any Federalist speaking in any of the ratification conventions in any of the states, or in a public lecture, or in a newspaper article – whatever. One Federalist who took your position. I want his name and the exact quotation.

If I'm so wrong, this challenge should be a breeze. If you evade this challenge, or call me names, or make peripheral arguments instead, I will take that as an admission of defeat.

To be sure, Levin could claim that the fact that many presidents have ignored the Constitution amounts to an implicit amendment of the Constitution, but I doubt that kind of left-wing argument is one a self-proclaimed "originalist" should be eager to embrace.

Incidentally, I was amused to see, in the comments section beneath Levin's piece, several of Levin's followers assume I must be a "liberal revisionist" historian because I hold the constitutional view of presidential war powers. The traditional conservative position, as Russell Kirk and others made clear, recoiled at a strong and independent executive, a fact that years of neoconservative reeducation of the masses has done much to obscure. I suppose Senator Robert Taft, known in his day as "Mr. Republican," was likewise a "liberal revisionist" for making, in 1950, the very same arguments I am advancing against Levin today?

In fact, when Taft denied that Harry Truman could commit troops to Korea without congressional authorization, his major intellectual opponents were left-liberal historians Henry Steele Commager and Arthur Schlesinger. Levin listeners, this is the side your host has placed you on: against the Senate's great twentieth-century conservative, and in support of the left-liberal historians who hated him. But here's the difference between them and Levin: years later they had the decency to admit they had been wrong on the facts, and that Taft had been right.

Levin says he is "embarrassed" for me, so transparently have I allegedly prostituted my historical scholarship on behalf of my political ideology. He must have an acute sense of embarrassment indeed, since it appears to paralyze his ability to respond with specifics when his position is completely destroyed. And indeed so non-embarrassed am I that I heartily encourage all the world to read all the original sources, mine and his, at TomWoods.com/Levin.

Perish the thought, but could it be that it is Levin, who supports the bipartisan foreign-policy consensus with such gusto, who has cherry-picked evidence from the historical record to suit his political position? That could be, but I doubt it. For that to be the case, there would have to be some evidence in the historical record to cherry-pick for his position in the first place.

March 27, 2011

39

HOW I SENT MARK LEVIN HOME CRYING

So Mark Levin responded to my challenge (see chapter 38). Did he find a Federalist who agrees with him that a president can launch a non-defensive war without consulting Congress? I was a real sport – I let him look through the ratifying conventions of every single state, and I also let him cite public lectures or newspaper articles. Really anything at all. Did he find someone, anyone?

Of course not. Instead, he pretends I am too stupid to understand his position: "I've explained my position on radio, on FOX, and on this site. I think it is extremely wise for a president to consult with Congress (well, not all 535 members but members in leadership positions) before launching non-defensive military actions for both policy and political reasons. In fact, most presidents claim to have done so in one form or another respecting most military operations. I cannot imagine any Federalist would have argued against a president consulting with Congress."

And I'm the one changing the subject? This is beyond belief.

Mark, the point is not and has never been whether it is *wise* for the president to consult Congress. The point is whether he is *allowed* to conduct offensive operations without consulting them. That is your position.

And I have shown that there is zero – *zero* – evidence that the Constitution allows this. Levin's ham-handed evasion of my challenge has only amplified my point. I am changing the subject, he says. Well, let's let the whole world look at what we've written – all of which is linked at TomWoods.com/Levin – and they may decide for themselves who is addressing the issue and who is running away from it. Levin's position is that the president may launch offensive operations without consulting Congress. I deny that this was any part of the original constitutional intent. That is the entirety of the disagreement between us. Whether it would be nice for the president to consult Congress, whether it's practical for him to do so, etc., are entirely irrelevant to a discussion of this specific issue. Those are forms of evasion, as Levin's own followers are capable of seeing.

I have already made clear that the president has the constitutional authority to engage in purely defensive measures. That's what George Washington said he was doing against the Indians. But when the issue of offensive operations against the Indians came up, he said he would have to consult Congress for that. Not too confusing.

Mark has no time for further exchanges – he is Mark Levin, remember – but he did have time, to show how unreliable I allegedly am, to dig up an article from six years ago by Marxist-turned-social-democrat Ronald Radosh. Radosh didn't like my *Politically Incorrect Guide to American History*, though I'm hardly surprised; most neocons, for all their talk, have a pretty conventional view of American history, and my book was much too politically incorrect for them. I dealt with my critics on that long ago (see "replies to critics" on the Articles page at TomWoods. com). On the About page of my website (TomWoods.com/about) one can find a series of endorsements of my work from periodicals like the *Journal of American History*, the *American Historical Review*, *Choice* (the review publication for academic libraries), and others, any one of whose opinions is worth a teensy bit more than that of Ronald Radosh, whoever he is.

One gentleman asked, without any invective or disrespect, if Levin would be willing to debate me, perhaps at the Reagan Library in California. That gentleman was simply deleted from Levin's Facebook page.

I win.

March 28, 2011

40

STATE NULLIFICATION:
ANSWERING THE OBJECTIONS

In January 2011 my book *Nullification* became notorious when it was linked to a bill that declared Barack Obama's health care law unconstitutional and therefore void and of no effect in the state of Idaho. (Other states had been introducing similar bills, but Idaho grabbed the media's attention.) Legislators had read it, the news media reported, and while Governor Butch Otter turned down a state senator's offer of a copy, that was only because he already had one. He had read it, too.

Naturally, the smear patrol went into overdrive. Why, this is crazy talk from a bunch of "neo-Confederates" who hate America! Anyone who has observed American political life for the past 20 years could have predicted the hysterical replies down to the last syllable – as I did in my book, as a matter of fact.

"Nullification" dates back to 1798, when James Madison and Thomas Jefferson drafted the Virginia and Kentucky Resolutions, respectively. There we read that the states, which created the federal government in the first place, by the very logic of what they had done must possess some kind of defense mechanism should their creation break free of the restraints they had imposed on it. Jefferson himself introduced the word "nullification" into the American political lexicon, by which he meant the indispensable power of a state to refuse to allow an unconstitutional federal law to be enforced within its borders.

Today, political decentralization is gathering steam in all parts of the country, for all sorts of reasons. I fail to see the usefulness of the term "neo-Confederate" – whatever this Orwellian neologism is supposed to mean – in describing a movement that includes California's proposal to decriminalize marijuana, two dozen states' refusal to abide by the REAL ID Act, and a growing laundry list of resistance movements to federal government intrusion.

As states north and south, east and west, blue and red, large and small discuss the prospects for political decentralization, the Enforcers of Approved Opinion have leaped into action. Not to explain where we're wrong, of course – we deviants are entitled at most to a few throwaway arguments that wouldn't satisfy a third grader – but to smear and denounce anyone who strays from Allowable Opinion, which lies along that glorious continuum from Joe Biden to Mitt Romney.

Anyone who actually reads the book will discover, among many other things, that the Principles of '98 – as these decentralist ideas came to be known – were in fact resorted to more often by northern states than by southern, and from 1798 through the second half of the nineteenth century were used in support of free speech and free trade, and against the fugitive-slave laws, unconstitutional searches and seizures, and the prospect of military conscription, among other examples. And nullification was employed not in support of slavery but against it.

When *Nullification* was released, here's what I predicted would happen: "If the book's arguments are addressed at all, they will be treated at a strictly second-grade level. (Official Left and Right agree on more than they care to admit, an unswerving commitment to nationalism being one of those things.) The rest of the so-called reply will run like this: Nullification is a secret plot to restore the southern Confederacy, and Woods himself is a sinister person with wicked intentions, before which all his fancy moral and constitutional arguments are nothing but a devious smokescreen."

Since that is indeed what has happened, I'm following up with this point-by-point reply to the standard arguments I knew would be trotted out against the idea. (My replies to these claims are discussed in much greater detail in the book.)

"Nullification violates the Constitution's Supremacy Clause."

This may be the most foolish, ill-informed argument against nullification of all. It is the reply we often hear from law school graduates and professors, who are taught only the nationalist version of American history and constitutionalism. It is yet another reason, as a colleague of mine says, never to confuse legal training with an education.

Thus we read in a recent AP article, "The efforts are completely unconstitutional in the eyes of most legal scholars because the U.S. Constitution deems federal laws 'the supreme law of the land.'" (Note, by the way, the reporter's use of the unnecessary word "completely," betraying his bias.)

What the Supremacy Clause actually says is: "This Constitution, and the Laws of the United States which shall be made in pursuance thereof…shall be the supreme law of the land."

In other words, the standard law-school response deletes the most significant words of the whole clause. Thomas Jefferson was not unaware of, and did not deny, the Supremacy Clause. His point was that only the Constitution and *laws which shall be made in pursuance thereof* shall be the supreme law of the land. Citing the Supremacy Clause merely begs the question. A nullifying state maintains that a given law is not "in pursuance thereof" and therefore that the Supremacy Clause does not apply in the first place.

Such critics are expecting us to believe that the states would have ratified a Constitution with a Supremacy Clause that said, in effect, "This Constitution, and the Laws of the United States which shall be made in pursuance thereof, plus any old laws we may choose to pass, whether constitutional or not, shall be the supreme law of the land."

Alexander Hamilton himself explained at New York's ratifying convention that while on the one hand "acts of the United States…will be absolutely obligatory as to all the proper objects and powers of the general government," at the same time "the laws of Congress are restricted to a certain sphere, and when they depart from this sphere, they are no longer supreme or binding." In Federalist #33, Hamilton noted that the clause "expressly confines this supremacy to laws made pursuant to the Constitution."

At North Carolina's ratifying convention, James Iredell told the delegates that when "Congress passes a law consistent with the Constitution, it is to be binding on the people. If Congress, under pretense of executing one power, should, in fact, usurp another, they will violate the Constitution." In December 1787 Roger Sherman observed that an "excellency of the constitution" was that "when the government of the united States acts within its proper bounds it will be the interest of the legislatures of the particular States to support it, but when it leaps over those bounds and interferes with the rights of the State governments they will be powerful enough to check it."

"Nullification is unconstitutional; it nowhere appears in the Constitution."

This is an odd complaint, coming as it usually does from those who in any other circumstance do not seem especially concerned to find express constitutional sanction for particular government activities.

The mere fact that a state's reserved right to obstruct the enforcement of an unconstitutional law is not expressly stated in the Constitution does not mean the right does not exist. The Constitution is supposed to establish a federal government of enumerated powers, with the remainder reserved to the states or the people. Essentially nothing the states do is authorized in the federal Constitution, since enumerating the states' powers is not the purpose of and is alien to the structure of that document.

James Madison urged that the true meaning of the Constitution was to be found in the state ratifying conventions, for it was there that the people, assembled in convention, were instructed with regard to what the new document meant. Jefferson spoke likewise: should you wish to know the meaning of the Constitution, consult the words of its friends.

Federalist supporters of the Constitution at the Virginia ratifying convention of 1788 assured Virginians that they would be "exonerated" should the federal government attempt to impose "any supplementary condition" upon them – in other words, if it tried to exercise a power over and above the ones the states had delegated to it. Virginians were given this interpretation of the Constitution by members of the five-man commission that was to draft Virginia's ratification instrument. Patrick Henry, John Taylor, and later Jefferson himself elaborated on these safeguards that Virginians had been assured of at their ratifying convention.

Nullification derives from the (surely correct) "compact theory" of the Union, to which no full-fledged alternative appears to have been offered until as late as the 1830s. That compact theory, in turn, derives from and implies the following:

(1) The states preceded the Union. The Declaration of Independence speaks of "free and independent states" that "have full power to levy war, conclude peace, contract alliances, establish commerce, and to do all other acts and things which independent states may of right do." The British acknowledged the independence not of a single blob, but of a group of states, which they proceeded to list one by one. Article II of the Articles of Confederation says the states "retain their sovereignty, freedom, and independence"; they must have enjoyed that sovereignty in the past in order for them to "retain" it in 1781 when the Articles were officially adopted. The ratification of the Constitution was accomplished not by a single, national vote, but by the individual ratifications of the various states, each assembled in convention.

(2) In the American system no government is sovereign, not the federal government and not the states. The peoples of the states are the sovereigns. It is they who apportion powers between themselves, their state governments, and the federal government. In doing so they are not impairing their sovereignty in any way. To the contrary, they are exercising it.

(3) Since the peoples of the states are the sovereigns, then when the federal government exercises a power of dubious constitutionality on a matter of great importance, it is they themselves who are the proper disputants, as they review whether their agent was intended to hold such a power. No other arrangement makes sense. No one asks his agent whether the agent has or should have such-and-such power. In other words, the very nature of sovereignty, and of the American system itself, is such that the sovereigns must retain the power to restrain the agent

they themselves created. James Madison explains this clearly in the famous Virginia Report of 1800:

> The resolution [of 1798] of the General Assembly [of Virginia] relates to those great and extraordinary cases, in which all the forms of the Constitution may prove ineffectual against infractions dangerous to the essential right of the parties to it. The resolution supposes that dangerous powers not delegated, may not only be usurped and executed by the other departments, but that the Judicial Department also may exercise or sanction dangerous powers beyond the grant of the Constitution; and consequently that the ultimate right of the parties to the Constitution, to judge whether the compact has been dangerously violated, must extend to violations by one delegated authority, as well as by another, by the judiciary, as well as by the executive, or the legislature.

"The Supreme Court declared itself infallible in 1958."

The obscure *obiter dicta* of *Cooper v. Aaron* (1958) is sometimes raised against nullification. Here the Supreme Court expressly declared its statements to have exactly the same status as the text of the Constitution itself. But no matter what absurd claims the Court makes for itself, Madison's point above holds – the very structure of the system, and the very nature of the federal Union, logically require that the principals to the compact possess a power to examine the constitutionality of federal laws. Given that the whole argument involves who must decide such questions in the last resort, citing the Supreme Court against it begs the whole question – indeed, it should make us wonder if those who answer this way even understand the question.

"Nullification was the legal doctrine by which the Southern states defended slavery."

This statement is as wrong as wrong can be. Nullification was never used on behalf of slavery. Why would it have been? What anti-slavery laws were there that the South would have needed to nullify?

To the contrary, nullification was used *against* slavery, as when northern states did everything in their power to obstruct the enforcement of the fugitive-slave laws, with the Supreme Court of Wisconsin going so far as to declare the Fugitive Slave Act of 1850 unconstitutional and void. In *Ableman v. Booth* (1859), the U.S. Supreme Court scolded it for doing so. In other words, modern anti-nullification jurisprudence has its roots in the Supreme Court's declarations in support of the Fugitive Slave Act. Who's defending slavery here?

"Andrew Jackson denounced nullification."

True, though Jackson was presumably not infallible. (Had nullification really been all about slavery, then Jackson, a slaveholder himself, should have supported it.) His proclamation concerning nullification was in fact written by his secretary of state, Edward Livingston, and that proclamation was, in turn, dismantled mercilessly – *mercilessly* – by Littleton Waller Tazewell. Today, Tazewell's reply is a Google search away.

"You must be a 'neo-Confederate.'"

I confess I have never understood what this Orwellian agitprop term is supposed to mean, but it is surely out of place here. Jefferson Davis, president of the Confederacy, denounced nullification in his farewell address to the U.S. Senate. South Carolina, in the document proclaiming its secession from the Union in December 1860, cited the North's nullification of the fugitive-slave laws as one of the grievances justifying its decision.

Don't expect critics of nullification to know any of this, and you won't be disappointed.

One of the points of my book *Nullification*, in fact, is to demonstrate that the Principles of '98 were not some obscure southern doctrine, but at one time or another were embraced by all sections of the country. In 1820, the Ohio legislature even passed a resolution proclaiming that the Principles of '98 had been accepted by a majority of the American people. I do not believe there were any slaves in Ohio in 1820, or that Ohio was ever part of the Confederacy.

"James Madison spoke against the idea of nullification."

More sophisticated opponents think they have a trump card in James Madison's statements in 1830 to the effect that he never intended, in the Virginia Resolutions or at any other time, to suggest that a state could resist the enforcement of an unconstitutional law. Anyone who holds that he did indeed call for such a thing has merely misunderstood him. He was saying only that the states had the right to get together to protest unconstitutional laws.

This claim falls flat. In 1830 Madison did indeed say such a thing, and pretended he had never meant what everyone at the time had taken him to mean. Madison's claim was greeted with skepticism. People rightly demanded to know: if that was all you meant, why even bother drafting such an inane and feckless resolution in the first place? Why go to the trouble of passing solemn resolutions urging that the states had a right that no one denied? And for heaven's sake, when numerous states disputed your position, why in the Report of 1800 did you not only not clarify yourself, but you actually persisted in the very view you now deny and which everyone attributed to you at the time? Madison biographer Kevin Gutzman (see *James Madison and the Making of America*, St. Martin's, 2012) dismantled this toothless interpretation of Madison's Virginia Resolutions in "A Troublesome Legacy: James Madison and 'The Principles of '98,'" *Journal of the Early Republic* 15 (1995): 569-89. Judge Abel Upshur likewise made quick work of this view in his 1833 study *An Exposition of the Virginia Resolutions of 1798*, excerpted in my book.

The elder Madison, in his zeal to separate nullification from Jefferson's legacy, tried denying that Jefferson had included the dreaded word in his draft of the Kentucky Resolutions. Madison had seen the draft himself, so he either knew this statement was false or was suffering from the effects of advanced age. When a copy of the original Kentucky Resolutions in Jefferson's own handwriting turned up, complete with the word "nullification," Madison was forced to retreat.

In summary, then, (1) the other state legislatures understood Madison in 1798 as saying precisely what Madison later tried to deny he had said; (2) Madison did not correct this alleged misunderstanding when he had the chance to in the Report of 1800 or at any other time during those years; and (3) the text of the Virginia Resolutions clearly indicates that each state was "duty bound" to maintain its constitutional liberties within its "respective" territory, and hence Madison did contemplate action by a single state (rather than by all the states jointly), as indeed supporters and opponents alike took him to be saying at the time.

"Nullification has a 'shameful history.'"

So we are instructed by the scholars who populate the Democratic Party of Idaho. Was it "shameful" for Jefferson and Madison to have employed the threat of nullification against the Alien and Sedition Acts of 1798? Was it "shameful" of the northern states to have employed the Principles of '98 against the unconstitutional searches and seizures by which the federal embargo of 1807-1809 was enforced? Was it "shameful" for Daniel Webster, as well as the legislature of Connecticut, to have urged the states to protect their citizens from overreaching federal authority should Washington attempt military conscription during the War of 1812? Was it "shameful" for the northern states to do everything in their power to obstruct the enforcement of the fugitive-slave laws (whose odious provisions they did not believe were automatically justified merely on account of the fugitive-slave clause)? Was it "shameful" when the Supreme Court of Wisconsin declared the Fugitive Slave Act of 1850 unconstitutional and void, citing the Kentucky Resolutions of 1798 and 1799 in the process?

May I take a wild guess that no Democrat in the Idaho legislature knows any of this history?

The "shameful history" remark is surely a reference to southern resistance to the civil rights movement, in which the language of nullification was indeed employed. The implication is that Jeffersonian decentralism is forever discredited because states have behaved in ways most Americans find grotesque. They *are* states, after all, so we should not be shocked when their behavior offends us. But this is apples and oranges. This outcome was possible only at a time when blacks had difficulty exercising voting rights, a situation that no longer obtains. Things have changed since Birmingham 1963 in other ways as well. The demographic trends of the past three decades make that clear enough, as blacks have moved in substantial numbers *to* the South, the only section of the country where a majority of blacks polled say they are treated fairly. It is an injustice to the people of the South, as well as an exercise in emotional hypochondria, to believe the states are on the verge of restoring segregation if only given the chance.

(By exactly the same reasoning, incidentally, any crime by any national government anywhere would immediately justify a *world* government. Anyone living under that world government who then favored decentralization would be solemnly lectured about all the awful things that had happened under decentralism in the past.)

As Michael Klarman of the University of Virginia showed in his book *From Jim Crow to Civil Rights*, what brought about desegregation was not the Supreme Court, whose orders were obeyed minimally if at all, but the Voting Rights Act of 1965, which involved enforcing the Constitution's Fifteenth Amendment.

Supporters of nullification do not hold that the federal government is bad but the state governments are infallible. The state governments are rotten, too (which is why we may as well put them to *some* good use by employing them on behalf of resistance to the federal government). We are asking under what conditions liberty is more likely to flourish: with a multiplicity of competing jurisdictions, or one giant jurisdiction? There is a strong argument to be made that it was precisely the *decentralization* of power in Europe that made possible the development of liberty in Western civilization.

This objection – why, an institutional structure was once put to objectionable purposes, so it may never be appealed to again – never seems to be directed against centralized government itself, particularly the megastates of the nationalistic twentieth century. I rather doubt nullification critics would turn this argument against themselves – by saying, for instance, "Centralized governments gave us hundreds of millions of deaths, thanks to total war, genocide, and totalitarian revolutions. In the U.S. we can point to the incarceration of hundreds of thousands of Japanese and a horrendously murderous military-industrial-congressional complex, among other enormities. Our federal government is so remote from the people that it has managed to rack up debts (including unfunded liabilities) well in excess of $200 trillion. In light of this record, what intellectual and moral pygmy would urge nationalism or the centralized modern state as the solution to our problems?"

In fact, anyone who argues that centralized states have been wonderful, progressive institutions when it comes to the minorities within their borders might consult the Armenians in Turkey, the Ukrainians in the Soviet Union, the Jews in Germany, the Asians in Uganda, or a whole host of other peoples who might have rather a different opinion.

"Nullification would be chaotic."

It is far more likely that states will be too timid to employ nullification. But the more significant point is this: if the various states should have different policies, *so what?* That is precisely what the United States was supposed to look like. As usual, alleged supporters of "diversity" are the ones who most insist on national uniformity. It says quite a bit about what people are learning in school that they are terrified at the prospect that their country might actually be organized the way Americans were originally assured it would be. Local self-government was what the American Revolution was fought over, but we're told this very principle, and the defense mechanisms necessary to preserve it, are unthinkable.

Part of the reason the idea of nullification elicits such a visceral response from establishment opinion is that most people have unthinkingly absorbed the logic of the modern state, whereby a single, irresistible authority issuing infallible commands is the only way society can be organized. Most people do not subject their unstated assumptions to close scrutiny, particularly since the more deeply embedded the assumption, the less are people aware it exists. And it is this modern assumption, dating back to Thomas Hobbes, that – whether they realize it or not – lies at the root of nearly everyone's political thought. Not only is this assumption false, but (as I discuss in the book) the modern state to which it gave rise has been the most irresponsible and even lethal institution in history, racking up debts and carrying out atrocities that the decentralized polities that preceded them could scarcely have imagined. Why it should be given the moral benefit of the doubt, to the point that all skeptics are to be viciously denounced, is unclear.

"The compact theory may apply to the first 13 states, but since all the other states were created by the federal government, we cannot describe these later states as building blocks of the Union in the same sense."

The Idaho attorney general's office tried making this argument against the Idaho health-care nullification bill. Superficially plausible, the argument amounts to a gross misunderstanding of the American system. Were the Idaho attorney general correct, American states would not be states at all but provinces.

The argument of the Idaho attorney general's office, in fact, amounts to precisely the Old World view of the nature of the state and the people that Americans fled Europe to escape. The *American* position has always been that an American state is created by the people, not the federal government. Jefferson himself amplified this point in the controversy over the admission of Missouri. The people of Missouri had drafted a constitution and were applying for admission to the Union. Were they not admitted, Jefferson told them, they would be an independent state. In other words, their statehood derived from their sovereign people and its drafting of a constitution, not the approval of the federal government.

"The Civil War settled this."

The Civil War was not fought over nullification, and as I've said above, at the time of the war it was the northern states that had much more recently been engaged in nullification. The legitimacy of nullification involves a philosophical argument, and philosophical arguments are not – at least to reasonable people – decided one way or the other by violence. No one would say, when confronted with the plight of the Plains Indians, "Didn't the U.S. Army settle that?" If the arguments for nullification make sense, and they do, that is what matters. Reality is what it is. The compact theory, from which nullification is derived, does describe U.S. history. There is no way to evade that brute fact.

My primary intention in writing *Nullification* was to resuscitate portions of American history which, having proven inconvenient to the regime in Washington, had slipped down the Orwellian memory hole. I wanted Americans to realize that illustrious figures from their country's past posed questions about the most desirable form of political organization – questions that today one is written out of polite society for asking. I wanted to make a case, backed by overwhelming historical evidence, that the inhumane system whereby a single city hands down infallible dictates to 310 million people is not a fated existence.

Jefferson and others proposed an alternative, one we might wish to revisit in light of how obviously dysfunctional the present system has become. Before this information can be put to much immediate use there is a good deal of educational groundwork to be laid. I intended the book to be a first step along the road back to sanity.

February 1, 2011

PART VII

WHEN LIBERTARIANS GO WRONG

41

WE'RE THE SWEETIE PIE LIBERTARIANS

I don't want to mention names here. This transcends names. This is a phenomenon I've witnessed many times over the years. It's the sweetie-pie libertarian syndrome.

The other day, an aide to a prominent American politician was the subject of an attack in the major media. Why, this person has said some things that all right-thinking people oppose! When he was a radio host, he was provocative! We've never observed this phenomenon before! And he thinks there might be some kind of objection to the Lincoln regime! Why, he must support *slavery*!

Now there are perfectly good reasons one might have to oppose the Lincoln regime. Lysander Spooner opposed it, and Spooner supported John Brown. (I suppose Spooner supported slavery?)

A few thoughts off the top of my head:

(1) Lincoln was a man of his time, which means he viewed large, centralized states as self-justifying goals. This was the age of centralization in Italy, Germany, and Japan, after all. Yes, large, centralized states can abolish slavery. They can also wage horrifying wars, carry out genocides, and erect massive police states. As many people were killed in World War I, the first great war of the world's centralized states, as there had been slaves in the South.

(2) The precedents set by Lincoln during the war have been exploited ever since by left-liberals and neoconservatives, who are all too glad to respond, when you object to some enormity of the War on Terror, "Why, *even Lincoln* did these things!"

(3) In every other country in our hemisphere in which slavery was abolished in the nineteenth century it was done peacefully, without 1.5 million people dead, wounded, or missing.

(4) The Lincoln legacy involves glorifying wars of nationalism and demonizing efforts at secession, wherever they may be and whatever the circumstances. To this day, Americans are taught to sympathize with central governments trying to keep territories from breaking away, and to look with disgust at smaller units seeking self-government.

(5) Lincoln is the creator of the centralized, imperial regime under which we live today, which is the real reason left-liberals and their neoconservative cousins will brook no criticism of the sixteenth president.

Now I am about to quote one of those Wicked Southerners, which will of course make me suspect of longing for slavery, but taking that risk I boldly proceed: Robert E. Lee told the great libertarian Lord Acton in 1866 that "the consolidation of the states into one vast republic, sure to be aggressive abroad and despotic at home, will be the certain precursor of that ruin which has overwhelmed all those that have preceded it."

If you are wondering how we got to our present condition, ponder that statement. Then consider the possibility that the great fratricidal war of American history might in its ultimate significance have amounted to something other than the cartoonish struggle of saints and sinners we encounter in the *New York Times*, or from so-called libertarian institutes.

There is much, much more that can be said about all this, but I've now reached my destination: what I find so interesting is the reaction by what we might call "official libertarians," or what Lew Rockwell calls "regime libertarians," to the attacks on this person. Now this person has said nothing that Walter

Williams, whom these very libertarians fawn over, hasn't said at one time or another. This person is consistently antiwar, which is more than we can say for many of the people with whom official libertarians consort.

But with attacks like this flying around, official libertarians do not miss the opportunity to inform the world – a world awaiting their announcements with bated breath, of course – that they themselves hold all the approved opinions about events in American history. Moreover, the opinions they hold today, while different in many ways from those of the *New York Times*, are still within the range of allowable opinion. So please, please do not include me in your condemnations, oh Mr. Nice Media Person, sir.

These are the libertarians who portray themselves as the abolitionists of today – an age when everyone in the world is an abolitionist. The real test is this: would you have been an abolitionist in the nineteenth century, when abolition parties received two percent of the vote, and lynchings of abolitionists were not unknown? What is the likelihood that someone so desperate to inform everyone that his views fall within the spectrum of allowable positions laid out by establishment opinion would have been – of all things! – an abolitionist, when it really counted?

These are what I am now calling the sweetie-pie libertarians. Why, Mr. Media Person, sir, I am just an innocent bystander in this whole mess! I favor liberty, but would I question the judgments of our esteemed historians (on a matter that might make me unpopular)? Never! I can overlook the pro-war positions of people I work with and praise, but someone who used insensitive language a few times ten years ago? Why, that's the greatest offense in the history of the world, Mr. Media Person, sir!

Then these libertarians pat themselves on the back for protecting libertarianism against the wacko extremists who question their eighth-grade textbooks. The sweetie pies assure us that by policing the thoughts of libertarians, they will make our philosophy more attractive to other Americans. Wherever would we be without their wise custodianship of our brains?

It's a good thing the sweetie pies have no sense of irony. No one has ever heard of any of them, and not one of them has a following worth speaking of. It was Ron Paul – who just spoke his mind regardless of focus groups, and who told Meet the Press that (for example) no, he doesn't believe the fourth-grade

Civil War narrative – who set the world ablaze with interest in libertarianism. No sweetie pie has had a billionth of the impact the rule-breaker Ron Paul has had.

Meanwhile, the sweetie pies, who are so anxious to protect libertarianism from people whose thoughts might soil it, utter not so much as a peep when their fellow sweetie pies ridicule the religious beliefs of a huge chunk of Americans, thereby alienating those people from libertarianism. This double standard is pretty much all you need to know about their solemn assurances that they're just trying to make libertarianism palatable to the public. Sure they are.

On the one hand, therefore, we have Ron Paul and his circle, which have converted more people (by orders of magnitude) to libertarianism than all the DC think-tanks put together. On the other, we have a handful of policy wonks protesting that they themselves are much better representatives of the cause. But no one can hear them over the cheers and huzzahs for Ron and his followers.

It's like an outraged Homer Simpson trying to tell Moe the bartender that he's just lost himself a customer, but Moe can't hear him over all the new customers he does have.

I'll end with this. One sweetie-pie organization thought it would dance all over what it assumed would be Ron Paul's grave several years ago when the media attacks on him had grown severe and relentless. We told you so, they said. This is why we stayed aloof from him. Got to keep the cause pure, you know!

But then, when they noted that the young people did not give a hoot what the media said about Ron, and that they themselves were like Homer in the bar, this organization sheepishly invited Ron to speak at a special event.

As Johnny Most used to say: justice prevails.

July 10, 2013

42

THE CENTRAL COMMITTEE HAS HANDED DOWN ITS DENUNCIATION

Julie Borowski, who goes by Token Libertarian Girl on YouTube, makes some good videos and is a smart libertarian. The other day, though, she ran afoul of the Libertarian Thought Police, Humorless P.C. Automaton division.

Julie made a video exploring why the libertarian movement attracts so few women. It is a two-minute video describing some of her anecdotal impressions, not a peer-reviewed journal article. She gave an incorrect answer, according to the Banishers. The correct answer, evidently, is that libertarians are mean and say mean things, and that this general libertarian perversity keeps women away. The possibility that any kind of difference between men and women might at least be partially responsible for the disparity is not even raised, needless to say.

Julie was thus subjected to the kind of stern ideological correction one would expect from leftists who have had their p.c. pieties challenged. This is no surprise, since these folks' criticism of other libertarians is that we don't embrace leftism with sufficient gusto.

I won't go through the whole dreary, predictable thing, which you can read for yourself (at bit.ly/commissars).

Among other things, Julie's critics say she "slut shames women who engage in casual sex." (Shows how sheltered I am: evidently there are people in the world who use the phrase "slut shames.") Doesn't Julie know that such behavior, far from being a "cause for shame," is just one of the "complex choices that smart, thoughtful women can and do make"?

And while of course the author of a blog post is not responsible for the comments readers leave, I found this one revealing: "Why does she [Borowski] rail against other women's choices? Surely a core libertarian value is neutrality between different conceptions of the good?"

Actually, no. I replied: "The core libertarian value is nonaggression. 'Neutrality between different conceptions of the good' has nothing to do with libertarianism. If you were truly neutral between different conceptions of the good, you wouldn't be arguing against Julie's conception of the good."

Unfortunately, this kind of thinking dominates a certain wing of the libertarian movement, which congratulates itself for its "thick" libertarianism, as opposed to the (I guess) thin kind embraced by the rest of us. Yes, yes, they concede, nonaggression is the key thing, but if you really want to promote liberty you can't just oppose the state. You have to oppose "the patriarchy," embrace countercultural values, etc.

Then, once libertarianism has been made to seem as freakish and anti-bourgeois as possible, these same people turn around and blame the rest of us for why the idea isn't more popular.

Physician, heal thyself.

Incidentally, by the reasoning of Julie's critics, one would be led to the equally patronizing conclusion that the reason there are so few female chess champions is that women can't succeed, or won't even try, unless everything is just so. Since male/female differences are ruled out, what other explanation is left? Not enough "role models" for women? Then how did anyone, anywhere, ever start doing anything?

George Mason University professor Bryan Caplan has also weighed in, suggesting that there may indeed be differences between men and women that might account for the discrepancy within libertarianism. (I can hardly wait for the shrill cries of "sexist" to overcome us all, though for various reasons I suspect Bryan will be allowed a pass.) Caplan writes:

> My study of personality psychology makes me one of the doubters. On the popular Myers-Briggs personality test, there is a *huge* Thinking-Feeling

gap between men and women. For men, the breakdown is roughly 60% Thinking, 40% Feeling. For women, the breakdown is roughly 30% Thinking, 70% Feeling.

This Thinking/Feeling disparity explains a lot about gender gaps in college major and occupation. There's every reason to think that this disparity can help explain gender gaps in political and social views.

To make a long story short: Thinking people tend to have "hard heads" and "hard hearts," while Feeling people have "soft heads" and "soft hearts." Unsurprisingly, then, Feeling people tend to hold more anti-market views. I've similarly found strong evidence that males "think more like economists." This gender belief gap increases with education, consistent with a simple model where male and female students gradually learn more about whatever their personalities incline them to study. . . ..

Libertarians can and should better market their ideas to women (and people, for that matter). But marketing can only do so much. Women really are more Feeling than men, and selling libertarianism to people with Feeling personalities is inherently difficult. [Internal hyperlinks removed.]

Julie's critics can't conclude their attack without unbosoming the lasting trauma of the whole episode for them: today, because of Julie's video, they're "a little embarrassed to admit" they're libertarians. Poor babies. To my knowledge, they have not expressed any embarrassment when libertarians have (for example) gratuitously insulted the religious beliefs of tens of millions of Americans in crude and ignorant ways. I suppose that's designed to bring people *into* the fold?

Obviously, what matters to these critics is not what will bring people to libertarianism or keep them out; if it did, the overall weirdness and reflexively anti-bourgeois posture of some of the loudest libertarians would be their first targets. What appears to matter is that on issues involving men and women (and other subjects, too, no doubt), the uttering of anything other than an exquisitely p.c. opinion is to be shunned as oh-so-embarrassing to libertarianism.

To my mind, this is the most interesting and revealing part of the whole episode – the double standard, the highly selective nature of the "outrage" on display. Violate p.c. decorum and you'll get a ponderous, humorless reprimand. Gratuitously trample on basic decency, making libertarians seem like anti-social losers, and…nothing.

I say hooray for Julie Borowski, who through sheer hard work has made herself an increasingly accomplished and significant figure among young libertarians.

January 4, 2013

43

HEY, EVERYONE, LOOK AT ME: I'M AGAINST SLAVERY!

In light of recent libertarian showboating I have composed this couplet:

Hey, reporter, look at me
I'm against slavery!

It took a lot of courage to oppose slavery in, say, 1855. It takes zero courage to oppose it today. This is one reason I am convinced that those who are most ostentatious in their aversion to slavery in 2013 are the least likely to have opposed it at the time. Their excessive eagerness to disassociate themselves from perceived "extremism" would not have served them well in the 1850s, when abolitionism, which had zero electoral success, was the most notorious extremism of the day.

Who in 2013 ever found himself dismissed from his post, or held up to scorn, for opposing slavery?

The most recent case is Jason Kuznicki, who unbosoms to the world his views on the War Between the States in a recent column. Among other things, Kuznicki writes: "Anyone who cares about human liberty – to whatever degree – ought to despise the Confederacy, ought to mock and desecrate its symbols."

Here, it seems to me, Kuznicki falls into the trap most left-liberals and neoconservatives fall into: he conflates government and society. The grotesque atrocities carried out during the war against a defenseless civilian population are too well known to need repeating. And unless we are going to fall for the crazy collectivism of so many Randians, who claim to be individualists while speaking of "terrorist countries," there were indeed innocent people in the South. If we look the other way at the butcheries to which they were subjected, we are no better than Donald Rumsfeld and his fake concern for collateral damage in Iraq.

If a man gave his life defending his home against invaders, who should care about the intentions of his government – of all things? He protected his family, and there is, therefore, nothing wrong with his descendants honoring his memory. It would be strange if they didn't.

Did the southern secession have something to do with slavery? Obviously. I see no reason not to take the secessionists at their word, and we are being dishonest if we do not acknowledge the references to slavery in the secession documents. But the war? The war was fought to prevent the secession, not to free the slaves. People who took up arms in the South did so because they were being invaded.

What exactly was a man supposed to do when Union armies went about setting fire to his town? "Mr. Union soldier, sir, I realize that I fall under your righteous wrath because of the geographical region in which I happen to reside, and because the rulers who – through no influence of mine – have come to rule this place have been said to have disreputable goals. Please do kill me on the spot, and burn all the buildings, and leave the children to scavenge for food – forced to eat even cats, dogs, and rats. I deserve this because of what my government has done."

Leave aside all the insufferable 21st-century respectable libertarian speechifying. It is not libertarian to expect someone to have said something as preposterous as this. People fighting to repel invaders are not automatons of the regime under whose banner they fight. They have their own reasons for doing what they do – not seeing their families tortured or starved to death being one of them.

It is also interesting to consider, as historian Clyde Wilson observes, the southerners who returned to the South from the North and West, so that they might share the southern people's fate during the war. Kentucky's Simon B.

Buckner gave up a fortune in Chicago real estate; George W. Rains of North Carolina left a prosperous iron foundry he had established in Newburgh, New York; Alexander C. Jones of Virginia resigned a judgeship in St. Paul, Minnesota, where he had lived twenty years; Joseph L. Brent of Louisiana gave up a lucrative law practice and leadership of the Democratic Party in Los Angeles. We are to believe that these people, and countless others besides, dropped everything and put their prosperous lives on indefinite hold in order to go fight for slavery? Who could be so blinded by prejudice as to persuade himself of such a ridiculous proposition?

Readers at Rachel Maddow's level will take what I am saying as a defense of the Confederacy. I don't defend any government, as anyone who glances at my work for five minutes can see, so it would be rather odd for the Confederacy to be the one government in human history for which I make an exception. What I am saying is that life is nearly always more interesting than a Washington policy wonk thinks — and thank goodness for that! It is not right, and ludicrously at odds with the libertarian spirit, to conflate government with the individuals who must live under it.

Do I stand to gain anything by writing this? Unlike Kuznicki, I say things that go against the grain even though I know they will yield me nothing but grief. I hope this means I would have opposed injustice when it counted and when it might have done some good, and not just 150 years later, when I safely say what everyone thinks, to the applause of the world.

July 13, 2013

PART VIII

BOOKS YOU MAY HAVE MISSED

44

CHRISTIANITY AND WAR

Several years ago, Congressman Sam Johnson (R-Texas) told parishioners at Suncreek United Methodist Church in Allen, Texas, something he had said to President George W. Bush: "Syria is the problem. Syria is where those weapons of mass destruction are, in my view. You know, I can fly an F-15, put two nukes on 'em and I'll make one pass. We won't have to worry about Syria anymore."

Johnson later claimed he'd been joking. But the congregation wasn't laughing – it was roaring with cheers and applause.

These were all Christians, you understand – you know, people who are supposed to be concerned about the wrongful taking of innocent human life.

It's not just Protestants; a substantial number of Catholics are guilty of the same cavalier attitude toward war, which is ipso facto just if waged by the U.S. government. They will spend their time tracking down whatever slivers of evidence they can find in support of their leaders' war propaganda, a practice they would have laughed at if they'd observed it in the Soviet Union. As a Catholic myself I have been mortified to think that a neoconservative death cult is what is being projected to the non-Christian world as Christianity.

This is why the second edition of Laurence Vance's *Christianity and War, and Other Essays Against the Warfare State* (which is nearly four times as long as the first edition) is at once both good news and bad news. The good news is the book itself, which eviscerates the self-justifying nonsense that passes for moral reflection among so many Christian supporters of war. The bad news is how rare such a book is these days: a theologically conservative Christian's powerful, unrelenting case against war, militarism, and an eagerness to believe whatever propaganda will promote war and cast those politicians who support it in a favorable light. And it is to conservative Christians that Vance directs the bulk of his appeal, since it is they, he finds, who most readily adopt the war propaganda that emanates from Washington.

It's one thing to describe someone as a voice crying in the wilderness, but that doesn't quite capture Laurence Vance and his work. Vance is a voice crying in a soundproof sarcophagus on the moon.

Vance is no pacifist and would not oppose Christian participation in the armed forces if the U.S. military were actually used for defensive purposes. But that has not been the case for quite some time, which is why two of the essays in this collection are provocatively entitled "Should a Christian Join the Military?" and "Should Anyone Join the Military?"

To those who urge participation in the state's wars on the grounds that Christians must obey the powers that be – an objection Vance evidently encounters quite a bit – Vance counters with the admonition to obey God rather than men. No one is exempt from moral censure on the grounds that he was just obeying orders. The issue is whether the orders are morally acceptable or not, and that question is not answered by anti-intellectual demands of obedience. Vance demands to know whether, on the grounds that one must obey the powers that be, such critics would kill their own mothers if ordered to do so by the state. I'm not sure I want to hear the answer.

Vance raises another good point: what about the soldiers of the enemy country? Are evangelicals prepared to say that those men are to be honored and respected as well, since they too are obeying the powers that be, namely their own rulers?

Evangelicals cite that verse, incidentally, not because they need to persuade themselves of the need to support the war, but in order to bully other Christians into doing so. Most evangelicals need little biblical encouragement to follow a position on war they have already adopted on other grounds. Apparently determined to live down to the *Washington Post*'s famous description of evangelicals years ago as "poor, uneducated, and easily led," they can't sign on fast enough to whatever immoral, harebrained military intervention their leaders urge them to support. Anyone who reacts otherwise must be a "liberal" who "hates America."

As for those who appeal to the Old Testament to prove divine sanction for war (for instance, the late Jerry Falwell in a bizarre article called "God Is Pro-War"), Vance joins other antiwar Christians in the obvious reply: "God commanded the nation of Israel in the Old Testament to fight against heathen nations (Judges 6:16), but George Bush is not God, and America is not the nation of Israel."

Not just among Christians but among conservatives more generally, all critical thinking and curiosity cease when the subject turns to war. Moral relativism and utilitarianism, which Christians supposedly oppose, take the place of serious moral argument. Vance describes the position simply: "Killing someone you don't know, and have never seen, in his own territory, who was no threat to anyone until the United States invaded his country, is not murder if the U.S. government says he should be killed." Behavior that Christians would never support in any other context suddenly becomes perfectly acceptable, even praiseworthy, simply because the state has declared that a war is under way. (That's what Voltaire meant when he said, "It is forbidden to kill; therefore all murderers are punished unless they kill in large numbers and to the sound of trumpets.") Many even seem to suspect the Christian orthodoxy of those who raise the subject of war as a moral question.

It was not always so. Vance includes an essay on the evolution of the Southern Baptists, who in the past have issued compelling statements about the moral and material catastrophes of war. These beautiful statements in behalf of peace weren't merely the perfunctory preambles that good taste demands before bringing out the war drums, as is so often the case today. Consider this single paragraph from a 1940 statement:

> Because war is contrary to the mind and spirit of Christ, we believe that no war should be identified with the will of Christ. Our churches should not be made agents of war propaganda or recruiting stations. War thrives on and is perpetuated by hysteria, falsehood, and hate and the church has a solemn responsibility to make sure there is no blackout

of love in time of war. When men and nations are going mad with hate it is the duty of Christ's ministers and His churches to declare by spirit, word, and conduct the love of God in all men. In time of war it is our Christian responsibility to prepare for peace. We would, therefore, urge our churches to think and work toward a Christian social order in which a just and lasting peace can be realized.

Now to be sure, Vance's is not the most elegant English prose you will ever read; there is little subtlety in his sledgehammer style. But there is nothing subtle about the subject matter, either, and if anyone can be excused some understandable exasperation, it is Vance, who has so often been shunned and condemned in Christian circles for his rational thinking and aversion to propaganda. (The typographical errors, which I'm sure will be corrected in the next printing, are less excusable; the United States is described as a "rouge" nation twice on the same page, for instance.)

The foreword to the second edition of *Christianity and War* is written by Mike Reith, a retired major in the U.S. Air Force. Reith was resistant upon reading Vance's work for the first time, but he finally had to admit to himself that Vance had the better of the argument.

Most describe it as a "loss of innocence" – that moment of enlightenment when we discover a painful truth of life. My loss of innocence is still ongoing. Vance has caused me to open my eyes. The result has been a discovery of the wonderful truths and economics of libertarianism, and a correction and deepening of my faith in and understanding of Christianity, and most importantly, the orthodox, historical, and biblical views of war.

"This book," Reith concludes, "is a clarion call that challenges the modern American church, the military member, and all citizens as to their beliefs concerning the historical and moral aspects of warfare. For me, it was literally life changing."

Few authors ever receive an endorsement like that. Fewer still actually deserve it. Vance's book is refreshingly – at times even shockingly – radical, but I am unable to identify any flaws in his unrelenting exposition. He says what all Christians, *especially* those who boast of their fidelity to the Bible, should be saying. I am not just delighted with *Christianity and War.* I am grateful for it.

November 1, 2008

45

THERE REALLY HAVE BEEN ANTIWAR CONSERVATIVES

Winston Churchill once described the Soviet Union as the only country in the world with an unpredictable past. It was an impressive racket, really, in which the official version of history changed in accordance with the political demands of the present. If something in the past discomfited the regime and its propaganda, then it never happened, or happened quite differently.

In our own country, teachers and ordinary citizens alike are expected to conform to the Official Version of our history. Book publishers, to be sure, do not conspire behind closed doors to come up with ways to enslave the American people to their government. But suppose they did, and American history textbooks were written for the express purpose of turning American students into zombies who mindlessly repeated government propaganda and believed the state existed to protect the common good. How would the books be any different?

For a maverick historian, though, an ossified Official History has a silver lining: he can make a career out of exposing and correcting it, or filling in the gaps that court historians choose to ignore. Until Bill Watkins' 2004 volume *Reclaiming the American Revolution*, for instance, there had not been a single book on the Virginia and Kentucky Resolutions of 1798 in a hundred years – as scores of studies of every bit of useless trivia lined the shelves.

Bill Kauffman has filled another such gap in delightful and dramatic style with *Ain't My America: The Long, Noble History of Anti-War Conservatism and Middle-American Anti-Imperialism.* Kauffman's book joins only a handful of titles on this interesting and important subject, including Justin Raimondo's excellent *Reclaiming the American Right: The Lost Legacy of the Conservative Movement,* Justus Doenecke's bland but useful *Not to the Swift: The Old Isolationists in the Cold War Era,* and Ronald Radosh's *Prophets on the Right: Profiles of Conservative Critics of American Globalism.* (Radosh, now a neoconservative, has doubtless repudiated this useful book, which is further indication of its worth.)

The figures and organizations Kauffman profiles do not fit into the received version of American history, in which only "leftists" who "hate America" might object to spending trillions of dollars feeding imperial ambition. The conservative John Randolph of Roanoke, who opposed the War of 1812, and Alexander Stephens, the Confederate vice president who had earlier opposed war with Mexico, are just two of the people discussed in *Ain't My America* who refuse to fit themselves into the proper categories.

A strange omission from this book is the War Between the States, for if violently suppressing the peaceful secession of sovereign states does not smack of imperialism –especially in the context of the nation-building nineteenth century – then nothing does. The depiction of that war as glorious and righteous is a central ingredient in the current regime's flattering portrayal of itself, and in the civic religion taught in the institutions of propaganda to which some still entrust their young. Robert E. Lee made the connection explicit, predicting that the "consolidation of the states into one vast republic" would produce an entity that was "sure to be aggressive abroad and despotic at home." This should have been perfect grist for Kauffman's mill.

The cross-ideological American Anti-Imperialist League, formed in the wake of the American acquisition of (among other territory) the Philippines following the Spanish-American War, is right up Kauffman's alley. He gives us lively vignettes of its more colorful figures, such as the laissez-faire businessman Edward Atkinson, who asked the War Department for some addresses so he could send his antiwar pamphlets to the troops.

Now once in a while the anti-imperialists are taken to task for their alleged lack of racial enlightenment (the pro-war forces, of course, being their usual models of toleration). This description of the anti-imperialists is not even accurate in the first place; Moorfield Storey, a leader of the NAACP, is one of many obvious counter-examples. But Kauffman, who is able to put such matters into perspective, suggests that mass murder may actually be a worse crime than racial insensitivity: "If neither side distinguished itself by the elevated moral standards of the twenty-first century, when all men are brothers and peace rules our planet, at least the anti-imperialists wanted to leave the Filipinos alone rather than conquer and slaughter them."

Along the same lines Kauffman cites Sen. James K. Vardaman of Mississippi, who like most Americans at the time believed neither in integration nor racial equality but who sacrificed his career for the cause of peace as Woodrow Wilson was pushing his country into the Great War. His friends tried in vain to persuade him to support the president, but he would not budge. Losing his Senate seat was as nothing, he said, compared to the lives and liberties that Americans would lose if the country entered the war. In 1918 he was defeated for re-election by Democrat Pat Harrison – who, by the way, was pro-war *and* pro-segregation. (Wilson himself was not exactly known as a champion of the oppressed black man, but is still ranked among the "near great" presidents; taking the country to war evidently covers a multitude of sins.)

Vardaman, says Kauffman, "understood that standing athwart the empire would destroy his career." How easy it would have been "to trim, to temporize, to dissemble, to quietly slip out of the peace camp and vote for Death. But to his eternal credit, he did not." As he left the Senate, Vardaman called on the nations of the world to abolish conscription and to establish national referenda to decide on war.

That latter suggestion would reappear in the 1930s in the form of the Ludlow Amendment, a proposed constitutional amendment that would have required just such a referendum in the United States. I once favored that solution as a way to keep the war machine in check, and I suspect Kauffman does as well. I was talked out of it by the argument that if a war should actually be approved by such a vote (and in the weeks leading up to it the machinery of propaganda would whir like never before), the referendum would then become a potent rhetorical weapon in favor of the war. The war would have all the sanction it could need; and we'd never hear the end of all the people-have-spokens.

The Ludlow Amendment, I suspect, would have been just another casualty of Donald Livingston's observation that most efforts to limit the central government's power usually wind up increasing it.

But if that proposal held more potential peril than promise, opponents of the warfare state in the 1930s possessed equal parts cleverness, cynicism, and dark humor. Kauffman reminds us of the Veterans of Future Wars, a group organized at Princeton University in 1936 that went on to boast 584 chapters around the country. Then there was the Association of Gold Star Mothers of Future Veterans, born at Vassar College, as well as the Foreign Correspondents of Future Wars, established at the City College of New York. This latter group proposed "to establish training courses for members of the association in the writing of atrocity stories and garbled war dispatches for patriotic purposes." If only our own opposition to war and propaganda could be half as inspired.

Thanks to Ron Paul's campaign the term "Taft Republican" is being tossed around once again, and Kauffman reintroduces us to the Ohio senator. Taft, known in his day as Mr. Republican, declared on the Senate floor in January 1951 that "the principal purpose of the foreign policy of the United States is to maintain the liberty of our people.... Its purpose is not to reform the entire world or spread sweetness and light and economic prosperity to peoples who have lived and worked out their own salvation for centuries, according to their customs, and to the best of their abilities." Taft identified the second goal of American foreign policy as peace. Writes Kauffman: "*Liberty* and *peace*; with those two words, [Taft] had placed himself as far outside postwar discourse as one could reasonably stand."

We are also treated to a sympathetic account of the anti-militarist side of Russell Kirk, whose seminal work *The Conservative Mind* became a revered text in the conservative canon. Among other things, Kirk was a staunch opponent of the first Persian Gulf War, writing privately to a friend that George H.W. Bush should be strung up on the White House lawn for war crimes. His lectures at the Heritage Foundation in the early 1990s decrying war and militarism were allowed, no doubt, only because the aging Kirk was considered too iconic not to be granted respect. Those speeches would never be permitted today, it hardly need be said, with war and bankruptcy now the most urgent conservative goals.

Kirk, who had earlier dismissed libertarians as "chirping sectaries," praised them in the 1990s for having an "understanding of foreign policy that the elder Robert Taft represented." That was a position he had long respected. In his 1951 biography of Randolph of Roanoke, Kirk spoke sympathetically of his subject's aversion to war and expansionism, for men of "sturdy conservative convictions…were naturally lovers of tranquility and foes of aggression." Skepticism of global intervention can also be found in 1954's *A Program for Conservatives*, a fact the conservative establishment does not typically go out of its way to point out.

Curiously, Ron Paul barely registers in *Ain't My America* – perhaps because, compared to the others featured here, he is already relatively well known. Kauffman instead interviews Congressman Jimmy Duncan (R-TN), who agrees with the Texas congressman that there was nothing conservative about the Iraq war. Duncan also has the crazy idea that the U.S. government might engage in too much military spending: "My goodness, we're spending as much as all other countries of the world combined on defense spending – and they always want more." This alone makes Duncan a "liberal," according to the automatons.

Kauffman's writing style is a perfect medium for transmitting the flavor of these times and the character of these men. The old republic practically courses through his veins, and the words flow effortlessly from his pen – even if they happen to be words like amaranthine, mephitic, esurient, and nepenthe. At times an understandable exasperation comes through. Thus: "War effaces and perverts everything that traditionalist conservatives profess. Every damn thing, from motherhood to the country church. And yet postwar conservatives, and especially the scowling ninnies of the Bush Right, revere war above all other values. It trumps the First Amendment; it razes the home; it decks the decalogue. And they don't care."

Nor do most Americans, if their voting patterns and apathy are any indication. "The American Century, alas, did not belong to the likes of Moorfield Storey, Murray Rothbard, or Russell Kirk," Kauffman laments. "But the American soul does."

I agree, or at least I want to. Ours is a great anti-colonial tradition, and our founders cautioned us about the perils of war and entangling alliances. Charles Pinckney warned his countrymen that global ambition was incompatible with republicanism. And the feisty individualism, the aversion to propaganda, and the plain-speaking common sense of the conservatives who populate Bill Kauffman's book have a distinctly American flavor.

Yet one nagging argument just won't go away: if this truly is the American soul, someone must have forgotten to tell the American people. William James, aghast at the colonial occupation of the Philippines that followed the Spanish-American War, declared that the U.S. had "puked up its ancient soul...in five minutes." That soul, such as it is, has been sold time and again. And not to particularly high bidders, either: what people possessed of an antiwar, anti-imperial soul, that wishes only to do justice and pursue the ordinary things of life, could have been led into an immoral absurdity like the Iraq war?

With very rare exceptions, Kauffman observes, the American people have never really been presented with a choice for or against the empire. All too true – but are the people really blameless here? Some of their stupid electoral decisions may be the result of an ignorance for which they are not entirely responsible, but what remotely educated or even half-conscious living being could consider John McCain a fit candidate for anything?

I'm not entirely sure why the old America is so unpopular, though part of the reason is that few Americans have been allowed to discover it. When they do, many want to recover it. That's why, if I were looking to transform a neoconservative into a normal human being, *Ain't My America* would be one of the first books I'd hand him in my proselytizing mission.

May 5, 2008

46

JAMES MADISON AND THE MAKING OF AMERICA

Kevin Gutzman's *James Madison and the Making of America* takes what we thought was a familiar story and gives it a fresh and important interpretation that challenges old orthodoxies and helps us better understand important episodes in American history.

For instance, proper credit for the world-historic Virginia Statute for Religious Freedom is at last granted not to its draftsman, Thomas Jefferson – who had his gravestone list the statute along with the Declaration of Independence and the founding of the University of Virginia as his proudest achievements – but to James Madison, who actually managed to get the statute enacted (and who would have nothing inscribed on his gravestone).

More significantly, we are treated to a precise and detailed description of Madison's evolving role vis-à-vis the drafting of the Constitution. At the Philadelphia Convention Madison had championed a much stronger central government, a veto over state laws, and a diminished role and significance of the states. He favored a national rather than a federal government, and one in which the states would be retained insofar as they might be "subordinately useful." His major proposals, including the veto of state laws, a legislature with plenary authority, and basing both legislative houses on population, were all rejected.

Madison may be known as the father of the Constitution, but Gutzman is having none of it. "Far from being the 'father of the Constitution,' Madison was an unhappy witness at its C-section birth. Perhaps he might be more appropriately called an attending nurse. He certainly did not think of it as his own offspring."

What emerged from the Philadelphia Convention was a federal government with enumerated powers, not a national government with plenary authority.

At that point there were two ways forward for the nationalists. One way was the approach of figures like Alexander Hamilton and John Marshall, who simply spoke and acted as if the federal Constitution drawn up in Philadelphia had been the nationalist creation with broad powers they favored rather than the limited, federal structure it turned out to be.

Marshall, for instance, would later make much of the fact that the Constitution nowhere said that the federal government possessed only the powers "expressly delegated" to it; the word "expressly" is not used, he said. But Marshall knew better. He was present at the Richmond ratification convention, where people were assured that the Constitution they were being urged to ratify would indeed grant the federal government only the powers "expressly delegated" by that instrument.

Madison took a more honest route. Although he preferred a national government, he acknowledged that such a thing was neither what had been drafted in Philadelphia nor what the people ratified in the conventions that followed. So he defended not what he wished had been ratified, but what had actually been ratified.

Already in the early 1790s Madison found himself in opposition to those who acted as if the federal government had been granted powers it surely had not been granted. He spoke out against the incorporation of a national bank and in opposition to Alexander Hamilton's use of the Constitution's "necessary and proper" clause in support of that bill. When Hamilton and his allies tried, in defiance of universal practice both in the United States and elsewhere, to derive powers from the Constitution's preamble, Madison reminded them that preambles merely state the ends of a document and do not assign powers.

Madison likewise opposed John Marshall's seminal decision in *McCulloch v. Maryland* (1819), which echoed the arguments of Alexander Hamilton for broad federal powers. The Supreme Court, warned Madison, had thereby given Congress power "to which no practical limit can be assigned." The Court's reasoning stood in defiance of the understanding by which Virginia had ratified the Constitution in 1788.

Gutzman's important account of Virginia's ratifying convention, heretofore confined to the professional journals, makes its first appearance in a scholarly book. The accepted version of American history holds that the doctrines of nullification and secession were the product of an extreme Antifederalist reading of the American political tradition. Gutzman shows that this rendering has things backward. It was supporters of the Constitution, eminent Federalists themselves, who in seeking to persuade skeptics to ratify, spelled out the limited nature of the federal government and the true meaning of ratification for Virginians. Virginia would be "exonerated" from the imposition of "any supplementary condition" upon them – i.e., the exercise of a federal power Virginia did not grant.

It was this Virginia understanding of the meaning of ratification that Madison defended in the famous Virginia Resolutions of 1798 and the follow-up Report of 1800, where the states as the parties to the federal compact were said to possess the sovereign right in the last resort to prevent the enforcement of an unconstitutional federal law. (Gutzman is unconvinced by Madison's later claims that he had never endorsed any such principle; Madison in retirement simply "mischaracterize[d]" the Principles of '98, Gutzman says.)

Although Gutzman provides some important and useful analysis of the better known entries of *The Federalist* that were drafted by Madison, he also contends that those articles by Publius (the pseudonym under which Madison, Alexander Hamilton, and John Jay wrote their 85 articles in support of the Constitution) have been overemphasized by historians in relation to their actual effect in the ratification struggle. Hardly anyone outside the range of the New York newspapers in which those essays appeared ever heard their arguments. By the time New York's ratification convention met, ten states had already ratified. New York had to decide whether it wanted to join North Carolina and Rhode Island as the only two states remaining outside the Union, and also faced the prospect of a secessionist New York City withdrawing from the rest of the state and ratifying the Constitution on its own. That, and not the arguments of those 85 essays, is what persuaded New York's convention to ratify, by a tiny margin.

Edward Lengel, editor of *The Papers of George Washington*, contends that *James Madison and the Making of America*, the featured selection of the History Book Club for February, promises to become the standard biography of this important man. Let's hope it does.

February 22, 2012

47

WHO WAS THE REAL THOMAS JEFFERSON?

No one doubts that our understanding of historical figures may need to be revisited from time to time. But academic specialists have been known to overreach. To portray a historical figure in a light exactly opposed to the popular impression and to how all other scholars have viewed him is far more exciting than repeating the boring conventional wisdom. And if you can contrive a case that an admired statesman from history actually supported your own views after all, all the better.

Poor Thomas Jefferson has suffered this kind of treatment at the hands of countless historians, and Marco Bassani, a scholar of the history of political thought, will have none of it. Bassani, an American-born professor teaching at the University of Milan, takes ruthless aim at what has been called the "scholars' Jefferson," who bears scant resemblance to the classical liberal figure of the popular mind. Jefferson is one of those cases in which – in terms of his views on property, states' rights, the Union, political majorities, and the Constitution – the earlier, conventional view was in fact the correct one. Bassani's wide-ranging knowledge of Jefferson scholarship serves him well in *Liberty, State, & Union: The Political Theory of Thomas Jefferson*, as he carefully describes and then refutes the competing schools of thought.

He begins with the controversy over "republicanism" and "liberalism" that erupted among historians of early America in the latter half of the twentieth century. The "republican" consensus that developed sought to downplay, and even to dismiss altogether, the role of classical liberalism in the tradition of John Locke from the formative influences of the revolutionary generation. In its place they substituted an ideology called "republicanism."

In colloquial usage, "republican" might be used to describe those who merely support a republican form of government, but that is not what the republican school had in mind. The republicanism those historians postulated was a full-fledged counter-philosophy that was said to describe the thinking of the revolutionary generation more faithfully than the limited-government classical liberalism everyone had thought to be at the center of early American thought. Republicanism, so formulated, placed the locus of true liberty and fulfillment not in the individual, private pursuit of one's ends, but in active participation in the *res publica*. The strict limitation of government power to the protection of person and property is not the central concern of the "republican" as it is of the classical liberal.

Bassani traces the path by which this interpretation of the revolutionary generation grew to the point that it came to dominate the profession, eclipsing rival versions of the revolutionary outlook and excluding Locke and natural law altogether.

The new consensus, in turn, tried to force the square peg of Thomas Jefferson into the round hole of "republicanism." Jefferson, it turned out, was no classical liberal after all; he, too, was a "republican." J.G.A. Pocock, the founder of the republican school, even tried to portray the Declaration of Independence as a document devoid of Lockean influences. Hannah Arendt, who anticipated many of the themes of the republican school, referred to the ward system that Jefferson spelled out in 1816 (in which most decisions would be made at the level of the ward, a part of a city) as evidence that he considered civic participation to be the highest source of human fulfillment. "The basic assumption of the ward system," she argued, "whether Jefferson knew it or not [!], was that no one could be called happy without his share in public happiness, that no one could be called free without his experience in public freedom, and that no one could be called either happy or free without participating, and having a share in, public power."

Forcing Jefferson of all people into this mold is no easy task, and all such efforts have been ludicrously strained. His political thought is certainly not centered on "republicanism," as understood by those historians. To the contrary, observes Bassani, Jefferson "spent his whole life on the reflection upon the best mechanism to curb and oppose the concentration of political power, both of government against individuals and of the union against the states." Little wonder that in recent years the historiographical pendulum has at last begun to swing the other way.

Some scholars have even called into question Jefferson's commitment to private property in the tradition of Locke. That effort seems doomed from the start. "Locke's little book on government [which includes a section on the natural right of property] is perfect as far as it goes," Jefferson said. He had in fact been accused of plagiarizing Locke's *Second Treatise* in the text of the Declaration of Independence: "There are certain principles in which all agree, and which all cherish as vitally essential to the protection of life, liberty, property, and the safety of the citizen." Jefferson likewise wrote that "a right to property is founded in our natural wants, in the means with which we are endowed to satisfy these wants, and the right to what we acquire by those means without violating the similar rights of other sensible beings." He added in 1816, "To take from one, because it is thought that his own industry and that of his fathers has acquired too much, in order to spare to others, who, or whose fathers have not exercised equal industry and skill, is to violate arbitrarily the first principle of association, 'the guarantee to every one of a free exercise of his industry, and the fruits acquired by it.'" Toward the end of his life, Jefferson remarked, "As to the general principles of liberty and the rights of man, in nature and in society, the doctrines of Locke, in his 'Essay concerning the true original extent and end of civil government' and of Sidney in his 'Discourses on government,' may be considered as those generally approved by our fellow citizens of [Virginia], and the United States."

Those who would question the view of Jefferson as a Lockean natural-rights theorist on property contend that he viewed property not as a *natural* right that may never be curtailed, but as a purely conventional right that individuals enjoy at the sufferance of the community. One way of advancing that claim is by making an argument from omission: in the Declaration of Independence, such critics point out, Jefferson substituted "pursuit of happiness" for "property" in the familiar triad of "life, liberty, and property." That is supposed to indicate that

Jefferson wished to remove property from the list of rights man enjoys by nature. Bassani takes on that argument convincingly, providing an impressive body of evidence showing that the enjoyment of property was one of the indispensable ingredients of a truly happy human life.

In order to posit any other Jefferson, revisionist scholars would have to produce a comparable body of statements to the contrary, or show why every existing statement in which Jefferson appears to describe property as a natural right must be given the opposite meaning. That, needless to say, they have not done. "The burden of proof," writes Bassani, "lies with those who espouse the bizarre picture of a champion of Lockean natural rights – considered by his contemporaries as the most representative of the ideas of an entire generation steeped in natural law tradition – denying property as a natural right. And the clinching evidence is lacking."

On the Constitution, Bassani acknowledges that Jefferson did endorse the work of the Philadelphia Convention – with reservations – but finds that his enthusiasm has been exaggerated. Jefferson spoke favorably of the Articles of Confederation, telling a correspondent that "the Confederation is a wonderfully perfect instrument, considering the circumstances under which it was formed." In November 1787, two months after the Philadelphia Convention had completed its work, Jefferson confided to John Adams that "all the good of this new constitution might have been couched in three or four new articles to be added to the good, old and venerable fabrick, which should have been preserved even as a religious relique."

To assess Jefferson's endorsement of the Constitution we need to bear in mind the very limited consequences that its ratification entailed in his view. In an era in which "Tenther" (i.e., a supporter of the Tenth Amendment to the Constitution) has, absurdly enough, become a term of derision, Jefferson's approach to the Union is a splash of cold water:

> The true theory of our constitution is surely the wisest & best, that the states are independent as to everything within themselves, & united as to everything respecting foreign nations. Let the general government be reduced to foreign concerns only, and let our affairs be disentangled from those of all other nations, except as to commerce, which the

merchants will manage the better, the more they are left free to manage for themselves, and our general government may be reduced to a very simple organization, & a very unexpensive one; a few plain duties to be performed by a few servants....

That, in turn, brings us to Bassani's discussion of states' rights, the topic on which Jefferson's thought seems to elicit the greatest consternation among purveyors of fashionable opinion today. ("States' rights," a phrase Jefferson himself used, is of course a shorthand term; Jefferson understood as well as anyone that states do not have rights in the sense that individuals do.) Jefferson was a principal architect of the compact theory of the Union, which conceives of the United States as a collection of self-governing, sovereign communities (the states). (More precisely, it is the *peoples* of the states who are sovereign; no *government* is sovereign in the American system.)

Those communities, according to the compact theory, have not forfeited their sovereignty by delegating a portion of their sovereign powers to a central government that is to act as their agent. The sovereign peoples of the states are *exercising* their sovereign powers when they apportion tasks among the state governments, the federal government, and themselves. They remain just as sovereign as before.

That it is the *peoples of the states* (often referred to in shorthand merely as "the states"), rather than an American people in the aggregate, who are sovereign is evident from history. The colonies-turned-states declared their independence from Britain as thirteen "Free and Independent States" that had "full Power to levy War, conclude Peace, contract Alliances, establish Commerce, and to do all other Acts and Things which Independent States may of right do." The British acknowledged the independence of those states by naming them individually. Article II of the Articles of Confederation declared, "Each state retains its sovereignty, freedom, and independence"; the states must have had that sovereignty to begin with in order to *retain* it in 1781, when the Articles officially took effect. And when the Constitution was to be ratified, it was ratified by each state separately, not in a single national vote. This simple historical overview establishes a very strong prima facie case that the states remained sovereign and were never collapsed into a single whole.

What that meant for Jefferson and many of the thinkers who followed in his footsteps was that in the last resort the states, the constituent parts (and creators) of the Union, had to have the power of nullification, the refusal to allow the enforcement of unconstitutional federal laws within their borders. When a conflict arises as to whether a particular power was delegated to the federal government or reserved to the states, the states must be the ultimate judges; they are the proper disputants in such a case. It would be logically backward for the principals to ask their agent whether that agent was intended to have a particular power.

The states need some kind of defense mechanism by which they can prevent the federal government from destroying the very system they themselves created. (James Madison insists on this point in his famous Report of 1800.) When the delegated powers are abused, recourse may be had to ordinary political remedies. But when the federal government exercises powers not delegated to it, a more direct and immediate response from the states is called for.

According to Bassani, the Kentucky Resolutions of 1798, which vindicate the compact theory – and which countless historians have tried to run away from – contain "the whole of [Jefferson's] theory of the federal union." Jefferson's draft even contained the word "nullification," which was later removed by a skittish legislature; it would later appear in the Kentucky Resolutions of 1799. It is exceedingly rare to encounter a historian or a political philosopher who approaches this document or its decentralist ideas with sympathy, so entrenched is nationalism in the popular mind. The usual response is to try to explain away Jefferson's position, downplay its significance, or portray it in an absurd light, often raising objections against it that Jefferson himself answered. Bassani, to the contrary, gives us one of the best short overviews of Jefferson's view of the states and the federal government readers are likely to encounter.

Although a popular audience can learn a great deal from *Liberty, State, & Union*, readers should understand that Bassani is looking to do much more than merely present the real Jefferson to interested laymen. He is seeking to overturn competing schools of thought on Jefferson that have emerged over the years, and he does so in careful and systematic fashion. In navigating the thickets of recent scholarship and uncovering the real Thomas Jefferson, Bassani is an outstanding guide.

March 27, 2012

PART IX

TALKING LIBERTY:
SELECTED TOM WOODS SHOW INTERVIEWS

(aired at TomWoodsRadio.com)

48

ARE THERE ANY GOOD ARGUMENTS FOR THE STATE? (WITH MICHAEL HUEMER)

Michael Huemer is a professor of philosophy at the University of Colorado at Boulder, and the author of The Problem of Political Authority: An Examination of the Right to Coerce and the Duty to Obey.

WOODS: Your book *The Problem of Political Authority* breaks new ground in the way it attacks a very, very important question. It's a question that so often goes unexamined – well, thanks to John Simmons it goes slightly less unexamined – but you subject it to relentless scrutiny in this book.

Before we get into the details of your arguments and the different chapters, I want you to take a minute to explain to the audience the overall project that you're engaged in and how you go about it.

HUEMER: There's this question about the nature of political authority. Political authority is a kind of hypothetical, moral property that the state allegedly has, which gives it a kind of different moral status from all other agents. Political authority is supposed to explain why it is permissible for the state to do so many things that are not permissible for any other agent.

So if I have a charity that I want to collect money for, it's not considered permissible for me to collect it by force. I can't go out and extort people and threaten to imprison people if they don't contribute to my charity. Even if it's a really good charity. But the state is allowed to do that. So there is a philosophical question of why they should be allowed to do that and nobody else is. A theory of authority is supposed to explain things like that.

At the same time, it's supposed to explain why we should obey the state when we wouldn't have to obey anyone else. If somebody else tells you, don't take these drugs because they're bad for you, it's generally thought that you don't have to obey them, but most people think that you have to obey the state when they tell you not to take certain drugs.

WOODS: In other words, we have come to accept that there's a double standard at work. That we all have to obey a certain moral code that we intuitively recognize. Yet we are willing to allow the state to get away with brazenly violating this all the time.

Now let me skip ahead to the very end of your book. I hate to give away the punchline for everybody, but I want them to know where you're headed. Where is this argument ultimately going to take you and the reader?

HUEMER: By the end of the book I have defended anarcho-capitalism. Basically, I think that we don't need a state.

The first half of the book is about why political authority is an illusion, that the state doesn't really have a different moral status from anyone else. The second half of the book is about how you could have a society that doesn't have a central authority structure and how it could work out okay.

WOODS: Now, as I said before we went on the air, I think I'd like to have you come back on another time and take on that section of the book. I've had Gary Chartier on in the past; I've had David Friedman. The program is no stranger to these topics. But you have a very good take on it and I want people to be exposed to it.

Let me just say in parentheses, though, I wonder what you would have to say to Bryan Caplan's criticism. He loves your book, but his criticism is that it's too abrupt. On the one hand, maybe people are willing to accept that your arguments against political authority are sound, but then pushing them right away into the deep end of anarcho-capitalism maybe is too abrupt. Maybe you needed to make the more moderate case first and then say, "Oh, and by the way, security services and legal services can be provided, too."

What do you think about that?

HUEMER: Yeah, well, maybe. Bryan's main criticism of my book is that there's not enough of it.

WOODS: That's not a bad criticism.

HUEMER: The first half the book is supposed to get you to moderate libertarianism like the minimal state. The second half of the book is supposed to get you the rest of the way. So, if you only read the first half of the book you wouldn't be shocked – well, actually, most people would be shocked.

WOODS: Right, right.

HUEMER: But ordinary libertarians would not be shocked, because the result of there not being political authority is not that you have to immediately abolish the state and all of its functions. The result is that the state simply has to operate by the same rules as everyone else. So, if you only read the first half of the book the result is that the state shouldn't interfere with any behavior that it would not be permissible for a non-state agent to interfere with.

WOODS: All right, so that really brings us to one of the key points of your book, which is that you're not going to spend time focused on the traditional libertarian approach of talking about the nonaggression principle and applying it in various situations, but rather a kind of – now forgive me if as a non-philosopher I'm using terms incorrectly – maybe a kind of moral intuitionism. The idea that there are some moral principles that, at least on a basic level, seem to be shared by almost everybody and if we can appeal to those – the same way that Robert Nozick, in *Anarchy, State, and Utopia* appeals to the idea that forced labor is wrong. I don't need to draw you a diagram about that. If I can show you that what the state is doing is akin to forced labor then I've made my case. Is that the kind of angle you're taking?

HUEMER: My approach is a little more concrete and specific than most libertarian arguments. I'm not claiming to have a general moral theory that tells you when any action is permissible or not. Many libertarians rely on this nonaggression principle as a kind of universal axiom. What I'm doing is relying upon judgments of what people would make in a concrete situation.

If I go to my neighbor next door and I bring my gun there and I demand that he contribute a certain amount of money to my charity, almost everyone will agree that that's wrong. We might not agree about why that's wrong, right? There are different moral principles that somebody could advance to explain why that's wrong, but almost everyone agrees that I can't do that. And then the strategy of argument is to just show that there's an analogy between that and something that the state is doing, namely taxation. I don't have to give a complete moral theory, and I think this is an advantage of the approach.

WOODS: Let's start going through some of the beginning of the book. When you're talking about social contract theory, although you're talking about it the way a philosopher would, these are arguments that a lay audience will find familiar. They are objections that on a lower level the average libertarian encounters all the time on Facebook and with friends and family: you obviously benefit from the state; if you don't like it here you might as well leave, but the fact that you're here and you're enjoying the benefits indicates that you have implicitly or tacitly consented.

We're all familiar with this sort of argument. It always struck me that this is one of the weakest arguments I think I've ever heard on behalf of anything, and yet it has such purchase on the public mind. How do you respond to it?

HUEMER: Going with the analogy strategy, let's say that the mafia has taken control of your neighborhood, and they're extorting money from you and you say to the mafia boss, "Please, stop extorting money from me; this is wrong." And the mafia boss says, "Well, you live in this neighborhood, we control the neighborhood and you live here so you're agreeing to have us extort money from you."

If somebody actually owned the neighborhood legitimately – they had acquired a property right by one of the accepted, legitimate methods – and then they said, "If you move in here then you have to do this," and then you signed a contract and moved in, then they'd have an argument that they can do whatever the contract said they can do. But, what you can't do is go to somebody who's living on their own property, which they own, and tell them that they have to move out of their property if they don't agree to your terms. You don't have the right to set terms on other people's use of their own property.

WOODS: Yeah, that's the key thing. I've had somebody raise an objection: if there were, somewhere in the world, a libertarian society – Somalia is the one that's always thrown at us – but if there were a place without a state, we as libertarians would be morally obligated to move there. But I don't see why we would because, as you say, if I own this property, I get to establish the rules on my property. For somebody else to come along and start badgering me – that person is the bully. Why would the bully have the moral benefit of the doubt?

HUEMER: You might say: no, the state should leave.

WOODS: Yeah, that's exactly my thought!

HUEMER: I and the state are not in agreement with each other; why don't they leave the territory?

WOODS: That argument has never worked, however, in practice. But in terms of the strict logic of it, I don't see what the problem is.

Now, you're also talking in the book about a hypothetical social contract, I suppose talking about the veil of ignorance, the "original position," the sort of thing that John Rawls might have advanced. Can you talk about that a little bit?

HUEMER: After philosophers figured out that there is no actual social contract – nobody actually agreed to it – then they moved to: well, maybe you would have in some hypothetical scenario.

It's a little hard to see how that's supposed to give any moral force. Here's an example. Let's say you're a doctor in a hospital and an accident victim has just been brought in. The accident victim needs immediate medical care; however, he is unconscious. Now, normally you need somebody's consent in order to give them medical care, but you can't get this person's consent, so what do you do? And the answer is you give them medical care anyway. And the rationale is, it's reasonable to assume that they would consent if they were able. Because most people would consent, and it's really genuinely necessary and so on. There is the efficacy of hypothetical consent.

This isn't going to work for the state and the social contract. It's not going to work for the state to say, "Well, you would have consented to have us."

First of all, in the case of the unconscious accident victim, it's actually important that the victim is unconscious, because if the victim is conscious you have to ask them. You can't just say, "Well, you would have consented, if I had asked you, right?"

Citizens of modern governments are not all unconscious. The government could ask them if they consent. The government chooses not to ask them because they're afraid of what their response would be.

WOODS: Yeah, there you go.

HUEMER: The consequence with you saying, "No, I don't agree," would be that you would have zero tax liability. Then quite a lot of people would say, "No, I don't agree." Then they would get a complete tax refund, right?

The other problem with the hypothetical consent theory is that when the philosopher argues that you would consent, they do that with a counterfactual assumption that your beliefs and values are different than what they actually are. Because there are certain people, namely like most libertarians, who would not consent. Or, at least, would not consent if they knew what the government was going to be like. So in order to make the argument that hypothetically we would consent to the state, you have to either ignore the libertarians or hypothetically assume that the libertarians had different beliefs than what they actually had. This doesn't really work. The appeal to hypothetical consent should be based upon the person's actual beliefs and philosophical values.

WOODS: Speaking of ignoring the libertarians, it's interesting that John Rawls during his public life, his life as a professor, seemed quite willing to engage people who disagreed with him from, let's say, a more left-wing perspective. I don't know if he ever interacted with G.A. Cohen, the Marxist philosopher, but people like that he was at least willing to talk to. Whereas you don't see a full-fledged response to a libertarian critique of Rawls.

Now can you talk about what was Rawls doing? What was wrong with his whole approach? There does seem to be a superficial plausibility to it. If I were behind a veil of ignorance and I didn't know if I was going to be male or female, or rich or poor, or black or white, or talented or untalented, maybe I would say, "Since I might end up being the lowest of the low, then the rule I would want governing society is that we should be as equal as possible, so that even if I am the lowest of the low, I won't be so low." What's the problem there? Because, as I say, there seems to be some superficial plausibility to it.

HUEMER: So here's another hypothetical: Let's say that there is a lottery and there's one particular ticket that if you have it you get a million dollars, and then the other tickets are all worth nothing. So I bought this lottery ticket. Suppose that I've just found out that it's the winner and is worth a million dollars. And then you come up to me and you say, "Mike, you paid three dollars for this lottery ticket. If you didn't know it was a winner you'd be happy to sell it to me for $10, right? So, you should sell it to me for $10."

Wrong. Now if I didn't know that it was a winner I'd sell it for $10, but that's completely irrelevant once I do know. And once I do know that it's a winner, of course I'm not going to sell it. There's no argument from justice that I'm morally obligated to sell it to you, right? No, I'm not obligated to sell it – it's not unjust for me to keep it.

This is kind of analogous: if I'm in society and I found out that I'm one of the winners, so to speak – that is, wealthy, I have talents that are socially valuable, I'm in a good position – it might be true that I would have agreed to a massive wealth redistribution if I didn't know I was going to be one of the winners, but that doesn't mean that in actual fact I should or that I'm obligated to agree to the wealth distribution once I know that I'm one of the winners.

WOODS: But, they could say to you that the talent you have – it could be a talent you have to work to cultivate – but even the very fact that you have this work ethic is also something that is unmerited and undeserved. You don't deserve it. Surely you should, as a morally reasonable person, want to share the fruits of it with people who don't have this beneficial endowment.

HUEMER: Yeah, yeah. Also irrelevant, right?

It's a controversial claim that you don't deserve your talents. You don't deserve the talents that you worked to cultivate, that's controversial, but it's irrelevant because you could take the clearest case of something that I don't deserve and I'm still not obligated to compensate other people. That's why the lottery example is good, because the fact that I won the lottery is just the clearest case of random fortune. Clearly I didn't deserve to win the lottery. It was just good luck. But I'm still not obligated to give away the money. So when you come to the controversial case where maybe my talents are a matter of luck or maybe I'm responsible for them, maybe not, even more clearly I'm not obligated to give away the fruits, the results from that.

WOODS: But, I wonder: what would Rawls say about a lottery ticket? Would he say that to some degree the difference principle requires that you give away at least some of that money?

HUEMER: Well, in fact you do have to give away some of it in taxes. Not sure what he would say. Should the state take away all of the lottery money? But, of course, that would just defeat the purpose of having a lottery. I think that Rawls's response to most of my hypotheticals would be: "Well, my philosophical principles only apply to the general political structure of society and they don't apply to cases involving individual people. So, if there's only two people my principles don't apply, so you can't use an analogy."

WOODS: And he also said the same sort of thing when you're dealing with one country versus another: that he's not willing to apply the difference principle when you're dealing with the Democratic Republic of the Congo and the United States. It seems to be morally arbitrary – although Thomas Nagel tries to rescue him from that – but that's getting us a little off topic.

Let me ask you about an objection I think a lot of American schoolchildren might have to what you're saying. And that would be: we live in a democratic society and we all collectively decided that people should be able to get a chunk of the fruits of your talents, or your lottery winnings, or whatever. We all freely decided that and you're part of that. You had your equal say and it just came out the other way. There's nothing wrong with that.

HUEMER: Well, usually the mere fact that a larger number of people wants to do something than the number of people that are opposed to it, doesn't mean that they have the right to do it, right? So, if there's some behavior that would normally violate somebody's rights it doesn't cease to be a rights violation just because more people support than oppose it.

For example, I go for drinks with some of my friends and at the end, after we've all run up a big tab and the question arises about who's going to pay for it. Suppose the majority of my friends vote that I should pay for everyone and I'm the only one who disagrees. Five people want me to pay for everyone, only I don't want to pay for everyone. Am I obligated to pay for everyone? No.

Are they ethically entitled to force me to pay for everyone? No.

So it's really unclear how the appeal to the opinion of the majority makes any difference. It could just be a few dollars and they still don't have the right to take my money. So it looks like majority will has very little moral force.

WOODS: People treat it, though, with a religious reverence. There are almost religious trappings around the process of voting – it's like a sacrament for some people. And yet, as you say, when you look at it closely what is it supposed to mean that more people want to do something than don't want to do it? Well, there *are* a lot of moral outrages that have occurred over the centuries that many more people wanted to engage in or connive at than not.

HUEMER: Right, so sometimes the majority is right, sometimes they're wrong, but the fact that the majority of people support something isn't very strong evidence that it is right. The fact that a narrow majority of people want drugs to be illegal really shouldn't change my mind to make me think, "Oh yeah, I guess drug use is really wrong."

WOODS: Let me jump in with what will probably be my last question as we wrap up here. I guess the answer to this question really requires the second part of your book, which is the discussion of the stateless society, how it would work, and answering objections that a lot of people maybe have, but I think a lot of people think so little about anarchism that they're not even really sure what the objections are. They just know that it would be crazy, and people would be getting shot all the time and all that, and you take that objection on pretty well. But the key objection, I think a lot of people ultimately have – once you've broken down all these other objections – that would remain with them is: even if I accept that what you're saying is right, that the state doesn't have a moral leg to stand on, if it turns out that the only way for civilized life to be possible is under the authority of the state, then you can take your highfalutin' philosophical arguments and go take a hike because we need the state to make civilized life possible.

HUEMER: As you say, the second half of the book deals with the question of whether you really need the state to make civilized life possible. Of course, the answer turns out to be no, but that's a long story. But even if you didn't buy the second half of the book there are still significant consequences of rejecting political authority. If you think that there's going to be some big disaster if we don't have the state, then we don't have to abolish the state, but still the state would have to be much more limited than most states in fact are.

So if the state is necessary to prevent constant violence then it's permissible for the state to do the minimum activities necessary to prevent that violence. But it's not permissible for them to go on and do all these other things: regulating drug use, having a space program, support for the arts, all of these programs that are not actually necessary for that central function.

February 19, 2014

49

THE UNFASHIONABLE DISSENTER: COPPERHEAD, THE MOVIE (WITH BILL KAUFFMAN)

Bill Kauffman is the author of numerous books, most recently Bye, Bye, Miss American Empire: Neighborhood Patriots, Backcountry Rebels, and their Underdog Crusades to Redraw America's Political Map.

WOODS: Bill, you may not know this, but the response from my listeners to your last appearance was just overwhelming. The consistent response I got was: I was unfamiliar with Bill Kauffman before and shame on me, but I love this guy – I can't believe how much I love this guy.

KAUFFMAN: Well, to know, know, know him is to love, love, love him, right?

WOODS: That's what I tried telling them: the response you are having is the perfectly human response when first encountering Bill Kauffman.

So I thought I'd have you back, Bill, especially because it's a particularly auspicious moment to do so: the *Copperhead* film that you played such an intimate role in is now available on DVD. This movie has Peter Fonda in it, and it has Ron Maxwell of *Gods and Generals* fame as the director. This is a big deal. How did this project get started? You just happened to know Ron Maxwell?

KAUFFMAN: Well, I did. Ron is probably the foremost cinematic interpreter of the Civil War, with *Gettysburg* and *Gods and Generals* – these two big-scale, epic films. I have known him for years, and we happened to be at breakfast like four or five years ago, and the night before he had spoken to the New Canaan Historical Society. I was up there because we had another project we were working on that was an abortive project – someday it may be revivified. But someone asked him, "Hey, when are you going to make another Civil War movie?" And he replied, "You know, I'd love to. I'm always looking for a topic, maybe something offbeat." And the next morning at breakfast I said, "Hey, you ever read this novella *The Copperhead?*" He said. "Oh, that's a fantastic book," and it was born there. *The Copperhead* was written by Harold Frederic, who is now a forgotten name in American letters, but at one point was considered one of the major American novelists. He was born in Utica, which I think is the literary capital of New York State. Certainly –

WOODS: Well, next to Batavia [TW note: Bill's hometown].

KAUFFMAN: Well, of course, so that's an exception, but pound-for-pound Utica is far more impressive than that city down there on the Hudson at the bottom of the state.

WOODS: Right.

KAUFFMAN: Frederic had been a boy during the Civil War, living in upstate New York, which was an area that as Edmund Wilson said was marked by a peculiar mixture of patriotism and disaffection. I think it's accurate to say that per capita we sent more boys to the Union army than any other region of the country, and yet it was also a hotbed of antiwar – or maybe not so much antiwar but anti-Lincoln sentiment. We elected a Democrat governor in 1862, Horatio Seymour, largely on the civil liberties issue.

Frederic had an odd life. He was an old-fashioned Jeffersonian Democrat. He was a friend of Grover Cleveland, Uncle Jumbo over there in Buffalo. He had been the London correspondent for the *New York Times* for a number of years. He died very young, under odd circumstances. It actually turned out he was a bigamist. He had two families in London, and he was staying with the Christian Science wife when he had a stroke, which was really a piece of bad luck: he was not treated. But she was tried for manslaughter. So he died scandalously.

And his works were forgotten. One of the books, *The Damnation of Theron Ware*, F. Scott Fitzgerald called the best American novel written before 1920, so he was not totally forgotten. But in the 1960s, the literary critic Edmund Wilson, also a native of the area around Utica, revived Frederic's Civil War stories. They came out in a new edition, and these stories are unlike any other Civil War stories in that they were about the home front in rural New York state. They don't have any Southern Dixie romanticism, nor do they have any of the northern "Battle Hymn of the Republic" triumphalist righteousness. They're stories about little communities, and the way these communities are changed and altered irreparably when young men are removed from the communities. Some of them will return home intact. Some will come home in pine boxes. Some will come home changed for the worse. And some, you never know what happens to them.

So these little hamlets, these interdependent communities of small farms and crossroads businesses, little Protestant churches, are shattered by the war. That's an aspect of war that our artists have tended to ignore – the domestic consequences. And that's what Frederic's stories are about, and that's what *The Copperhead* is about, and that's one thing that I think really attracted us to the story. [TW note: The book is called *The Copperhead*, and the film is called *Copperhead*.]

WOODS: When I interviewed you about this around the time the movie was coming out in theaters – I talked to you about it when I was filling in for Peter Schiff – I noted that there's a speech in it, a small soliloquy, let's say, delivered by the protagonist, where he's speaking to the Peter Fonda character, and he's defending himself. The protagonist is not in favor of the war. He would like to see peace reestablished. And there are some people who find this hard to understand. We're fighting for the Union. Don't you value the Union? And he basically says, look, there are so many things I value more than I value the Union, and he looks at his friend and he says, you know what? I value *you* more than I value the Union. It was this whole thing about preferring things that are close and tangible to things that are distant and abstract. As we were watching it, I turned to my wife and said, "Bill wrote that speech. There's no question in my mind that's Bill Kauffman through and through." (laughs)

KAUFFMAN: (laughs) Yeah, we try to avoid – I hate message movies, you know, where they pound you over the head.

WOODS: Oh, they're the worst; right.

KAUFFMAN: And this is not at all a message film, but yeah, I confess that I did write that little soliloquy.

WOODS: But I will say in your defense, though, it's not John Galt's 40-page speech.

KAUFFMAN: (laughs) Well, we should probably explain to the listeners that the very term Copperhead was a derisive, serpentine epithet applied to those northerners who were against the war. And the Copperhead of our film is a small farmer in upstate New York, an old-fashioned Jeffersonian Democrat who's certainly not pro-slavery. Most Copperheads weren't. Although, obviously in the southern parts of Indiana and Ohio you had a lot of people who were socially very close to the South, had family ties there. And a lot of those people were, say, indifferent to the suffering of black bondsmen and bondswomen. That was not the case in upstate New York. There the opposition tended to be centered in old-fashioned constitutional Democrats. Whether they were right or wrong, or misguided, or prescient is for the viewer to decide. But anyway, the war comes, and even though the war is far away, the war comes home as it always does. This formerly substantial man of the community is ostracized and made a pariah. His son ends up running off to join the Union army. So his family is riven, much as the community is riven, and thereupon unfolds a tale of recovery and redemption and violence and vengeance and the salvific properties of love.

WOODS: There is a moment in the film I won't give away in which something happens that is entirely shocking. You can see maybe the film is building to it.

You know there's tension in the town. You know that people don't much care for this guy's political views. But then something happens that is so jarring that you sit right up and pay attention.

Bill, let me change my line of discussion here, because I want to tell you that what impresses me about this is that it's not difficult to put together a Civil War movie in the sense that you have a ready audience for it. People eat it up. People love that era. People can't get enough Civil War movies. But they expect them to follow a certain line. They expect it either to be a military film, which this is not, or they expect it to repeat the standard pieties about the war that we've all imbibed, and yours throws them a curveball.

KAUFFMAN: It does, and in that sense it is subversive, I would say, but also is there any kind of political message to the film? I mean, other than love thy neighbor, which is as radical a message now as it was a couple thousand years ago. But it would be about tolerating dissent. Now, movies or plays, pieces of art about dissent, they always, I think, flatter the author and they flatter the audience.

WOODS: Yeah.

KAUFFMAN: Because, of course, all right-thinking people are on the side of the dissenter.

WOODS: Right.

KAUFFMAN: You know, who is being persecuted by the narrow-minded peasants, or the clerics who deny that the Earth is round, or that it orbits the sun, or that there's such a thing as evolution, and it's just such a cheap and easy pose to stand at this distance of time with Galileo, or –

WOODS: I know, right!

KAUFFMAN: Or Scopes, or the witches of Salem – oh, you're against witch burning!

WOODS: I know, boy, what moral courage you've shown in 2014 to be against witch burning! (laughs) [TW note: The accused witches were in fact executed by hanging, not burning, but you understand the point.]

KAUFFMAN: (laughs) Exactly. In our film, the protagonist in a sense, who is in many respects a flawed man, is standing up, speaking against the war, which is now hallowed. He is critical of Lincoln, who I think by most twenty-first-century lights is the greatest American hero. So it makes it more difficult: okay, Mr. Free Speech, Mr. Oh, I'm for the First Amendment, oh, I may disagree with what you say, but I defend to the death your right to say it: are you going to stand with this man? You know, who's taking on probably the most hallowed cause in American history, the Civil War? It makes it much more difficult, and I think it introduces a lot of complexities into it.

His chief antagonist, Jee Hagadorn, who is brilliantly played by Agnes Macfadyen – I should say, Abner [the protagonist] is played by Billy Campbell in a really powerful, understated performance – Hagadorn is an abolitionist, and so he is, I think, unquestionably right on the central moral question of the age, the immorality of slavery. The great, big failing of this country was the failure to have liberated the slaves, not only many decades earlier but also peacefully. And yet Hagadorn, the abolitionist, is also a fanatic, and like any fanatic, political fanatics, religious fanatics, he subordinates personal relationships to a cause, and that cause eventually becomes an abstraction. So he becomes the kind of guy – he only can see a forest. He can't see the individual trees.

Now, again, in a conventional film Hagadorn should have been impeccable and Abner Beech, the antiwar guy, should have had a Snidely Whiplash mustache, and he should have kicked the dog, and he should have been smoking cigarettes and whatever other signifiers you have now of a villain. But that's not the case in this film or in the story upon which it's based. That's one of the things that I think makes it something that people, when they see it, most of them are affected by it and they talk about it.

And certainly Abner Beech is not flawless, because he suffers also in a sense from Hagadornism in that he, too, comes to subordinate his family to the personal cause, the antiwar cause. So it's kind of a complex film, I think, and we're proud of it. It didn't exactly set the box office on fire, but it played in about 100 cities, and now it's on DVD and Blu-Ray, and should be in your friendly neighborhood video store, or even better, you can buy it.

WOODS: What was your exact role in the film? Did you adapt the screenplay from the original work?

KAUFFMAN: Yes, I did. I wrote the screenplay, so it was an adapted screenplay, and Ron Maxwell, the director, was a tremendous mentor. We followed the novella somewhat closely. Although, actually, about halfway through we branch off. The book ends very badly. I don't know what happened. Maybe Frederic was tired. I have no idea. It's inspired by the book, largely based on the book, but if you read the novella, which I encourage folks to do, there are a fair number of differences.

WOODS: Where did you guys film it?

KAUFFMAN: It was filmed actually up in where of course you would expect an American Civil War movie to be filmed, in Canada.

WOODS: Oh, that's funny! I didn't realize that. Why?

KAUFFMAN: Yeah, I was hoping it would be filmed, actually, in a historical site in upstate New York, but for tax reasons it was filmed in the province of New Brunswick – actually, for more than tax reasons. They filmed it at a place called King's Landing, which is a treasure of Canada, I would say. It's a living history museum, where the architecture and layout is mid-nineteenth century North American. So it was the perfect spot to film, and it was a fantastic set. They tell me it would have cost $30 million to build a set like this, but it was there for us to use.

WOODS: Wow! Beautiful! Well, you can't argue with that.

KAUFFMAN: Although the funny thing is, at the last minute, maybe two and a half months or so before the film was released, the producers, who were fantastic people, said, "You know what? We need a brief scene at the beginning of the film." So that's actually the one scene that I didn't write. Ron wrote it. And it's the very first scene in the movie, and it was filmed, since you can't really film anything in the provinces in early March, it was actually filmed in southern California, doubling for upstate New York.

WOODS: How about that!

KAUFFMAN: But you can't see any palm trees or anything like that in the background.

WOODS: Oh, that's funny. When huge movies come out, YouTube has a channel that puts out everything wrong with them. It finds all the anachronisms, and you know, the guy's wearing three pens in his pocket in one shot, and then the very next shot he's got only two. So mercifully, you will not be subjected to that. I think they would have spotted the palm tree.

KAUFFMAN: They would have, yeah, yeah, and I hope they won't find too many anachronisms. The biggest anachronism, usually, in a historical movie is, again, the author doesn't want to be thought to in any way share the social conventions or whatever of the time, so there's always this auctorial alter ego. So you have a movie set in the 1830s where you'll have a female character who has the attitudes of a twenty-first-century screenwriter. And that to me is a true anachronism.

WOODS: In *Amistad*, for example, there are scenes in which black people are sitting in a courtroom observing the trial, which goes to show they are more interested in political correctness than they are in really showing what conditions were like. You think black people would have been allowed in a courtroom in Connecticut? There's no way! But, of course, we have to make it seem like these were the good guys – and there were some good guys, yes, but you can't pretend that society was a way that it wasn't unless you just want to use "the North" as against the traditional foil, "the South," thinking of them as these gigantic blobs, these gigantic aggregates that have no actual people in them.

KAUFFMAN: Right! Right! And so again, all the complexity and contradiction gets washed out – the Unionists in the South, the antiwar folks in the North. I actually live about 20 miles north of what was really the cradle of political abolitionism in America – Warsaw, New York, where the Liberty Party was formed. And these were, to me, some of the great heroes of American history. I mean, they took a very unfashionable position, and they were motivated by, I think, Christian concerns. They had a two-pronged approach: moral suasion, and the enactment of personal liberty laws – which I know you've written about, Tom – which were essentially defying the Fugitive Slave Act. This was one of the strategies to end slavery peacefully.

WOODS: As a party, they got about two percent of the vote. This is why, Bill, this particularly sticks in my craw: today, we have a number of libertarians who are dying to let the establishment know that, yeah, we favor free trade and low taxes, *but please, please don't call me an extremist, oh, good* New York Times *reporter, sir; I want you to know that I hold all the fashionable opinions on everything, and I am deeply opposed to slavery. And these other libertarians, I think secretly they support it because they've said unkind words about Lincoln. But I am really against slavery!*

What I have sometimes said, Bill, is that I consider it exceedingly unlikely, given that two percent of the vote went to the Liberty Party 150 years ago, that people today who devote themselves to assuring everybody that they hold all the officially approved opinions would have been among that two percent. In that day, they would have been assuring everybody they held the officially approved opinion that they were, of course, opposed to the Liberty Party and the extremists who belonged to it!

KAUFFMAN: Right! Anathematizing of Gerrit Smith and all these I think really heroic figures.

WOODS: Bill, were you actually on set when they were filming?

KAUFFMAN: Yes, I was. They filmed for about seven weeks. I was there off and on for about four weeks. On the set of a well-planned movie there's not a whole lot for a writer to do, but once in a while they'd say, hey, we need a little transition scene here for tomorrow, and I had a little cubby hole, and it was fun because it was from like a 1930s movie – "Get me a rewrite!" So I get in there and pound out the scene. I was really impressed by the competence and the dedication of – these crews are phenomenal. It's a really complicated undertaking with many hundreds of parts to put one film together, but this worked very well, and I think it shows on the screen. I like the film a lot.

WOODS: You know, Bill, I was asking not so much – it hadn't occurred to me that there would be a need, let's say, for an impromptu drafting of a short scene, but just that this was in some ways your baby, having done the screenplay, and it just might be fun to go and observe it, whether or not they really needed you there.

KAUFFMAN: Oh, yeah, absolutely it was. You hear a lot of stories – writers tend to be whiners, as you know, Tom.

WOODS: I refuse to believe that.

KAUFFMAN: I think people who write films sometimes, I've heard a number of horror stories about how all these vulgar philistines ruined my vision, etc. But in this case, Ron Maxwell and the cast and crew – I can't imagine it having turned out better. There might be one or two little things where I wish this scene stayed, and this scene didn't, but I can't complain. It was a great experience.

May 2, 2014

50

THE MYTH OF THE RULE OF LAW
(WITH JOHN HASNAS)

John Hasnas is associate professor of business at Georgetown University's McDonough School of Business, and visiting associate professor of law at Georgetown University Law Center. He is the author of Trapped: When Acting Ethically Is Against the Law.

WOODS: Some years ago I read your article "The Myth of the Rule of Law." Let me tell you: I emphatically and indignantly rejected the thesis of this article. I could not accept it. And I think, judging from the tone of the article, that's the response you were expecting from a lot of people. I was already more or less a libertarian, and yet I thought what you were saying was so out of bounds, even though I couldn't refute it. It ate away at me for years until finally I said, "All right, that Hasnas is right after all." I want other people to have their eyes opened the same way that mine were.

Let's start off by having you explain the myth of the rule of law, that is to say, what it is that people think of when they hear this very attractive sounding phrase, "the rule of law."

HASNAS: Okay, I'll try to do that, but you are asking me about an article that is now rather old, so I will do my best to recall what I said in it. I have to say that I appreciate your reaction. I find that, with regard to my work, if someone agrees with me in less than two years, I know they are not thinking about it deeply enough.

WOODS: Well, thanks. (laughs)

HASNAS: The article, "The Myth of the Rule of Law," does require a bit of explaining. There's a widespread belief in the philosophical community, and I believe also reflected in the general community, that the outcome of legal cases is controlled by the language of the rules of law. This is encapsulated in the phrase "the rule of law and not men," which suggests that the law is a neutral and objective set of rules that regulates human behavior, that there is always one right answer to legal controversies, and that legal outcomes are not merely a matter of human whim in which one group of people control the behavior of others. Now, there are many ways that the phrase "the rule of law" is used, but this is the meaning I explore in the article you ask about.

My article argues that this widely held belief is a myth, at least when applied to the law that comes from legislative bodies, and to some extent even when applied to the law that comes out of common law courts. The article argues that when human beings make the law, it's the human beings that control others, not the rules themselves. The article illustrates this with several examples.

The most familiar example I use is the First Amendment to the United States Constitution. The language of the First Amendment states, "Congress shall make no law abridging the freedom of speech or of the press." If it was the language of the Amendment that controlled outcomes, then almost everything that most people believe about the First Amendment – including libertarians – would be wrong.

For instance, if I ask most people whether the Congress can pass a law prohibiting someone from revealing military secrets in a time of war, they usually say yes. But that means that they are interpreting the word "no" to mean "some." If I ask people – especially libertarians – whether the President can issue an executive order that bans criticism of his administration, most people say no. But that means that they are interpreting "Congress" to include the President. Does the First Amendment prohibit laws against flag burning? Many people say it does. But then they are interpreting speech and press to include any type of expressive conduct.

Every single word in the Amendment is being interpreted to reflect the pre-existing political or ethical beliefs of the speaker. As a libertarian, I tend to interpret the First Amendment to create the greatest possible protection for freedom of expression that I can imagine. On the other hand, people who disagree with me – people who are advocates of campaign finance reform and think that the rich shouldn't be allowed to spend large sums to advocate their political positions – will read the same language and come up with an entirely different interpretation.

It's not the words that are controlling the results, it's the presuppositions of the individuals who are making the decision. Now, with regard to constitutional law, that is the Supreme Court. With regard to ordinary state-level law, it's state appellate courts. But as long as human beings are making the decisions, it's always the rule of some people over others. It's never the rule of objective, impersonal law that somehow exists out there.

WOODS: What I like about this First Amendment example is that you're saying that if we take a statement that we're all familiar with, and whose meaning we all think we know, and then we note just how broadly it's interpreted by so many people in ways that clearly depart from that text, well, if the First Amendment, which is a canonical statement, can be interpreted in such varying ways, then what hope have we for just the ordinary case?

In the article you give numerous examples – I won't ask you to try to recall them now – in which you are disputing the claim that every time there's a legal dispute, there is, at least according to the myth of the rule of law, anyway, a single, determinate outcome that is demanded by words on a page. For instance, I recall one of the examples having to do with somebody having something that was of indeterminate worth. He didn't know how much it was worth, so he sold it for $100. And then it turned out to be an item of priceless value, so he sued to invalidate the contract. It turns out that even a matter like this, where there would be a law for how to deal with such situations, you can still find precedents that would go both ways.

HASNAS: You're right. I'll have to be careful now to guard against my professorial tendency to go on too long on somewhat arcane subjects. The part of the article you're referring to deals with legal cases that would be obscure to the lay person, but would be familiar to anyone who has taken a first-year law school course in contracts. The cases you referred to relate to a rule of contract law that is well known to first-year contracts students – the rule that states that when two parties to a contract are both mistaken about an essential aspect of the subject of the contract, the contract is rescindable; that is, it's not a valid contract. That's the rule of mutual mistake. But what does it mean to say both parties are mistaken? Consider the following two cases. In the first, a woman finds an interesting-looking rock, and brings it to a dealer. Neither party knows what type of rock it is, and the dealer pays her $1 for the rock. The rock turns out to be a rough diamond worth $700. The woman sues to rescind the contract and get the diamond back, but the court rules that there was no mistake. Both parties knew they were bargaining about a rock of unknown value. Since there was no mutual mistake, the rule of law implies that the contract is not rescindable.

In the second case, an individual buys a painting at an auction for $100. The painting turns out to be a lost masterpiece worth much more. The seller sues to rescind the contract. In this case, the court finds that there was a mutual mistake about the subject of the contract because both parties believed it was a cheap work of art when it was actually a lost masterpiece. Therefore, the contract is rescindable.

What determines these cases is not the language of the law. What matters is whether the decision-maker thinks it is fair to uphold the contract or not. In the legal system, there are always enough precedents so that you can find a good argument for a conclusion that you believe to be just. No one is manipulating things for nefarious purposes. Most judges – most decision-makers – want to do what they think is just and right, and we have enough precedents in our law that will allow them to find an argument for whatever result that is.

The explanation of why the Anglo-American legal system has this indeterminate character is that it's actually a combination of two legal systems that were merged in the nineteenth century. One was common law courts, in which the rules of common law were applied. The other was the courts of equity, in which principles of equity designed to relieve injustice were applied. The principles of equity were applied when the rules of common law produced unjust or overly harsh results. In such cases, the principles of equity would undo unjust results of the common law. When the common law courts were merged with the courts of equity, both the rules of common law and the principles of equity were being applied within a single legal system. The result is that both a rule of common law and a principle of equity that will undo that rule are available to the decision-maker, which allows the decision-maker to appeal to whichever he or she believes will produce a just result.

So, despite the logical form of judicial rulings, the rules are not controlling anything. What determines the outcome are the beliefs about justice of the people in the role of decision-maker. My article points out that in these circumstances, there are only two options. One is to engage in the political struggle to control the people making the decisions in order to have the law interpreted in the way you believe appropriate. The other is to shrink the realm of legal decision-making as much as possible and leave most of human activity in the realm of private decision-making.

WOODS: So in other words, you're saying that the reason that, let's say, court decisions are not completely random or completely unpredictable is not that there's the rule of law keeping them semi-determinate or predictable, but that probably the judges have at least some ballpark resemblance in their visions of what is just, and that's what drives whatever stability we see in the law. Is that what you're claiming?

HASNAS: Yes, that's very well put. That is precisely what I am claiming. When I say that the rule of law is a myth, or that the law is indeterminate, all I am saying is that the rules are not controlling things. Something else is. But that doesn't mean that law is unpredictable. It's perfectly predictable based on the beliefs that the people in the decision-making role share. If almost all of our judges are, let's say, wealthy, Bostonian, Harvard graduates, they will all have a common background, and you can bet that the outcome of cases will be perfectly predictable and fairly uniform. Note that a major complaint over the last few decades has been that the law is becoming scattershot; it's becoming more and more unpredictable. Well, that corresponds to a time period in which we've been attempting to diversify the bench – to get judges with different backgrounds from different socioeconomic classes. This diversification makes it less likely that the judges will share the same predispositions, and, as a result, the law will become less predictable.

Of course, even with the recent diversification, to become a judge, one must hold a fairly conventional set of political beliefs. Someone like me, a professor who writes articles like the one you read, will never be appointed a judge. My position is too far outside the range of what's conventionally acceptable. What controls the outcome of legal cases is not the rules of law, but the common belief structure of the people invested with decision-making capacity.

WOODS: I can still anticipate an objection, though, and it's one that you've anticipated in your article: couldn't we somehow word the congressional legislation or just word the legal principles in such a way that a diversity of interpretations would be impossible, so that we could really put a straightjacket around judges?

HASNAS: The answer to that is no. What language could be clearer than "Congress shall make no law abridging the freedom of speech and of the press"? Or another example I use in the article is the text of the Civil Rights Act declaring it to be illegal to discriminate on the basis of race, sex, religion, or national origin. This is pretty clear language. Yet look at the range of interpretation it has given rise to since 1964.

My favorite example in the article is one designed to appeal to libertarians. Most libertarians adhere to the principle that contracts that one voluntarily enters into without fraud or duress should be binding. I then discuss another case from my first-year law student days: the case of Agnes Syester. Agnes was a lonely 68-year-old widow who was recruited for dance lessons by Arthur Murray Dance Studios. Arthur Murray had an interesting way of recruiting customers. It would go through obituary columns, and then send coupons for free dance lessons to widows. When these lonely, little old ladies would come in for their lessons, the studio would have handsome, young dance instructors dance with them and compliment them on their dancing. On the basis of this sales technique, Agnes Syester signed up for three lifetime memberships and essentially signed over her life savings to Arthur Murray Dance Studios. Now there was no fraud in this case. No one lied to Agnes about the terms of the contracts. No force was used. Agnes voluntarily entered into each of her contracts. And yet, the outcome is completely unfair.

Would we really want legal language that required contracts to be enforced no matter how unfair they were? Agnes's contract is a pretty clear example of a contract voluntarily entered into without fraud or force, so under the rule she should have to turn all of her money over to the Arthur Murray Dance Studio. I wouldn't want to live under a legal system that produces such a result, and our legal system doesn't. It is to avoid such results that it contains the principles of equity.

Even if it were possible to express the law in language so definite that there could be no disagreement about what it meant, we would not want a legal system that achieved certainty at the cost of justice. The purpose of the legal system should be justice, not certainty. You could have a really, really certain legal system which is highly oppressive. But such a system is not desirable. So if you want a just system, you're going to have to accept the fact that human beings are imperfect in many ways, and you're going to need some flexibility in the system.

WOODS: Why are people taught to believe in the rule of law? This is what really blew me away. If it clearly does not correspond to reality, what's the benefit to the regime of encouraging us to think that there's a rule of law?

HASNAS: Indeed. In the past, why were people taught to believe in the divine right of kings? Because if they believed that God endowed a king with the power to tell them what to do, they would obey. If we can be made to believe that the dictates of our politicians are actually statements of an objective, impersonal law, we are more likely to obey them. We will do what those in power want us to do.

Another example I used in the article, I got from watching the old movie *Gandhi*. The British – who are basically very moral people – were willing to assault Indians who just wanted to make salt in their own country. The movie dramatizes the scene of British soldiers striking down defenseless people. Why? Why would ordinarily decent human beings do that? Well, they wouldn't, unless they could be convinced that what they were doing was not oppressing an indigenous population, but upholding the rule of law.

The myth of the rule of law will lead the public to conspire in all kinds of oppressive conduct that the government wants to engage in. It's hard to explain why the people of the southern states during the civil rights era would accept extremely racist behavior by their political leaders, considering that they were not all racists, unless they thought that what they were doing was upholding the rule of the democratically enacted law.

I live in a small community around a lake, which has a community website. One day, a resident began cutting down trees on her own property, which, because they were so close to the lake, was a violation of law. The website erupted in anger. Everyone was up in arms, and wanted to have this person arrested. Residents arranged to meet the authorities in the street in front of the tree cutter's home to ensure that this violation of the objectively enacted rules of law was punished. There was no question about what would be just to the individual. All that was discussed was the importance of upholding the rule of law.

No oppressive government can survive if it has to use force to get people to obey its commands. What government must do is get the people to buy in, to voluntarily support their own oppressors, or the system will collapse. The divine right of kings served this purpose in the past; the idea of the rule of law does so now. When only a small minority challenges the myth, there is no effect. But just as was the case with regard to the divine right of kings, if the majority begins to question the myth, the power structure would soon collapse.

WOODS: We're just about out of time, but give us an overview of what your ultimate conclusion is, that if you want to solve this problem, it has to be solved not by trying to change the wording of the law or other fruitless efforts like that. It has to be solved in a much, much more radical way than even some libertarians may be prepared to concede.

HASNAS: Yes, I advocated a radical solution in the original article. But let me offer a slightly more moderate response here. In the intervening years, I wrote two additional articles: "The Depoliticization of Law" and "The Obviousness of Anarchy."

Both of these articles suggest that an anarchic system need not be a radical one. We needn't look for something wildly different from what we have now. We live in a system that's been governed by common law for over 1000 years. And the rules of common law – rules that evolve in response to actual human conflicts – provide all of the underlying contract, tort, and commercial law that we need to have a prosperous society. So a non-political legal system that would preserve freedom already exists. All we have to do is peel away the legislative overlay created by politicians. You never hear of people going to war over the rules of contract law, because that's law that evolved from human interaction designed to settle disputes without violence and to produce peace. We have an entire system of law that works well to produce cooperation and prosperity that already exists. We don't need anything more radical than to simply go back to the underlying system of common law to create a much more libertarian society.

May 6, 2014

51

WAR AND THE FED (WITH DAVID STOCKMAN)

David Stockman, director of the Office of Management and Budget under Ronald Reagan, is the author of The Great Deformation: The Corruption of Capitalism in America *He operates the website and blog David Stockman's Contra Corner.*

WOODS: You gave a speech earlier this year on the Federal Reserve and the warfare state, and what I found interesting in it, among many other things, is that you showed that it's not just the old story that the Fed enables the warfare state – although that's a story that can't be told often enough, and most people don't know anything about it. But it's also that it was under the conditions of war that the Fed itself grew, the Fed itself developed further what its role in the economy – which was initially a very modest one – was going to be. Now you have all this demand management and everything else going on. This really had roots during wartime. Can you talk a little bit about both angles of that?

STOCKMAN: Sure, I'd be happy to, and I elaborated this more in the longer article I wrote that appeared on my blog called David Stockman's Contra Corner. But you have to go back all the way to World War I, to 1913, to the enactment of the Federal Reserve Act on Christmas Eve that year, practically. And the interesting thing is that the Fed was not authorized in that fundamental change in our monetary system to buy government debt, to be intervening in the bond market or the money markets, to be active in Wall Street in any way. Instead, it was to be a banker's bank that passively supplied liquidity when country banks, or city banks, or reserve banks came forward with good collateral and were willing to pay a penalty rate of interest on top of what – and this is really important – the free market was setting. So that was the scheme: the banker's bank, there was no Keynesian macro-management of the economy, no Humphrey-Hawkins or targets for unemployment, or inflation, or housing starts, or anything else. It was to be essentially a market-driven liquidity mechanism.

Now, why did that change? It changed fundamentally because of the accident of World War I and the huge mistake that was made by Woodrow Wilson when he decided that the European war, which was nearing exhaustion in 1917, was something that we needed to jump into. And when we did, there was a massive war finance. Interestingly enough, and I laid this out in my book, Tom, and I just feel like mentioning it again: on the eve of World War I, we had $1 billion of national debt only. It was 4% of GDP. It had not increased since the Battle of Gettysburg, if you can imagine, more than a 50-year period. And suddenly, they had to finance $20 or $25 billion – a 20-fold increase in the national debt. It couldn't be done overnight, on the spot – another huge part of the mistake Wilson made. And so they drafted the Fed into the service of financing the massive emission of war bonds.

And that's where it all started. The Fed's mission fundamentally changed. It got into the bond market. It got into the interest rate setting and impacting business. It got into the fiscal management side of our whole economy, and it took obviously decades and decades for mission creep to go from that start during World War I to what we have today. But, of course, I think there is a continuous thread there, a continuous history, and with each pulse of the warfare state problem we've had, then going to World War II, and then the Cold War, and even now with these ridiculous interventionist wars, the Fed has been called into service to finance the government debt on the cheap, and so therefore, people tolerate the wars and the cost of the wars that we don't need, because essentially it's being financed with free money from the Fed.

WOODS: David, I noted in that speech you even used the word "genocide," at least borderline genocide, when talking about the U.S. role in the Vietnam War. Now I can't imagine that using that language would have landed you a position in the Reagan administration. So sometime between then and now you changed your views of the warfare state. When and how did that happen?

STOCKMAN: Well, that's an interesting question, Tom, but in a sense I didn't. I started out life as a student at Michigan State University in 1964 to 1968. I became rabidly antiwar. I was an SDSer. [TW note: SDS stands for Students for a Democratic Society.] I fell for the whole sort of radical line, but ironically, they were correct about our intervention in Vietnam. It was a tremendous mistake. I never changed my mind about that, frankly.

WOODS: Wow! Okay.

STOCKMAN: And then I ran for Congress, and I ran as a conservative – because I was: I was a free-marketer from southwestern Michigan. I proved my mettle because I voted against the first Chrysler bailout – not just the second one, the first one. But the opposition candidate I had basically ran against me on the grounds that I had a red file with the Michigan State Police.

Now, I bring this up because in 1980 I was then nominated by President Reagan to be budget director. Some enterprising reporter found out about the red file. They immediately raised the issue and tried to create a crisis, and you know, sort of put me in the penalty box. And he said he did that when he was a young man; I had a lot of crazy ideas, too.

WOODS: (laughs) That's good.

STOCKMAN: In other words, I have been skeptical all the way through about our interventionist, aggressive foreign policy. It's been one mistake after another. Vietnam, as I now can clearly see and something that I continue to blog about every day on my blog, David Stockman's Contra Corner, was just the first step in a multitude and in a long-running history of interventions in places where the true security of the American people was not at issue. And once you got that machine going – and Eisenhower warned us about it, as you well know, in his famous farewell address in 1960 about the military-industrial complex – once that machinery gets in motion and has the resources that it does – really, I figure the total warfare state today costs nearly a trillion dollars when you count all the debt that's been used to finance it, $150 billion that the Veterans Administration costs us today because of all the wounded and the harmed veterans that have come back from these unnecessary wars. When you put it all together – foreign assistance, and security aid, and the Pentagon budget per se, and all the spy state apparatus, the intelligence agencies – it's a trillion dollars, a massive amount of resources, hundreds of thousands of civilian employees, millions in the private sector directly or indirectly benefited, all looking for a mission to keep the thing going. And that's why I continuously try to say to conservatives and libertarians that the warfare state is every bit as much statist as is the welfare state, and that we have a dual challenge in trying to bring government to heel and get back to some kind of productive and prosperous capitalist system in America. We have to tame both the welfare state and the warfare state.

Unfortunately, I think we're losing the battle. I don't want to be a pessimist, but when you look around and you see the Republican Party has so completely capitulated to the neocons and the warfare state apparatus that it's no wonder they're not credible when they say we need to shrink the welfare state. And frankly, Tom, that's something that I faced day after day in the battle for the budget during the Reagan Administration: we couldn't persuade even the middle-of-the-road Republicans in the House to do what was necessary to begin to shrink the domestic budget, because they just kept whining about the massive Reagan defense buildup. Which frankly, as I lay out in my book *The Great Deformation*, was a huge mistake, unnecessary and left us with this huge, conventional war machine that has been used to invade all the areas of the world – Iraq, Afghanistan, Somalia, and everywhere else that we shouldn't have been involved in.

WOODS: I'm always interested in people who move from one worldview to another. So before we move on, I can't help asking: in your own transition from your SDS days to your days in the Reagan Administration, is there anything in the arguments that reached you that might be useful for us today in trying to make arguments with the Left? What was it that made you say, doggone it, I think I'm wrong on something important here?

STOCKMAN: Yeah, I was really wrong on the mechanics of democracy. I was right on the war and the imperialist foreign policy. I clearly didn't understand economics. I was a college kid. Although in those days you didn't get student loans and grants. You had to work 20 or 30 hours a week to keep going at a state college like Michigan State. But where I was wrong was on the mechanics of democracy. The Left insisted that voting didn't mean anything, that parliamentary democracy was a bourgeois illusion, all of those arguments, and that you had to take the fight directly to the streets. Well, to a point that seemed almost necessary to stop the Vietnam War with the protests, and I went to the marches on the Pentagon and a lot of other places.

But where it triggered an inflection point for me was in 1969, when it started to get violent, and you had the Weathermen come along. And I was a student at Harvard Divinity School then, frankly – I don't mind admitting this – hiding out from the draft, because I got a deferment. I wasn't going to go to South Vietnam on McNamara's invitation. Anyway, I lived right near Divinity Hall, and next door was the ROTC building. And the radicals burned down the ROTC building. That was like a wake-up call. It just struck me: what am I doing here? How can I possibly identify with people who randomly and wantonly decide that this property is going to be destroyed in order to make a statement?

So I began to retract rather dramatically. The violence at the Chicago Democratic Convention in the summer also turned me off. And then I happened to get – and I'll just throw this in as long as we're talking about it – a very profound mentor at the time whom you wouldn't recognize today as a conservative; I wouldn't, either. But it was Daniel Patrick Moynihan. Actually, I was his live-in house man in Cambridge. But he became a great mentor to me, and he was a conservative in the democracy side of it if not in what I would call the economic policy or welfare state side of it. And I learned a lot from him. I learned that you could be an intellectual and you didn't have to be left.

You asked me for the key point, and that was the thing that Daniel Patrick Moynihan did for me. Until then, I thought people on the right were basically mental midgets, and that if you were a real thinker, and you read a lot of books, and you went deep into history, and you dug into the library, which is what I did in those days, you had to be left because thinkers were left. What I discovered while I was at Harvard Divinity School and under the tutelage of Pat Moynihan – who eventually got me a job on Capitol Hill, and that's how I started in political life – was that you could be an intellectual, you could be a thinker, you could be steeped in history and in theory, and you didn't have to be on the left. So I think that's the real answer to your question.

WOODS: It's interesting you say that. We have a guest who's on this program from time to time, Bill Kauffman, who worked for Senator Moynihan for some time, and even though Bill's not a liberal and he's not a Democrat, he speaks very fondly of him, so to have two people I respect say that, well, all right, I'm willing to consider there might have been a decent person over in that institution.

I have a couple of things more that I want to make sure I hit with you, and one of them you might think is unfair, and you may want to pass or punt on it, and I would not think the less of you for it. But I feel compelled as a good journalist to ask. You worked in the Reagan Administration, and there is a wide array of testimonies about Reagan the man. You hear people say, he seemed very amiable on TV, but he was of middling intelligence, just a guy who more or less understood the big picture and that was it. Then you get other people who say he was very hands on, he knew all the details, he dominated the meetings. And then you get still others who say: I was at the meetings, and he was shockingly uninformed. Where does your recollection come down in that?

STOCKMAN: Ah, good question. I would sort of come out in a fourth category. I would say he was quite well informed, but his education, particularly on economic matters, was pre-1930. And since I went through the exercise of writing this whole book and digging back into the 1920s, and the real cause of the Great Depression, and what the world used to look like pre-1914, and with the liberal international order – of the real meaning of the word liberal – and the gold standard, I suddenly realized late in life that that was the view that Ronald Reagan had of the world. That's what he learned in his student days, and he never changed when the Keynesians took over, let's say, the intellectual brief in Washington, for economic policy anyway, after the 1950s. So a lot of people misunderstood his old worldview, old liberal worldview of economics, for lack of information, or lack of knowledge, or lack of intelligence. I think that was wrong.

But secondly, he was quite passive. He knew a lot. He could defend the position if pushed hard, but he was quite passive in the to and fro inside the administration. And as a result of that, the administration was really run by Deaver, Baker, and Meese. It wasn't that he didn't make decisions, but he was the decision-maker of last resort when it got down to two irreconcilable but easily separable choices. But those are about the only choices he made. I don't necessarily fault him for that: Jimmy Carter was in all the details, making all the choices, and that was totally unsuccessful.

So generally what I liked about Ronald Reagan was he had a tremendous temperament. He had a willingness to listen to people. He gave people an opportunity to do their job. So there are pluses and minuses, but I think a lot of the conventional stereotypes, negative or positive, really don't capture the more complex reality that existed.

WOODS: All right, let's jump ahead to the present day, then. What is your assessment of the economic picture today? That, of course, is what you get asked every time you're invited on the radio: where are things today? Especially given that we have heard some people say, look, you doom-and-gloomers, things are turning around, and things are turning around under the aegis of Janet Yellen and Barack Obama, so on what ground can you complain? Are things in fact turning around?

STOCKMAN: Well, the point is it's exactly what they were saying when we had this allegedly Goldilocks economy in 2005, 2006, and 2007. You can go back and replay some old CNBC tapes, and you'll get the same numbers coming up on the unemployment rate or the number of existing homes that were sold last month. We're in a serial bubble cycle created by the central banks that seem to last four or five years. They inflate the financial system to a fare-thee-well as Greenspan did during dot-com, as Greenspan did with Bernanke's help at the end during the housing and credit bubble, and as we're now doing during the Bernanke, Yellen period, what I call wealth effects, or risk asset bubbles. And they take a while to fully unfold. They do allow the economy to get up off the floor after a crash and revive itself. I don't think all this money printing and zero interest rates have anything to do with the economy inching forward at 1 or 2 percent a year. That's just a natural regenerative power of the private, capitalist system, even as hampered and impaired as it is by government policy. But at some point these bubbles become so fantastic – and I think we're getting close now, if you look at valuations in all the risk-asset markets, and the Russell 2000 trading at 85 times earnings and so forth – that when they crash it creates a sudden crash of confidence, and then economic activity freezes up, and we go into another down cycle.

It shouldn't happen. There is no reason why we have a monetary central planning agency, a monetary politburo inflating, and reflating, and reflating our financial system with cheap money, and zero interest rates, and massive bond buying. This is all wrong. We really need to go back to the banker's bank, where we started our conversation this afternoon. And I can tell you one thing: if we did, we wouldn't be going into the seventh year running of zero interest rates, effectively, in the money markets. They were set there by the Fed, the fed funds rate, which everything else prices off from for short-term interest rates, in December of 2008. And here we are mid-2014, entering year six of the so-called recovery, and they are still at zero. In a free market, where savers and borrowers were meeting and finding the requisite price, the market would be clearing at a lot higher levels, and with higher interest rates there would not be nearly as much carry-trade speculation. Zero money market rates are the mother's milk of gambling and speculation in the financial markets, and the Fed is massively empowering people to speculate. That's why we get the bubbles. That's why we get the busts. That's why we get the destructive cycle that we're in today.

June 24, 2014

52

THE AMERICAN REVOLUTION: THE REAL ISSUE (WITH KEVIN GUTZMAN)

Kevin Gutzman, a professor of history at Western Connecticut State University, is the author of The Politically Incorrect Guide to the Constitution, James Madison and the Making of America, *and (with me)* Who Killed the Constitution? The Fate of American Liberty from World War I to Barack Obama.

WOODS: We're gearing up for another Independence Day, so it seemed like a good idea to have you on to talk about the American Revolution. By an interesting coincidence, your course on the American Revolution is now available at LibertyClassroom.com. So all the stars are in alignment for you to be back here as a guest.

Let's start off with an overview of what you're basically saying. The course is "The American Revolution: A Constitutional Conflict." In what sense is it a constitutional conflict? People might be inclined to think: there is no U.S. Constitution yet at that point, so what can he mean?

GUTZMAN: Well, the conflict between the colonies and the mother country was over the shape of the British constitution. The British, for their part, were insisting on the newfangled product of the Glorious Revolution, which was parliamentary sovereignty, that claimed, as they said in the Declaratory

Act of 1766, that Parliament was entitled to legislate for the colonies "in all cases whatsoever." On the other side, one had the North American colonists, who were insistent that, no, the Glorious Revolution had not wiped clean the slate of all the precedents showing that they had various corporate rights, that is, that the colonies had a right to be taxed only by their own representatives, that the colonists had the right to trial by jury, that they had the rights of Englishmen, as kings had repeatedly insisted they would always have. So essentially what happened was that once the debt that accrued during the Seven Years War led Parliament to try to impose new taxes on the colonists, the colonists responded by saying, well, constitutionally you're not entitled to do that – which the mother country found to be nonsense in light of the claim that Parliament could legislate in all cases whatsoever. So that, to my mind, is what the American Revolution was about, and ultimately on the battlefield the American colonists vindicated their claim that they had local rights to self-determination essentially in each colony, now state.

WOODS: You and I are fans of Jack Greene, the colonial historian, who's written an awful lot about the constitutional angle of this particular conflict. As a matter of fact, he has a book that summarizes a lot of his work on this: *The Constitutional Origins of the American Revolution.* I really got to know his thesis in his other book *Peripheries and Center.* But Greene says that as early as the Stamp Act crisis in 1765 you've already got being articulated at least among some colonists the idea that this is not just about no taxation without representation. It's about no legislation without representation. You can see in Patrick Henry's resolves and in a few other places that there are some people who are willing to go that far, and then by the time you get to the Coercive Acts, a lot of people are willing to go that far.

GUTZMAN: Well, that's true, and that's the case I make in the new LibertyClassroom.com course. This should be unsurprising to anybody who is familiar with my training, since my graduate school adviser was Peter Onuf at the University of Virginia, and Onuf's graduate school adviser was Jack Greene at Hopkins, so I came by this honestly. I think the best book on the general subject is Greene's *Peripheries and Center,* which to my mind makes an irrefutable case.

Now the reason that this is an interesting take on things is because the overwhelming preponderance of product being poured out by academics these days concerning the American Revolution is based on the unholy academic trinity of race, class, and gender. So you have all kinds of arguments that, no, it was really the Indians who caused the American Revolution, or it was unhappiness about the uppitiness of indentured servants that led to the American Revolution, or in some other way it was about keeping down the lower classes.

I reject that summarily. I don't think those arguments have any real weight. I think actually there is a kind of laying out the thesis ahead of time, and then going out to try to find evidence to prove it in most of these studies. It seems to me that we can profit by taking at face value what these people were saying, which was: we don't want you to try to tax us because we think it's unconstitutional. As you say, during the conflict over the Stamp Act, the famous Stamp Act Congress-adopted resolution said that they could only be legislated for and taxed by their own representatives. They could not be represented in Parliament, and that meant that only their colonial legislatures could adopt such measures. Really, this argument didn't change from 1765. It was just that people had not recognized that there was no way to reconcile the two contending positions in 1765.

WOODS: And that leads me to a follow-up question. In my old teaching days, I would occasionally ask students, was such-and-such event inevitable, and the answer was always yes. No student can conceive of events ever having turned out differently from how they actually did. But I wonder if here we have a genuine case of something that *was* perhaps inevitable. The way I understand it is that there are two competing views of the British constitution and of this implicit, evolving, imperial constitution. On the one hand you have the American view, which is that the British constitution is a matter of, certainly some documents, to be sure, but also customary practice, and for a century and a half the customary practice has been self-government on internal affairs for the colonies. Parliament, in turn, regulates trade and external affairs, foreign policy. An implicit understanding was worked out. This is the colonists' view.

Parliament, for its part, acknowledges that this is indeed the customary way things have gone, but insists that that doesn't mean the Parliament therefore has no right to interfere in the internal affairs of the colonies if such intervention should be necessary. So on the one hand you have parliamentary supremacy. On the other hand you have this older, seventeenth-century view of the British constitution that the colonists have, that the British have to abide by traditional practice. Obviously these two are at odds with one another, because what if Parliament violates traditional practice? That to me seems like an inevitable conflict. Or was there some way out?

GUTZMAN: Well, what happened after the fighting started was that the British actually offered to turn things back to the *status quo ante*. They offered, in other words, to repeal the taxing measures and agree not to try to tax anymore. I guess another way of saying that is it finally became clear to people in authority in Great Britain how they had been benefiting from having these colonies even without taxing them, which was something that they had apparently not taken too seriously before.

One thing, too, that we have to notice here is something to do with the personalities involved. King George, although he was in the same office as the current British monarch, had a completely different kind of function from the one that Elizabeth II has today. We didn't actually know this until the 1990s, because while in America we have official documents being disclosed almost immediately when the president leaves office, in England it's a family, so King George's private correspondence was not actually made public until over two centuries after the Revolution ended. When it became public, everybody could see that George actually had been the one manipulating the politicians and repeatedly, for example, rejecting Lord North's attempts to resign because he had decided that the war was pointless, that it couldn't be won. Before that, King George was the one who insisted that, for example, a tax on tea be kept when the Townshend duties were repealed, and so on. He was the one who insisted at an early stage that either the North American colonies were subject to Parliament or they were completely independent, which also was the position that Governor Hutchinson had taken in Massachusetts in disputing the question of Parliament's authority in the late 1760s.

So I think if there had been a king who was not quite so insistent on the principle of the thing, it's possible that they could have just skated by without noticing this disagreement. That actually was the way that the British constitutional system had worked before. It was just about habits, practices, customs – whatever we've done, that's what we're supposed to do. And here we have this unhappy decision of the Parliament in 1766 to say no, we're not going to have just the *modus vivendi* that we don't ever think we have to describe. Instead, we're going to lay out a firm set of principles, and you have to adhere to them, whatever you think.

So I guess the short of it is today – and if you ask me next week, I might give you a different answer – but I do think today that it could have been avoided if only people in authority in Britain had noticed that they really were benefiting from having these North American colonies, and if they had given any thought to the possibility, which they don't seem to have considered a possibility, that they might actually lose the Revolution and find the colonies had become independent – I think that was something they didn't really take seriously as well.

WOODS: Kevin, let's go back to the colonists' understanding of their own position, and here I want to introduce Richard Bland's view, because he has an interesting take. He's not alone in this; Jefferson had a similar view. I want to talk about his take regarding the relationship between the colonies and the King as opposed to the relationship, if any, between the colonies and Parliament. How does he spell out the origins of American settlement?

GUTZMAN: Well, first, Richard Bland was a burgess, senior burgess, when Jefferson entered the House of Burgesses in the 1760s, and actually he was Jefferson's cousin, an elder cousin, a prominent person in the burgess system. You're asking me how he understood the relationship between the colonies and the mother country?

WOODS: Yes.

GUTZMAN: Okay, well, the way he explains things in a pamphlet, a very important pamphlet which Jefferson later would call the first accurately to describe the situation, was that the North American colonies had been founded by colonists who had come to North America in exercise of the natural right to emigrate. This was Bland's great invention. The idea of a natural right to emigrate was a completely foreign idea, as far as I know, to anybody in the world at the time. In World War II, in America, we had a shameful episode where the government jailed Japanese Americans, essentially, during the war because they accepted, more or less, the Japanese government's position that you could not become a former Japanese. If you were Japanese by blood, you were Japanese.

And that was essentially the way that the English understood Englishness, too. You could not become a former Englishman. If you moved to France, lived there for 70 years, and died in your 90s, thinking yourself French, speaking only French, having become a Catholic – they still thought of that as an English grave in France. But Bland said that everybody had a natural right to emigrate, that the fact of having been accidentally born somewhere did not mean that you were morally compelled to remain in that state. So he said the people who had come to North America had come in exercise of this right, which meant that as they left Britain, they sloughed off any responsibility they had had to King-in-Parliament. Now he said, of course, there was a relationship between the British and the North American colonies, and that's through the King, whom they have voluntarily accepted as their own King when they had the option of doing so, having entered into the state of nature by emigrating.

So as far as he was concerned, the relationship was one of sufferance, or lawyers would say it was defeasible. In other words, if this functionary who was in that position in relation to the colonies at their will ceased to fulfill his function, they could, at will, replace him with someone else. Jefferson, of course, later would lay this out very strongly in his *Summary View of the Rights of British America*, but although Jefferson took an impertinent tone in his pamphlet in 1774, it was essentially the same position, and this would become the American position. By the time Jefferson drafted the Declaration of Independence and took that position – which was essentially that the only relationship between the mother country and the colonies legally was the King, therefore, ignoring Parliament throughout the Declaration of Independence – that had come to be the position basically of all the Whigs in North America, that Parliament was just a foreign legislature.

WOODS: Kevin, assuming we can look at this dispassionately as scholars, how do you assess the plausibility of that claim?

GUTZMAN: It's pretty weak. The idea that the government of England, or in regard to later colonies, Britain, had nothing to do with establishing the colonies, is just unfounded. There were repeated instances in the colonies in which the mother country provided men, materiel, money, whatever kinds of resources, obviously military protection, superintendents of various kinds, throughout the colonial period. Now, of course, they were not doing what they decided to do after the Seven Years' War, which was wholesale to remake the North American government, to remake the constitutional system, to regularize it, and to take steps to subordinate New York, and Massachusetts, and whichever other colonies came to mind. But it's certainly not true that these people in North America were entirely separate from Britain or that they had no relationship to the Parliament.

WOODS: Well, there was certainly no British authority who thought that that was what was taking place when the colonists, or the would-be colonists, emigrated.

GUTZMAN: No, and we don't have any reason to think that the colonists thought that, either.

WOODS: It seems to me it's not even necessary to make this argument in order to advance the colonial position. You can simply make the traditional constitutional claims that we were making at the beginning. This additional claim is superfluous, isn't it?

GUTZMAN: Well, yeah, notice it's a different claim from the one that Henry made in the resolution, as you mentioned before. There he referred to the charters and to the commissions of various royal governors brought to North America when they became governors of Virginia and so on, and besides, traditional practice between Virginia and the mother country. He laid out a classic English lawyer's argument, which of course you'd expect, since he was an English lawyer.

WOODS: I want you to talk about Gordon Wood for a minute. He has a book *The Radicalism of the American Revolution*. What's the thesis of that book? I have a feeling that I've read somewhere that you don't think much of it.

GUTZMAN: Well, the thesis is that the American Revolution was the most radical thing that ever happened. It led to a society that was completely unlike any that had ever been known before. So basically the working out of equality in America over time was all the legacy of the American Revolution.

WOODS: What's your thought about that?

GUTZMAN: Well, it is a grand exercise in *post hoc, ergo propter hoc*, that is, essentially everything that's happened since can be traced to the Revolution. Therefore, the Revolution is responsible for all of it. There's no way to disprove *post hoc, ergo propter hoc* except to say there's no way to prove it, either. It's just an assertion. So he shows you that in time you'd have more or less direct election of presidents instead of having the electoral college. Well, this results from the American Revolution. And in time you have black people given the vote and made equal citizens; this is the result of the American Revolution. You have all kinds of social leveling, and you have a big, administrative state and so on, and anything that happened after the Revolution is a result of the Revolution. So I find it not very interesting, really. It's just a grand fallacy.

WOODS: But you know what, Kevin? It sounds like what a lot of historians implicitly believe and say about America: that as America becomes more egalitarian, it's living up to its original promise. For example, my Ph.D. dissertation adviser, Alan Brinkley at Columbia, who was an awfully nice guy on a personal level, wrote a textbook called *The Unfinished Nation* – by which, of course, he means that egalitarianism has not fully triumphed in every nook and cranny of society, so therefore it's unfinished. It's the same kind of permanent revolution idea that I guess is implicit in the Gordon Wood book.

GUTZMAN: Well, yeah, and of course, the ultimate manifestation of this tendency is the Marxist historian Eric Foner's book on the Reconstruction period, when he basically decried the postwar Republicans for not having enough dekulakization in the South. It's called *Reconstruction: America's Unfinished Revolution*.

WOODS: That's right.

GUTZMAN: So he wants the full Stalinist program, and he's dissatisfied that it wasn't all implemented at the same time.

I did not know Gordon Wood's book was coming out. When I first saw it was in a bookstore. I happened to be there with somebody else. I think this was in the spring of 1992, if I'm not mistaken. Seeing the book, reading its title, I said to her: this is going to win all kinds of prizes. And why was that? Just from the title you could tell that the whole point of the book was to say that people who have said that the American Revolution was about conserving local self-government, it was about conserving what was under attack from a distant state – these people are wrong, and so whatever the merits, or lack of merit of the book, it's going to win. Because historical prizes are generally based on the politics of the book. And that, it turns out, is exactly what the book is. I do think Gordon Wood's first book, *The Creation of the American Republic*, is an outstanding book, and I quite like his Franklin biography, but this one is just tendentious. There's nothing else to say about it. I think it's not even really very interesting.

June 30, 2014

PART X

BACK TO BASICS

53

LIBERALISM IN THE CLASSICAL TRADITION

This is the introduction I wrote for the new Mises Institute edition of Ludwig von Mises's classic book Liberalism *(1927).*

Any political philosophy must address itself to a central question: under what conditions is the initiation of violence to be considered legitimate? One philosophy may endorse such violence on behalf of the interests of a majority racial group, as with the National Socialists of Germany. Another may endorse it on behalf of a particular economic class, as with the Bolsheviks of Soviet Russia. Still another may prefer to avoid a doctrinaire position one way or another, leaving it to the good judgment of those who administer the state to decide when the common good demands the initiation of violence and when it does not. This is the stance of the social democracies.

The liberal sets a very high threshold for the initiation of violence. Beyond the minimal taxation necessary to maintain legal and defense services – and some liberals shrink even from this – he denies to the state the power to initiate violence and seeks only peaceful remedies to perceived social ills. He opposes violence for the sake of redistributing wealth, of enriching influential pressure groups, or trying to improve man's moral condition. Civilized people, says the liberal, interact with each other not according to the law of the jungle, but by means of reason and discussion. Man is not to be made good by means of the prison guard and the hangman; should they be necessary to make him good, his moral condition is already beyond salvage. As Ludwig von Mises puts it in this seminal book, modern man "must free himself from the habit, just as soon as something does not please him, of calling for the police."

There has been something of a renaissance in Misesian studies in the wake of the financial crisis that first gripped the world in 2007 and 2008, since it was followers of Mises who had the most compelling explanations for economic phenomena that left most so-called experts stammering. The importance of Mises' economic contributions to modern-day discussion is apt to make us overlook his contributions as a social theorist and political philosopher. The republication of *Liberalism* helps to rectify this oversight.

The liberalism that Mises describes here is, of course, not the "liberalism" of the United States today, but rather classical liberalism, which is how the term continues to be understood in Europe. Classical liberalism stands for individual liberty, private property, free trade, and peace, fundamental principles from which the rest of the liberal program can be deduced. (When the first English edition of *Liberalism* appeared in 1962, Mises published it under the title *The Free and Prosperous Commonwealth*, in order not to confuse American readers who associated liberalism with a creed very different from the one he championed.)

It is no insult to Mises to describe his defense of liberalism as parsimonious, in the sense that, following Occam's Razor, he employs on its behalf no concepts not strictly necessary to his argument. Thus Mises makes no reference to natural rights, a concept that plays a central role in so many other expositions of liberalism. He focuses primarily on the necessity of large-scale social cooperation. This social cooperation, by which complex chains of production function to improve the general standard of living, can be brought about only by an economic system based on private property. Private property in the means of production, coupled with the progressive extension of the division of labor, has helped to free mankind from the horrific afflictions that once confronted the human race: disease, grinding poverty, appalling rates of infant mortality, general squalor and filth, and radical economic insecurity, with people often living one bad harvest away from starvation. Until the market economy illustrated the wealth-creating possibilities of the division of labor, it was taken for granted that these grotesque features of man's condition were the fixed dictates of a cold and merciless nature, and thus unlikely to be substantially alleviated, much less conquered entirely, by human effort.

Students have been taught for many generations to think of property as a dirty word, the very embodiment of avarice. Mises will have none of it. "If history could prove anything in regard to this question, it could only be that nowhere and at no time has there ever been a people which has raised itself without private property above a condition of the most oppressive penury and savagery scarcely distinguishable from animal existence." Social cooperation, Mises shows, is impossible in the absence of private property, and any attempts to curtail the right of property undermine the central pillar of modern civilization.

Indeed Mises firmly anchors liberalism to private property. He is all too aware that to champion property is to invite the accusation that liberalism is merely a veiled apologia for capital. "The enemies of liberalism have branded it as the party of the special interests of the capitalists," Mises observes. "This is characteristic of their mentality. They simply cannot understand a political ideology as anything but the advocacy of certain special privileges opposed to the general welfare." Mises shows in this book and throughout his corpus of work that the system of private ownership of the means of production redounds to the benefit not merely of the direct owners of capital but indeed to all of society.

There is, in fact, no particular reason that people in possession of great wealth should favor the liberal system of free competition, in which continuous effort must be exerted on behalf of the desires of the consumers if that wealth is not to be whittled away. Those who possess great wealth – especially those who inherited that wealth – may in fact prefer to inhabit a system of intervention, which is more likely to keep existing patterns of wealth frozen. Little wonder that American business magazines during the Progressive Era are replete with calls for replacing laissez-faire – a system in which no one's profits are protected – with government-sanctioned cartel and collusion devices.

Naturally, given Mises' emphasis on the centrality of the division of labor to the maintenance and progress of civilization, he is particularly outspoken regarding the evils of aggressive war, which on top of its physical and human toll brings about the progressive impoverishment of mankind by its radical disruption of a harmonious structure of production that spans the entire globe. Mises, who rarely minces words but whose prose is generally elegant and restrained, speaks with indignation and outrage when the subject turns to European imperialism, a cause on whose behalf he will admit no arguments whatever. Just as his student, Murray Rothbard, would later identify war and peace as the foundational issue of the whole liberal program, Mises likewise insists that these questions cannot be neglected – as they so often are by classical liberals in our own time – in favor of safer, less politically sensitive issues.

The principal tool of liberalism, Mises maintained, was reason. That does not mean Mises thought its entire program must be carried through by means of dense and elaborate academic treatises. He greatly admired those who brought its ideas to the stage, the silver screen, and the world of published fiction. But it does mean that the cause must remain rooted in rational argument, a much sounder foundation than the fickle irrationalism of emotion and hysteria by which other ideologies seek to stir the masses. "Liberalism has nothing to do with all this," Mises insists. "It has no party flower and no party color, no party song and no party idols, no symbols and no slogans. It has the substance and the arguments. These must lead it to victory."

Finally, a brief word on the translation. Ralph Raico's elegant rendering of Mises' words not only conveys the author's ideas with precision and care, but also preserves his unique and captivating prose style. Readers of Mises' later works, many of which appeared originally in English rather than in translation, will be struck by how skillfully Raico has captured the voice they discover in those books.

We ought to rejoice at the publication of the Mises Institute's new edition of this old classic, particularly at such a perilous moment in history. With fiscal crises and the hard choices they demand threatening a wave of civil unrest across Europe, the impossible promises made by cash-strapped welfare states are becoming increasingly obvious. As Mises argued, there is no stable, long-term substitute for the free economy. Interventionism, even on behalf of such an ostensibly good cause as social welfare, creates more problems than it solves, thereby leading to still more intervention until the system is entirely socialized, if the collapse does not occur before then.

Mises' position runs counter to those who held that the market was indeed a place of rivalry and strife in which the gain of some implied losses to others. One thinks, for example, of David Ricardo, and his contention that wages and profits necessarily move in opposite directions. Thomas Malthus warned of a population catastrophe, which implied a conflict between some individuals (those already born) and others (the alleged excess who followed later). Then, of course, there was the entire mercantilist tradition, which viewed trade and exchange as a kind of low-intensity warfare that yielded a definite set of winners and losers. Karl Marx set forth a classic statement of inherent class antagonism on the market in *The Communist Manifesto*. Even older than these figures was Michel de Montaigne (1533–1592), who argued in his essay "The Plight of One Man is the Benefit of Another" that "no profit can possibly be made but at the expense of another." Mises later called this view the "Montaigne fallacy."

For the sake of civilization itself, Mises urges us to discard the mercantilist myths that pit the prosperity of one people against that of another, the socialist myths that describe the various social classes as mortal enemies, and the interventionist myths that seek prosperity through mutual plunder. In place of these juvenile and destructive misconceptions Mises advances a compelling argument for classical liberalism, which sees "economic harmonies" – to borrow Frédéric Bastiat's formulation – where others see antagonism and strife. Classical liberalism, so ably defended here by Mises, seeks no coercively derived advantage for anyone, and for that very reason brings about the most satisfactory long-run results for everyone.

July 16, 2010

54

INTERVIEW WITH THE *HARVARD POLITICAL REVIEW*

I graduated from Harvard in 1994. In August 2011 I consented to an interview with the Harvard Political Review. *I was interviewed by Naji Filali. I reproduce it below.*

Harvard Political Review: To start this off, here is a rather simple question: how was it to attend Harvard University as a libertarian intellectual and when did your views take shape? You concentrated in history, so did you ever get into disagreements with professors who offered a different interpretation of events?

Thomas Woods: I entered Harvard as a middle-of-the-road Republican, the very thing that drives me most berserk today. I began to move in a libertarian direction with the passage of time. The intellectual climate of Cambridge could be stifling, and indeed it began pushing me even farther in the other direction. By the time I completed the Ludwig von Mises Institute's summer Mises University program (which introduces students to the Austrian School of economics, which has enjoyed quite a renaissance since its economists predicted the Panic of 2008) in 1993, I was a full-fledged libertarian, which with the exception of a few phases and deviations here and there, is what I have remained to this day.

I learned a lot from my professors at Harvard, and did not consider myself an aggrieved party unjustly put upon by left-wing radicals. To be sure, a few people on the faculty simply had to be avoided; they disgraced the institution by more or less openly using the classroom as a propaganda machine. I found out about them and avoided them.

At the same time, though, I did have to learn an enormous amount on my own. You are not going to read Murray N. Rothbard's book *America's Great Depression* at Harvard, for instance, even though in a just world you would. But the Harvard library system was a great place for someone to be an autodidact.

HPR: The debate over the national debt has been quite vociferous of late in Congress, and does not seem to have any end in sight, even with the most recent compromise, if you will. However, members of the Cato and Ludwig von Mises Institutes, along with many in the Tea Party, demand deeper budget cuts that a good portion in Congress have yet to acknowledge; a glance at the failing of Rep. Paul Ryan's (R-Wis.) modest plan is all the proof one needs. This raises the question: what are the ramifications of Congress's relative intransigence for our future as a nation?

TW: I don't see it as a question of intransigence because I don't think the general public wants serious cuts. Even the vast majority of self-identified Tea Party voters want entitlements off the table. As for the rest of federal spending, *The Economist* did a poll of Americans in late 2010 in which respondents were asked which in a list of spending categories they would cut. The only one that a majority of Americans would cut was foreign aid, which amounts to a fraction of one percent of the federal budget. In no other area did even 30 percent of Americans say they wanted cuts. That means default. What else could it mean?

The politicians are not defying public opinion. They are reflecting it. With the unfunded liabilities of Social Security and Medicare in excess of twice the GDP of the entire world, this has to end badly. And how is the federal government going to fund trillion-plus annual deficits as far as the eye can see? Because that's what we're going to have. Even if the phony $4 trillion spending cut we've heard about were to be implemented, that's spread out over ten years, which means $400 billion a year. That's not even one third of the current deficit. And the cuts won't be evenly spread out over ten years. They will be back-loaded.

Since no Congress can bind a future Congress on spending, they are meaningless. Whenever you hear the words "over ten years" in a budget debate, substitute the word "sucker."

HPR: As a senior fellow at the Mises Institute, you have your fingers on the pulse of current policy debates. Which policy debate has interested you the most and what is your proposed solution to it?

TW: At the Mises Institute we are not keen on the term (or the concept) "public policy." According to Lew Rockwell, the Institute's founder, "Among the greatest failures of the free-market intellectual movement has been to allow its ideas to be categorized as a 'public policy' option. The formulation implies a concession that it is up to the state – its managers and kept intellectuals – to decide how, when, and where freedom is to be permitted. It further implies that the purpose of freedom, private ownership, and market incentives is the superior management of society, that is, to allow the current regime to operate more efficiently."

In other words, the very notion of "public policy" assumes that people's lives and property are to be disposed of by the political class in pursuit of the goals of that class. This we reject on moral (and economic) grounds.

I think of myself not as solving society's problems one at a time via well-formed "public policy" but as doing what I can to pursue justice. And yet, as luck would have it, justice does indeed wind up solving problems far better than busybodies or central planners ever could. That's the implicit lesson of *Rollback*, my latest book. In this connection I also recommend Jeff Tucker's engaging new book, *It's a Jetsons World: Private Miracles and Public Crimes*.

HPR: You have argued ardently for states' rights in your book *Nullification*, and the uphill battle between Virginia's Attorney General and the federal government will certainly be crucial to the states' rights movement. Yet, we have always been taught that the Supremacy Clause of the United States Constitution readily dismisses any individual state's nullification attempt. Why do you feel that the states' rights argument is sound, given the counter-argument?

TW: This particular argument is in fact quite weak, so I don't find it threatening to my view. It's the kind of argument a law professor would make, and I don't mean that as a compliment.

Thomas Jefferson was not unaware of, and did not deny, the Supremacy Clause. His point was that only the Constitution and *laws which shall be made in pursuance thereof* shall be the supreme law of the land. Citing the Supremacy Clause merely begs the question. A nullifying state maintains that a given law is not "in pursuance thereof" and therefore that the Supremacy Clause does not apply in the first place.

Such critics are expecting us to believe that the states would have ratified a Constitution with a Supremacy Clause that said, in effect, "This Constitution, and the Laws of the United States which shall be made in pursuance thereof, plus any old laws we may choose to pass, whether constitutional or not, shall be the supreme law of the land."

I think there are stronger arguments against nullification than the misplaced one from the Supremacy Clause. But I have replied to those as well. (See my NullificationFAQ.com, published in this book as chapter 40.)

Discussing state nullification in front of progressives is, unfortunately, like waving a crucifix before Dracula. Despite its horrific persecutions of minorities, its totalitarian revolutions, and even its genocides, they demand we believe the centralized modern state is a wonderful, progressive force. Whoever questions it is a crank.

But why is it obvious that centralization is a progressive's friend? The New Left had its doubts about that. And would it really be a tragedy for the Patriot Act to be defied? How about the grotesque injustices that go on every day in prosecuting the federal government's war on drugs? What if the states could have nullified the incarceration of the Japanese in America during World War II?

The New Left historian William Appleman Williams once said that the closest we ever came to having truly humane communities in this country was under the Articles of Confederation. Kirkpatrick Sale, who famously wrote *Human Scale*, insists that issues of size also apply to political units. This strain of progressivism is all but extinct. It has been replaced by left-nationalists who make excuses for Barack Obama no matter how many times he betrays their alleged principles. A single city hands down infallible decrees for 310 million people, and we are to believe this is the most humane form of political arrangement. The old progressive slogan *question authority* is long, long gone. Practically no conventional belief is ever seriously questioned by progressives.

HPR: The 2012 race is beginning to heat up, and unlike 2008, libertarians have two Liberty-minded candidates: Ron Paul *and* Gary Johnson. Do you foresee this choice as dividing libertarians and inimical to the "liberty movement" or as an encouraging harbinger of things to come?

TW: It hasn't been a big issue so far. I myself support Ron Paul, but I respect Gary Johnson for the courageous positions he has taken.

HPR: Your writings have at times reflected your religious convictions as a Roman Catholic. How does your faith impact your understanding of government, and do you think it adds to or detracts from your policy interpretations?

TW: I don't think it requires much beyond the simple exercise of reason to perceive the gross injustices and immorality that permeate – indeed define – the regime in Washington. To be sure, the Catholic intellectual tradition includes a commitment to subsidiarity, which teaches that tasks ought not to be delegated to distant authorities unless more local institutions are absolutely incapable of carrying them out, as well as the just war tradition, by which the federal government's foreign interventions may be held up to informed moral scrutiny. But as I say, we are dealing with thievery and killing on so grand a scale that it would take a concerted effort not to see it.

I wrote about some of these questions in my 2005 book *The Church and the Market: A Catholic Defense of the Free Economy.*

HPR: Thanks again, Dr. Woods, for being so availing of your time with us today.

August 16, 2011

AFTERWORD

HOW I EVADED

THE GATEKEEPERS OF APPROVED OPINION

My last book was published in 2011. Since then, I've devoted myself to three projects: my weekday podcast, the Tom Woods Show (TomWoodsRadio.com); my educational website LibertyClassroom.com; and the Ron Paul homeschool program (RonPaulHomeschool.com). In each case I'm circumventing the usual means of information transmission to reach the public directly – bypassing the mainstream media with my show, academia with my Liberty Classroom, and school boards with my homeschool courses.

The Tom Woods Show (TomWoodsRadio.com) aired for the first time on September 23, 2013. Every day I cover an interesting topic related to the broad subject of liberty. The program runs about 25 to 30 minutes – perfect for commuters, I think. Check out the archive, with hundreds of episodes, all free, at TomWoodsRadio.com. You can even get a free e-book of transcripts of all the interviews I did in 2013 – a veritable primer on liberty in and of itself – at TomWoods.com/woodsbook.

Meanwhile, in 2012 I developed a separate project, LibertyClassroom.com, out of frustration at the kind of history and economics people were generally learning in high school and college. I have no control over the composition of college faculties. What I do have control over are my own time and efforts.

I wanted an adult enrichment site for people who'd like to learn the real thing, but don't really have time and lack reliable sources.

At LibertyClassroom.com, people can download courses that can be watched or listened to (we have both video and audio files for every lecture) on a computer or on mobile devices. We have Q&A forums in which you can ask faculty your questions. We also offer recommended readings, and host a monthly live video session with faculty. Every year we add several more courses to our offerings.

As of this printing we have ten courses: U.S. History to 1877, U.S. History Since 1877, Austrian Economics: Step by Step, American Constitutional History, Western Civilization I, Western Civilization II (these are not my courses for the Ron Paul Curriculum; these are much shorter courses, taught by Professor Jason Jewell), Introduction to Logic, History of Political Thought, The American Revolution: A Constitutional Conflict and John Maynard Keynes: His System and Its Fallacies.

Just for reading this book, you can get 50 percent off a year's subscription at LibertyClassroom.com with coupon code DISSENT (all caps).

The third project has been by far the most time consuming, but I feel certain it will have the most lasting effect: the Ron Paul homeschool program.

Ron had been wanting to create a homeschool program since at least 2008, when he first raised the idea with me. He thinks of it not just as an effective way to carry on the ideas he has promoted all his life; it is, to his mind, truly indispensable. If the tradition of thought that he represents is not handed on and cultivated, it will wither away.

As parents, though, we're interested in more than just advancing ideas. We want our children to get the best education they can. I am convinced that students who use our curriculum will get both.

When students complete the program at RonPaulHomeschool.com, they will know an enormous amount about the freedom philosophy – because, unlike the traditional classroom setting, we also present the other side of the story. How many times have you read something by Ron Paul or a Ron Paulian scholar about history, or economics, or government, that you didn't learn in school? How many great thinkers have you discovered in adulthood who were never introduced to you as a student?

Students in this program won't have the same problem. The people, events and perspectives left out of the usual presentations of this material will actually be taught to them. They'll graduate knowing who Ludwig von Mises and Frederic Bastiat were, which is more than we can say for more than 99 percent of high school (and even college) graduates today.

In addition to getting an education in which the freedom perspective is systematically incorporated rather than ignored or presented in caricature, students will also:

(1) learn how to speak in public with confidence;
(2) become a good writer – a skill few adults share;
(3) learn (with their parents' permission) how to run a blog and a YouTube channel;
(4) learn how to start a home business.

Our students won't just have a lot of valuable knowledge, in other words. They will be effective communicators in speech and in print, will have a leg up on their peers in promoting themselves and their work online, and will have absorbed a healthy entrepreneurial spirit.

Each of these courses consists of 180 video lessons, plus reading and writing assignments. I am preparing four courses: three full-year courses, and one half-year course. My courses also include an audio file for each lesson so parents, too, can listen during their commutes to what their students are learning.

I'd like you to see the titles of the lessons, at least for my half-year course on government, pitched to ninth graders. (N.b.: None of my courses are taught at a level that would insult the intelligence of an adult who wants to learn as well. You will not feel talked down to if you take my courses, I promise.) I'll leave out the subheadings that organize the various parts of the course; trust me, therefore, that there's an overall coherence to the order of the lessons.

Lesson 1: Introduction
Lesson 2: Natural Rights Theories I (High Middle Ages to Late Scholastics)
Lesson 3: Natural Rights Theories II (Locke)
Lesson 4: Natural Rights Theories III (more recent theories)
Lesson 5: Week 1 Review

Lesson 6: Locke and Spooner on Consent
Lesson 7: The Tale of the Slave
Lesson 8: Human Rights and Property Rights
Lesson 9: Negative Rights and Positive Rights
Lesson 10: Week 2 Review

Lesson 11: Critics of Liberalism: Rousseau and the General Will
Lesson 12: Critics of Liberalism: John Rawls and Egalitarianism
Lesson 13: Critics of Liberalism: Thomas Nagel and Ronald Dworkin
Lesson 14: Critics of Liberalism: G.A. Cohen
Lesson 15: Week 3 Review

Lesson 16: Public Goods
Lesson 17: The Standard of Living

Lesson 18: Poverty
Lesson 19: Monopoly
Lesson 20: Week 4 Review

Lesson 21: Science
Lesson 22: Inequality
Lesson 23: Development Aid
Lesson 24: Discrimination
Lesson 25: Week 5 Review

Lesson 26: The Socialist Calculation Problem
Lesson 27: Working Conditions
Lesson 28: Child Labor
Lesson 29: Labor and Unions
Lesson 30: Week 6 Review

Lesson 31: Health Care
Lesson 32: Antitrust
Lesson 33: Farm Programs
Lesson 34: War and the Economy
Lesson 35: Week 7 Review

Lesson 36: Business Cycles
Lesson 37: Industrial Policy
Lesson 38: Government, the Market, and the Environment
Lesson 39: Prohibition
Lesson 40: Week 8 Review

Lesson 41: Taxation
Lesson 42: Government Spending
Lesson 43: The Welfare State: Theoretical Issues
Lesson 44: The Welfare State: Practical Issues
Lesson 45: Week 9 Review

Lesson 46: Price Controls
Lesson 47: Government and Money, Part I
Lesson 48: Government and Money, Part II
Lesson 49: Midterm Review
Lesson 50: Week 10 Review

Lesson 51: The Theory of the Modern State
Lesson 52: American Federalism and the Compact Theory
Lesson 53: Can Political Bodies Be Too Large?
Lesson 54: Decentralization
Lesson 55: Week 11 Review

Lesson 56: Constitutionalism: Purpose
Lesson 57: The American Case: Self-Government and the Tenth Amendment
Lesson 58: The American Case: Progressives and the "Living, Breathing Document"
Lesson 59: The American States and the Federal Government
Lesson 60: Week 12 Review

Lesson 61: Monarchy
Lesson 62: Social Democracy
Lesson 63: Fascism I
Lesson 64: Fascism II
Lesson 65: Week 13 Review

Lesson 66: Marx I
Lesson 67: Marx II
Lesson 68: Communism I
Lesson 69: Communism II
Lesson 70: Week 14 Review

Lesson 71: Miscellaneous Interventionism: Postwar African Nationalism
Lesson 72: Public Choice I

Lesson 73: Public Choice II
Lesson 74: Miscellaneous Examples of Government Activity and Incentives
Lesson 75: Week 15 Review

Lesson 76: Industrial Revolution
Lesson 77: New Deal I
Lesson 78: New Deal II
Lesson 79: The Housing Bust of 2008
Lesson 80: Week 16 Review

Lesson 81: Are Voters Informed?
Lesson 82: Is Political Representation Meaningful?
Lesson 83: The Myth of the Rule of Law
Lesson 84: The Incentives of Democracy
Lesson 85: Week 17 Review

Lesson 86: The Sweeping Critique: LeFevre
Lesson 87: The Sweeping Critique: Rothbard
Lesson 88: Case Study: The Old West
Lesson 89: Economic Freedom of the World
Lesson 90: What Have We Learned?

My Western Civilization I course covers Western history from the ancient world through 1492. When high schools offer Western civilization at all, they cover it all in one year. Ron Paul's program covers it in two: one year for Western Civ I, and one for Western Civ II.

I have a sense that a lot of adults feel they should know something about Aristotle, or the Renaissance, or indeed about a whole host of topics that run through the history of Western civilization. Here's how an adult can learn them painlessly, and how a student can acquire a command over material most adults won't know.

Here's a taste of the topics covered: the ancient Hebrews, Greek drama, Greek science, Greek art, Socrates, Plato, Aristotle, Alexander the Great, the Hellenistic world, the rise and expansion of Rome, Roman literature and art, the rise of Christianity, early Christian texts (New Testament, Didache, Apologists), monasticism, Diocletian, Constantine, Rome and the barbarians, Augustine, Charlemagne, the Carolingian Renaissance, Islam, Byzantium, medieval art, feudalism, William the Conqueror, the Great Schism, the Gregorian Reform, the medieval Church, sacraments and liturgy, the Crusades, the Magna Carta, the growth of the English and French monarchies, the rise of the universities, Scholastic philosophy, Thomas Aquinas, just war theory, the cathedrals, the Holy Roman Empire, Dante and the *Divine Comedy*, Marsilius of Padua, the Avignon papacy, the Hundred Years War, the Great Western Schism, the Renaissance, humanism, and the Age of Discovery.

If you'd like to see the list of topics for all of my courses (two of which are complete as of this printing, and two are in process), you can do so at TomWoodsHomeschool.com. They are also offered through Ron Paul's K-12 curriculum at RonPaulHomeschool.com.

Finally, the easiest and neatest way to get my stuff is by supporting my show at SupportingListeners.com. I don't give away umbrellas, like PBS. I am so genuinely thrilled and honored when people help me out, I'm inclined to just give away lots and lots of things, worth as much as or more than what people contribute.

Yes, the gatekeepers still exist. The gates are still standing. But as a friend of mine puts it, the walls themselves have come down. These three ways are how I am conveying ideas that people won't hear about through conventional outlets. Instead of cursing the world and how unfair it is, I'm just producing my own content – a lot of it.

If you enjoyed this book, I think you'll enjoy these things. Look around at TomWoods.com, the central location for everything I do, and let's set fire to that index card of allowable opinion.

ABOUT THE AUTHOR

 Thomas E. Woods, Jr., is a senior fellow of the Ludwig von Mises Institute and host of the Tom Woods Show, which broadcasts every weekday at TomWoodsRadio. com. He holds a bachelor's degree in history from Harvard and his master's, M.Phil., and Ph.D. from Columbia University. Woods has appeared on CNBC, MSNBC, FOX News Channel, FOX Business Network, C-SPAN, and Bloomberg Television, among other outlets, and has been a guest on hundreds of radio programs, including National Public Radio, the Dennis Miller Show, the Michael Reagan Show, the Dennis Prager Show, and the Michael Medved Show.

Woods is the author of twelve books, including the *New York Times* bestsellers *Meltdown: A Free-Market Look at Why the Stock Market Collapsed, the Economy Tanked, and Government Bailouts Will Make Things Worse* and *The Politically Incorrect Guide to American History*. His 2004 book *The Church Confronts Modernity*, published by Columbia University Press, received critical acclaim throughout the historical and theological journals. Woods' books have been translated into Italian, Spanish, Polish, German, Czech, Portuguese, Croatian, Slovak, Lithuanian, Russian, Korean, Japanese, and Chinese.

Woods edited and wrote the introduction to five additional books: *Back on the Road to Serfdom: The Resurgence of Statism, We Who Dared to Say No to War:*

American Antiwar Writing from 1812 to Now (with Murray Polner), Murray N. Rothbard's *The Betrayal of the American Right*, *The Political Writings of Rufus Choate*, and Orestes Brownson's 1875 classic *The American Republic*. He contributed the preface to *Choosing the Right College* and the forewords to Ludwig von Mises' *Liberalism* and Abel Upshur's *A Brief Enquiry into the True Nature and Character of Our Federal Government*. He is also the author of *Beyond Distributism*, part of the Acton Institute's Christian Social Thought Series.

Woods' writing has appeared in dozens of popular and scholarly periodicals, including the *American Historical Review*, the *Christian Science Monitor*, *Investor's Business Daily*, *Catholic Historical Review*, *Modern Age*, *American Studies*, *Intercollegiate Review*, *Catholic Social Science Review*, *Economic Affairs* (U.K.), *Quarterly Journal of Austrian Economics*, *Inside the Vatican*, *Human Events*, *University Bookman*, *Journal of Markets & Morality*, *New Oxford Review*, *Catholic World Report*, *Independent Review*, *Religion & Liberty*, *Journal of Libertarian Studies*, *Journal des Economistes et des Etudes Humaines*, *AD2000* (Australia), *Christian Order* (U.K.), and *Human Rights Review*.

Woods won first prize in the prestigious Templeton Enterprise Awards for 2006, given by the Intercollegiate Studies Institute and the Templeton Foundation, for his book *The Church and the Market*. He was the recipient of the 2004 O.P. Alford III Prize for Libertarian Scholarship and of an Olive W. Garvey Fellowship from the Independent Institute in 2003. He has also been awarded two Humane Studies Fellowships and a Claude R. Lambe Fellowship from the Institute for Humane Studies at George Mason University and a Richard M. Weaver Fellowship from the Intercollegiate Studies Institute.

Woods lives in Topeka, Kansas, with his wife and five daughters, and operates TomWoods.com.

Made in the USA
Middletown, DE
03 June 2022